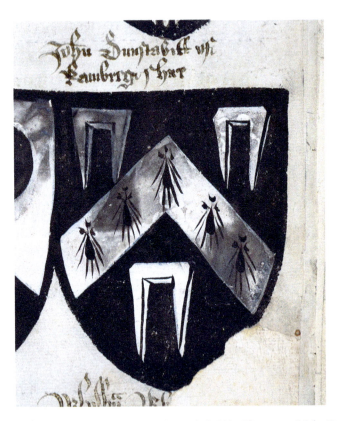

Frontispiece London, College of Arms, MS M. 10, f. 113r. The arms of John Dunstaple (Dunstabill) of Cambridgeshire (sable chevron ermine between three staples argent), painted *c.* 1480, Reproduced with permission.

Angel song

Although medieval English music has been relatively neglected in comparison with repertoire from France and Italy, there are few classical musicians today who have not listened to the thirteenth-century song 'Sumer is icumen in', or read of the achievements and fame of fifteenth-century composer John Dunstaple. Similarly, the identification of a distinctively English musical style (sometimes understood as the *contenance angloise*) has been made on numerous occasions by writers exploring the extent to which English ideas influenced polyphonic composition abroad. *Angel Song: Medieval English music in history* examines the ways in which the standard narratives of English musical history have been crafted, from the Middle Ages to the present. Colton challenges the way in which the concept of a canon of English music has been built around a handful of pieces, composers and practices, each of which offers opportunities for a reappraisal of English musical and devotional cultures between 1250 and 1460.

Lisa Colton is a Senior Lecturer in Music at the University of Huddersfield, where she is also director of the Centre for the Study of Music, Gender and Identity. Her research interests focus on early and contemporary music from historical, critical and analytical perspectives. Lisa Colton's publications have included articles on medieval motets, manuscript sources, Judith Weir and Lady Gaga. She has co-edited two essay collections: *Gender, Age and Musical Creativity* (with Catherine Haworth), and *Sources of Identity: Makers, owners and users of music sources before 1600* (with Tim Shephard).

Angel song
Medieval English music in history

Lisa Colton

First published 2017
by Routledge
2 Park Square, Milton Park, Abingdon, Oxon OX14 4RN

and by Routledge
711 Third Avenue, New York, NY 10017

Routledge is an imprint of the Taylor & Francis Group, an informa business

© 2017 Lisa Colton

The right of Lisa Colton to be identified as author of this work has been asserted by her in accordance with sections 77 and 78 of the Copyright, Designs and Patents Act 1988.

All rights reserved. No part of this book may be reprinted or reproduced or utilised in any form or by any electronic, mechanical, or other means, now known or hereafter invented, including photocopying and recording, or in any information storage or retrieval system, without permission in writing from the publishers.

Trademark notice: Product or corporate names may be trademarks or registered trademarks, and are used only for identification and explanation without intent to infringe.

British Library Cataloguing-in-Publication Data
A catalogue record for this book is available from the British Library

Library of Congress Cataloging-in-Publication Data
Names: Colton, Lisa, author.
Title: Angel song : Medieval English music in history / Lisa Colton.
Description: Abingdon, Oxon ; New York : Routledge, 2017. | Includes bibliographical references and index.
Identifiers: LCCN 2016025717| ISBN 9781472425683 (hardback) | ISBN 9781315567068 (ebook)
Subjects: LCSH: Music--England--500-1400--History and criticism.
Classification: LCC ML286.2 .C65 2017 | DDC 780.942/0902--dc23
LC record available at https://lccn.loc.gov/2016025717

ISBN: 978-1-472-42568-3 (hbk)
ISBN: 978-1-315-56706-8 (ebk)

Typeset in Times New Roman
by Florence Production Ltd, Stoodleigh, Devon, UK

Contents

List of figures		vii
List of tables and musical examples		viii
Acknowledgements		ix
	Introduction: 'Merrie England', cultural memory and the writing of English musical history	1
1	'The greatest musical curiosity extant': 'Sumer is icumen in' and the canon of English music	13
2	*Anglicus angelicus*: Was English music political?	39
3	Authorship, musicianship and value in medieval English history	65
4	Who was John Dunstaple?	85
5	The idea of English music: Identity, ethnicity and musical style	117
6	*Contenance angloise*: A reappraisal	133
	Epilogue	149
	Appendix A: John Dunstaple and other relevant people in historical records	153
	Appendix B: Hertfordshire Record Office MS 44505	163
	Appendix C: Property owned by John Dunstaple and his heirs	169
	Bibliography	171
	Index	187

Figures

1.1	Dante Gabriel Rossetti, *My Lady Greensleeves* (1859)	16
1.2	Dante Gabriel Rossetti, *My Lady Greensleeves* (1863)	17
1.3	*Sumer is icumen in* (1920)	18
1.4	Speculative earlier version of 'Sumer is icumen in'	25
3.1	Richard Rolle as depicted in a fifteenth-century collection of his works	71
4.1	London, Metropolitan Archives, Husting Roll 175 (16)	96
4.2	Broadfield manor house	101
4.3	Family of John Dunstaple, Esquire, of Steeple Morden in Cambridgeshire	102

Tables and music examples

Tables

A.1	John Dunstaple, musician	153
A.2	John Dunstaple listed as Armiger or Esquire	154
A.3	Probably John Dunstaple Esquire	156
A.4	Other John Dunstaples	156
A.5	Richard Hatfield	157
A.6	Thomas Hatfield	157
A.7	Edward Hatfield	159
A.8	Margaret Hatfield/Hyde (née Margaret Dunstaple)	159

Music examples

2.1	*Civitas nusquam conditur*/T. *Cibus esurientum*/ *Cives celestis curie*	49

Acknowledgements

The research undertaken in the preparation of this book has taken me to numerous archives and libraries in order to track down manuscripts, catalogues and elusive secondary literature. I extend particular thanks to London Metropolitan Archives, York Minster Library, the Borthwick Institute of Historical Research, the Bodleian Library, Merton College Library, Durham Cathedral Archives, Hertfordshire Record Office, the British Library, the University of York and the University of Huddersfield; many institutions have also made their holdings available online, either independently or via www.diamm.ac.uk (an invaluable resource).

The University of Huddersfield has awarded me two periods of sabbatical leave – allowing precious time to think and write – as well as financial assistance for purchasing and reproducing images, and for travel. I am grateful to the Arts and Humanities Research Board for financially supporting my doctoral research, during which I was able to examine nearly one hundred manuscript sources of medieval English music. As a Visiting Scholar at St John's College, Oxford, in the summer of 2008, I enjoyed access to the manuscript and secondary resources that were needed for efficient archival and historiographical work.

Angel Song: Medieval English music in history has been strengthened by many stimulating discussions at conferences and colloquia, especially at the Medieval and Renaissance Music Conference (Med-Ren), and the International Medieval Congress (University of Leeds), at which various early ideas were trialled as papers. In particular, my work on 'Sumer is icumen in' benefited from sharing initial ideas at Med-Ren, at the conference Britten in Context (Liverpool Hope University, 2010), and at various university research seminars. Chapter 3 was strengthened following discussions at a conference on medieval British liturgical manuscripts at Trinity College, Dublin in 2015, hosted by Ann Buckley. Chapter 4 was significantly developed after the presentation of my initial findings at Med-Ren, and by the invitation to speak at the Medieval and Renaissance Music Seminar convened by Margaret Bent (All Souls College, Oxford). These papers offered opportunities to discuss my work with specialists on fifteenth-century English music, Latin, liturgical history and archival research; my thanks here go particularly to Allan Barton, Margaret Bent, Roger Bowers, James Cook, Leofranc Holford-Strevens, Robert Nosow, Anna Sander, Peter Wright and Magnus Williamson, some of whom read drafts and offered constructive feedback.

x *Acknowledgements*

Chapter 5 developed from a paper delivered at the American Musicological Society Annual Conference, New Orleans in 2012. I wish to make particular mention of the positive impact that modest grants from learned societies have made to specialist conferences and study days relevant to this book; in particular, the Plainsong and Medieval Music Society, the Royal Musical Association and British Academy series *Early English Church Music*.

I extend further thanks to those who have read or heard drafts of work-in-progress and offered constructive advice, notably Margaret Bent, Roger Bowers, Ann Buckley, Helen Deeming, James Cook, Pat Cullum, David Howlett, Robert Nosow, Magnus Williamson and Peter Wright. Margaret, Roger and Peter offered detailed advice on draft material related to John Dunstaple at various stages of the project. John Bryan, Sonia Colton and Heidi Johnson read draft chapters in the final stages of the book and responded with typically sage and constructive comments. Kind colleagues have answered queries along the way; particular thanks in this regard to James Blasina, Karen Cook, Leofranc Holford-Strevens, Stephen Mossman and Ian Walshaw. Helen Deeming, John Haines, Kate Maxwell, Robert Nosow and Anna Zayaruznaya sent me sections of their own work in advance of publication, for which I am very grateful. Many moments of serendipity have occurred during conferences or through informal discussion with friends; my thanks in such matters extend to more names than can reasonably fit into this section, but include Cheryll Duncan, Barbara Eichner, J. P. E. Harper-Scott, Catherine Haworth, Emma Hornby, Sarah Johnson, Ken Kreitner, Elizabeth Eva Leach, Christian Leitmeir, Melanie Marshall, Paul Schleuse, Thomas Schmidt, Tim Shephard and Laurie Stras. My particular thanks go to Laura Macy, who encouraged me to write this book in the first place, and to Emma Gallon, who took on the project in the final stages of publication. All remaining infelicities in matters of detail or judgement within this book are mine alone.

My final thanks go to Heidi Johnson, to our children Agent G and Agent B, and to our family and friends for helping to keep the academic world in perspective.

Introduction
Merrie England, cultural memory and the writing of English musical history

In January 1993, Founders' Day at Bournemouth School for Girls was marked by the performance – by all 800 girls and accompanied by a band of wandering instrumentalists – of the medieval English song 'Sumer is icumen in', filling the Bournemouth Winter Gardens with sounds of the distant past. It was a performance that, shunning authenticity, evoked the Merrie England familiar to the pupils, such as me, who had watched *Robin Hood: Prince of Thieves* (1991) – a Hollywood blockbuster and medieval fantasy whose commercial success was based on a combination of lead actor Kevin Costner's appeal and Bryan Adams's ubiquitous ballad '(Everything I do) I do it for you'.

In their selection of 'Sumer is icumen in' to mark this annual ceremony, the music staff at Bournemouth School for Girls added it to the end of a recent performance history that included 'Sound the Trumpet' from Henry Purcell's *Come Ye Sons of Art*, the 'Alleluia' from Mozart's *Exultate Jubilate*, the chorus 'Freude, schöer Götterfunken' from Beethoven's Symphony No. 9, and a choral version of 'Penny Lane' by The Beatles. Such repertoire choices were broadly representative of conventional Western musical history; they helped to forge a connection between past and present, while developing a sense of musical nostalgia for pupils whose earliest personal memories dated only to the late 1970s. But times change. Although the majority of pupils and parents had welcomed the choice of other instrumental and choral items, the use of 'Sumer is icumen in' was met with puzzlement. Why would we be required to sing a linguistically obscure, ancient and apparently trite song about the summer season? 'Sumer is icumen in' had featured in the music-making of this and similar grammar, private and public schools for decades, but, by the end of the twentieth century, its cultural implications – Britishness, English musical innovation, nostalgia for a national, rural past – were sliding into obscurity. Dislocated from its recent historical performance context, 'Sumer is icumen in' no longer held much relevance beyond the romanticised medievalism that the performers at Bournemouth School for Girls knew from *Robin Hood: Prince of Thieves*.

Step back a few decades and the picture would have been quite different. In the 1960s, classical music permeated popular and national culture in ways that reflected a shared public knowledge of music history, albeit one that relied on a particular level of education and, by implication, class. There was no hiding the

2 Introduction

learnedness of *Beyond the Fringe*, in which the satirical effect of Dudley Moore's performance at the piano required the audience's familiarity with the musical style of Beethoven, Britten, Schubert and Weill, and even the vocal mannerisms of Peter Pears. The post-concert discussion with Arthur 'Two Sheds' Jackson, a fictional composer of contemporary music, in *Monty Python's Flying Circus* (1969) lampooned similar cultural territory. Quotations and covers of classical music pervaded pop music in the same period, from the frequent appearance of the distinctive timbre of the harpsichord in song scorings by The Beatles, Van Morrison, The Kinks, Simon and Garfunkel, the Beach Boys and many others to more unusual projects such as Dusty Springfield's 'Don't Speak of Love' (1968, but not released until *Something Special*, 1998), a surprisingly powerful torch song version of the finale from Richard Wagner's *Tannhauser*. Within progressive rock – a genre whose origins in the 1960s were closely associated with a middle- and upper-class, white male demographic – bands demonstrated exceptional virtuosity in the arrangement and performance of classical concert repertoire. To take one example, Emerson, Lake and Palmer's album *Pictures at an Exhibition*, a transcription and reinterpretation of Mussorgsky's work of the same name, reached the album chart top 10 in both the UK and the USA in 1971–2.

Knowledge of English classical music had been stimulated in part by the Festival of Britain in 1951, a series of exhibitions and events that gloried in cultural, scientific, architectural and geographical achievements, and which included an array of festivals that drew on music, ancient and modern. The programme booklet for a series of concerts by English composers from 1300 to 1750 was illustrated by a colour manuscript image of 'Sumer is icumen in' on its front cover. The York Mystery Plays – a fifteenth-century dramatic cycle of Bible stories, revived for the first time as part of the Festival – were accompanied by the original music of Leeds-based composer James Brown (1923–2004), whose score included arrangements of medieval music, then considered 'traditional', such as 'Angelus ad Virginem' and settings of lyrics originally by Chaucer.[1] The middle decades of the twentieth century, especially after 1945, featured a significant revival of interest in medieval culture, leading to the fictional representation of figures like Robin Hood or Joan of Arc on stage and screen.[2] Academic interest likewise increased, encouraged by a mixture of nationalist sentiment, the rediscovery of additional source materials, and the work of charismatic performers. Particularly important in this respect was Noah Greenberg (1919–66), whose direction of New York Pro Musica's production of the *Play of Daniel* at the Cloisters in the 1950s did much to portray medieval music as vibrant, exotic and engaging.[3] The British equivalent, in terms of musical energy and celebrity status, was David Munrow (1942–76), whose talent for presenting the unfamiliar with personality and dynamism was evident in his concert, studio and television performances.[4] Early instruments offered a window into an unacquainted past, as well as a diversion from standard concert repertoire. The concept of medieval music as a repertory and as a practice was therefore stimulated and consolidated during the 1950s and 1960s, a time when university music departments were growing, and the production and dissemination of recordings was expanding rapidly. As Haines reminds us, the expression 'medieval music', although widely used today, 'did not become common coin until after the Second World War, with university programs devoted to the study and performance of music from the Middle Ages'.[5]

The Western musical canon, as conveyed in histories, recordings and concert performances, remained focused on Austro-German repertory of the eighteenth and nineteenth centuries. However, its origins, in British texts at least, were portrayed as distinctly English: 'Sumer is icumen in' and the contrapuntal language of John Dunstaple were placed together at the head of the canon as a whole, inviting parallels with Britain's imperial history. All historical writing has the potential to indulge in nostalgia, fantasy and stereotype. But to what extent did the positioning of English musical innovation, as articulated by writers in the nineteenth and early twentieth centuries, continue to govern subsequent discourse on medieval music, especially considering that much primary material has come to light only over the past century? The standard narratives about English music – some of which I challenge in this book – have in fact remained fixated on a set of mythologies around which any significant new material has subsequently been woven. The effect has been one of distortion: with the old stories difficult to set aside, more disparate sources, traditions and practices have been side-lined. The fact that English writers, from the Middle Ages to the recent past, have often been responsible for the construction of their own mythology has largely been overlooked.

Looking at key works in the musicological literature after 1950 can reveal some of their common themes and preoccupations. Frank Harrison's *Music in Medieval Britain*, for example, is essentially a history of liturgical music; it remains a comprehensive and authoritative text on the subject. Plainchant and monophonic song for the liturgy have typically been discussed in separate publications to those that have dealt with polyphony, allowing a continued elision of the history of music with the history of composed polyphonic song, acknowledging some notable exceptions.[6] Focused studies of English plainchant sources have greatly enhanced our knowledge of musical practices in religious establishments served by men and by women.[7] The English carol was the focus of a flurry of activity during the middle decades of the twentieth century, after which very little work was published on this genre, perhaps as a result of its lack of clear relationship with the liturgy, individual composers or institutions.[8] Recent work by David Fallows and Louise McInnes has reasserted the value of the carol, not only in the history of English music but in relation to music more generally, illustrating its fundamental relationship with non-musical elements of the liturgy (such as sermons), and its interaction with other sacred and secular musical forms and practices.[9]

Some polyphonic genres have been studied in more critical detail than others: questions relating to genre, form, notation, text and transmission have been explored in book-length studies of English motets, conductus and settings of the Ordinary of the Mass.[10] There has been little analytical engagement with pre-1420 English motets in the way that has proved successful with French music; the rich interplay of music and text is no less a hallmark of English examples than their continental counterparts, and this is something considered more fully in the present book, especially in Chapter 2.[11] In 1993, Reinhard Strohm made the point that 'popular, secular and instrumental music in England has not been thoroughly investigated', which to a large extent is still the case.[12] This is partly because, as Lefferts has lamented, few examples of folk or popular music from England have survived, and even the extant English-texted songs may not have been part of vernacular culture.[13] Only in relatively recent studies have aspects of performance been seriously addressed and preconceptions challenged about how medieval music should be realised.[14] Even John Caldwell's *Oxford History of English Music* has been criticised for sidelining 'social, political and ideological concerns', and being in effect a quasi-canonic 'history of high art music [. . .] as if these pieces existed in a world populated only by professional musicians and their patrons'.[15]

A particular problem for all writers stems from the anonymous nature of the repertoire: without the 'personality' of Guillaume de Machaut, to choose a fourteenth-century French example, it is difficult to deal with questions of subjectivity, intention or meaning with any confidence. The relatively small quantity of British sources preserved, in comparison with those from France or Italy, compounds the problem. As a result of changing modes of notation and of deliberate acts of destruction, no substantial volume of English polyphony survives from the later Middle Ages between the Winchester Troper (*c*. 1000) and the Old Hall Manuscript (early fifteenth century). Indeed, many hundreds of liturgical books were destroyed during the Reformation.[16] Where collections of material do appear to be complete in themselves, such as in the case of miscellanies that include one or more musical items, they are usually modest and reveal remarkable variety, especially in comparison with continental collections of organum, motets or trouvère song. It has become commonplace to mourn the paucity of the surviving material: Sanders once characterised thirteenth-century English music as a series of 'pitiful scraps and fragments'.[17] Lefferts has attributed the general lack of studies of English music to 'the vagaries of musical scholarship . . . the lack of sizeable integral manuscripts, the anonymity of English composers, and the apparent diversity and obscurity of their working environments'.[18]

There are clear indications that interest in early English music is in a healthy state, not least in growing areas of the discipline such as the reception of early music, the history of recordings and the history of performance.[19] The *Cambridge Companion to Medieval Music* included a valuable chapter on England, dealing with monophonic and polyphonic repertoire, in which Lefferts noted the common treatment of English music as peripheral to that from the European mainland. However, the considerable research undertaken since the Second World War had revealed a much fuller sense of the 'dimensions, vigour and creativity of medieval English musical life', matched by the growth of a back catalogue of recordings of the repertoire by performers such as Gothic Voices, the Hilliard Ensemble and Anonymous 4.[20] Finally, it is worth noting the significant advantage for scholars of the publication of editions, research blogs and digital images online over recent years. The most notable of these resources is the Digital Image Archive of Medieval Music, which makes it possible to study and compare the sources of English music still held across the length and breadth of Britain and internationally, and for scholars to respond dynamically to the identification of new music, to requests for assistance or to work-in-progress shared online. The result is a discipline that is increasingly enlivened, nimble and collegial. It is timely, then, for the present book to look back, in order to support the growing work in medieval music, and to negate the temptation for studies to fall into the same comfortable tales about the role and practice of music in Merrie England.

Retelling the stories of medieval English music

This book is stimulated by a desire to explore the ways that the stories of English medieval music have been constructed, received and transformed, to reveal the mythologies of Merrie England that continue to pervade recent discourse. My aim is to reappraise medieval English musical history, challenging assumptions, authorities, champions and legacies. There can be no single, authoritative chronology in English music; there remain many histories of English music waiting to be told. Instead, I will reveal common trajectories within music-historical writing in distant and more recent pasts, identify contradictions and open up avenues for future scholarship. While I may not always focus on what Kingsley Amis's Lucky Jim would have referred to as the 'strangely neglected topics', as outlined in the discussion above, it is certainly hoped that such work might be more possible as a result of the present study.

The structure of this book is thematic rather than strictly chronological, but it may be useful to note the majority of its source materials focus on the period from 1260 to 1460. Within English musical history, there are few precisely datable Significant Musical Events With Repercussions (to paraphrase Swanson), and indeed the death of Dunstaple in 1453 – sometimes used as a convenient borderline in the fifteenth century – is one of the events whose date is challenged in this book.[21] The earlier boundary line takes its signal from the provenance of 'Sumer is icumen in'; there is little doubt, for example, that in locating the genesis of modern music 'in England as far back as 1260', musicologist Edward J. Dent was alluding to this rota, widely accepted at the time as leading the canon of Western art music.[22] The song provides a valuable case study of how mythology functions; Chapter 1 traces how the piece achieved such a status, and how it served competing agendas, especially during the twentieth century.

Chapter 2 focuses on questions of politics, sanctity and identity in the thirteenth and fourteenth centuries. English song has commonly been viewed as separate from the country's political history, so – given the fundamental focus of the present book on music in relation to national history – it is worth pausing now to consider what can be gained from reassessing the role of music in developing understandings of nationhood. Although some may be troubled by the potential anachronism of discussing nationalism, Lavezzo and others have identified 'in medieval culture evidence of political structures – as well as structures of feeling – that anticipate the nation-state and the nationalist discourses of modernity'.[23] Emerging exemplars of Englishness were forged alongside and through musical creative products such liturgical song and motets. Far from being a stable category,

'English' historical identity was shaped from a morass of virile virgins, strong women, peaceful kings and mythical heroes. For English musicians and their patrons, or the monastic or secular institutions in which they lived and worked, the composition of liturgical music could be both a spiritual and a political act. The Latin-texted motet, a form that persisted in English sources at the expense of the cultivation of vernacular polyphonic song during the fourteenth century, was richly capable of channelling ideas of spiritual, regional or national identity, not least in motets that venerated English saints (or saints adopted as 'English') and were therefore part of their cults. Katherine Lewis has argued that:

> The value of studying a saint's cult lies not only in what it can tell us about the beliefs and practices associated with the veneration of the saint, but in the light it sheds on a whole range of matters pertaining to the society in which the cult flourishes.[24]

A study by Roman Hankeln has explored this point in relation to *historiae* ('liturgical chant cycles composed in honour of saints'), recognising that 'in celebrating patron saints, historiae simultaneously express the self-worth, values and ideals of communities', an idea that is compelling when applied also to votive music more generally, songs composed with the purpose of adding to the worship of holy figures.[25] As Hankeln, whose focus was on imagery of violence in medieval saints' offices, goes on to argue:

> It must be recalled that, in the Middle Ages, the saints functioned as figures manifesting religious and political ideals in concentrated form. Saints' legends concern key positive values, but they also established boundaries, reinforced stereotypes of the enemy and legitimated them, all against a broader Christian backdrop.[26]

English polyphony was part of that same devotional context, and drew readily and with poetic licence on the hagiographical materials available; many motets also incorporated liturgical quotation, not least through the manipulation of a preselected cantus firmus. In reference to medieval chronicles, Thorlac Turville-Petre has reflected that 'the form that a nation takes is justified by the history of its territory, people and institutions, so that writing history is fundamental to the establishment of national identity'.[27] Motets praising nationally significant figures were an important subset of that writing. The medieval English state emerged during the thirteenth and fourteenth centuries, and the king and his dynasty were at the heart of the representations of nationhood. Robert Davies concludes that although 'nation-states are ultimately mythological constructs', the country's 'cultic figure was quite simply the king of the English, *rex Anglorum*', a noble status shared by several of the saints worshipped in song.[28]

The notoriously problematic and nebulous idea of Englishness pervades this book, and is considered in critical detail in Chapter 3. 'Englishness' is loaded with many intractable historical associations, not least in today's political climate, and its meaning is made more ambiguous by loose application in every field since its first appearance in language. This originates in part from the historically slippery labels of England and Britain, which held very particular meanings in medieval writing at various times. As early as the tenth century, Ealdorman Aethelweard announced that Britain 'is now called England (*Anglia*), thereby assuming the name of the victors (*nomen victorum*)'.[29] Osbert of Clare, the prolific twelfth-century author, mourned the Norman Conquest as follows:

> And Great Britain [*maior Britannia*] herself, wet with the blood of her sons, burdened with sins, succumbed to a foreign race, who despoiled her of her crown and sceptre [. . .]. Therefore, after the death of the glorious king [Edward the Confessor], unhappy England [*infelix Anglia*] sustained this disaster, and today suffers a degradation ruinous to the native English [*innatis Anglis*].[30]

It is clear from historical writings of the later Middle Ages that an ambitious power plan transformed the nation so that Britain was rebranded as England, by virtue of the political power of the English throughout the four countries and peoples of the British Isles. But even by the end of the period treated in this book, England and Britain were neither stable nor consistently used labels. In the late fifteenth century, for example, the author John Capgrave wrote of 'Brytayn, the londe in whech we dwelle', yet it is impossible to say where he drew his own physical and imagined boundaries.[31] Britain's origins were seen to lie in the hero Brutus who settled on the island in ancient times, but Britons were only one people of many that influenced the mixture of nationalities over the subsequent ages. The fourteenth-century translator of *Brut* had put it as follows, emphasising the importance of immigration and noble bloodlines to early commentators:

> Þe grete lordes of Engeland were nouȝt alle of o nacioun, but were mellede wiþ oþere nacions, þat is forto seyn, somme Britons, somme Saxones, somme Danois, somme Peghtes, some Frenchemen, some Normans, somme Spaignardes, somme Henaudes, some Flemyngus, and of oþere diuerse naciouns, þe whiche nacions acorded nouȝt to þe kynde bloode of Engeland.

> The great lords of England were not all of one nation, but were mixed with other nations, in other words, some Britons, some Saxons, some Danish, some Picts, some Frenchmen, some Normans, some Spaniards, some Hainauts, some Flemings, and of other diverse nations, which accorded not to the natural blood of England.[32]

Musicologists have used the word 'English' to mean various things, and some have used expressions that avoid the term altogether because of its problematic nature.[33] In studies of medieval literature, the adjective 'English', when used to describe writing, lyrics or verse, applies exclusively to the substantial corpus of lyrics in Middle English. However, the majority of pre-1500 English music is anonymous, most of it is in Latin, and some is in French. It is only on the basis of a combination of evidence relating to textual and musical style, notational features or extra-musical evidence of provenance that one is able to claim that there is such a thing as an English repertory at all.[34] The word 'British' has sometimes been used, though occasionally only as a veil in discussions that, in fact, only explore English sources. During the Middle Ages, there was 'no such nation as "Britain"'.[35] Any term inevitably brings its own cultural baggage, but I have chosen to use 'English' and 'England' for this book, not least because these words were used as powerful tools throughout the Middle Ages by those who forged national identity through various cultural media. The ambiguity of how it felt to identify as English was challenged and focused through the products that redefined England's present through its cultural and religious past. The very construction of what it meant to be English, how this was expressed in music, and how the repertoire has subsequently been historicised, lies at the heart of many of the arguments presented here.

What does Englishness mean in relation to musical language and style? Writers with a nationalist agenda have sometimes sought to distinguish English stylistic features from those found in the music of other countries. A purpose of such analysis has been to demonstrate the influence, or the separatism, enjoyed by English musicians at various times. In some writings, it is possible to see a collapsing together of technical aspects of musical language and elements of ethnicity, not only of the composers responsible for creating music but also of the music so created. Moreover, previous focus on the role of 'great composers' within historical narratives – a linear impression that linked John Dunstaple to later masters such as Bach, Mozart and Beethoven – has cast anonymously preserved music, the musical contributions of women, improvised music and of what might be understood as amateur music-making further into the shadows.

The cult of authorship did not really exist for English music during the period 1260–1460, and certainly did not function in the same way as in later centuries. The problems of authorship – of claiming it, requiring it, understanding it – are the focus of Chapters 3 and 5 in particular. In many cases, we have only a limited knowledge of individual musicians, their working lives and the repertoire for which they were responsible. For some composers who held what must have been important musical posts – as chaplains for noble patrons, for example – there exist few or no pieces of music. The converse is true for John Dunstaple, many of whose works survive in English and continental sources, but whose biography remains obscure and problematic. The documents explored in Chapter 4 offer new evidence that both reinforce some biographical facts about the John Dunstaple for whom we have most evidence – a highly honoured esquire in the service of the nobility – while also destabilising the majority of this man's biography, since the documents reveal him to have died six years later than the composer's tomb apparently recorded. In this way, I take the opportunity to engage in what is quite firmly situated, methodologically, in historical musicology, as well as using the results of this enquiry to challenge our assumptions about the lives, careers and reputations of fifteenth-century English composers.

Chapter 6, '*Contenance angloise*: A reappraisal', takes a fresh look at an old musicological chestnut: the use of Martin le Franc's phrase as potentially suggestive of a host of ideas and practices in the fifteenth century. Variously understood as a style, compositional technique, as a nod to rhetoric, a manner of performance, and so on, (the) *contenance angloise* has been mapped onto particular musical devices. It is also used as evidence to link Dunstaple with a 'new' way of writing in the 1430s, an approach to musical language that has been understood to have influenced Dufay and other continental masters. A number of scholars have challenged the idea that such a shift in musical style occurred in the 1430s, or even that this is what le Franc and, later, Tinctoris were describing. However, in offering a further reading of le Franc's lines, I decouple *contenance angloise* from anything specifically musical or stylistic, suggesting that the phrase had a strong resonance for fifteenth-century readers with hagiographical writings that positioned Dunstaple and his fellow English composers with a native, Christian liturgical practice that went back to St Augustine and St Gregory, from whom sprung close identifications between Englishness and sanctity.

Angel Song: Medieval English music in history interrogates the country's musical history, assessing how musical debate has reflected broader culture attitudes. What would an account of early English music look like *without* prioritising 'Sumer is icumen in' as a masterwork? Is it possible or necessary to embrace the modern notion of decentering the author (or composer) in a predominantly anonymous repertoire? What if the few details we have of John Dunstaple's biography are challenged in the light of new evidence? Is it possible that the phrase *contenance angloise* reflected something other than a national musical style? The significance of the present book lies in its re-evaluation of these and other crucial questions from diverse historical and critical perspectives, including original archival work, to reach new answers.

Notes

1 Transcription of interview with James Brown (Leeds, 26 April 2002). York Mystery Plays Archive, www.yorkmysteryplays.org, Recording Reference: INT/08.
2 John Haines, *Music in Films on the Middle Ages: Authenticity vs. fantasy* (New York: Routledge, 2014).
3 Kirsten Yri, "Noah Greenberg and the New York Pro Musica: Medievalism and the cultural front," *American Music* 24 (2006): 421–44; John Haines, "The Revival of Medieval Music." In *The Cambridge History of Medieval Music*, 2 vols, edited by Mark Everist and Thomas Forrest Kelly (Cambridge: Cambridge University Press, 2017).
4 See Edward Breen, "The Performance Practice of David Munrow and the Early Music Consort of London." (PhD diss., King's College, London, 2014).
5 Haines, *Music in Films on the Middle Ages*, 4–5.
6 An important publication to embrace both chant and polyphony was the collection Susan Rankin and David Hiley eds, *Music in the Medieval English Liturgy* (Oxford: Clarendon Press, 1993), including a posthumous contribution from Frank Harrison.
7 Anne Bagnall Yardley, *Performing Piety: Musical culture in medieval English nunneries* (New York: Palgrave Macmillan, 2006); Matthew Cheung Salisbury with Andrew Hughes and Heather Robbins, *Cataloguing Discrepancies: The printed York*

10 *Introduction*

   breviary of 1493 (Toronto: University of Toronto Press, 2011); Matthew Cheung Salisbury, *The Use of York: Characteristics of the medieval liturgical office in York* (Borthwick Institute, University of York, 2008); Matthew Cheung Salisbury, *The Secular Liturgical Office in Late Medieval England (Medieval Church Studies)* (Turnhout: Brepols, 2015); Matthew Cheung Salisbury, Sally Harper and John Harper eds, *Lady Mass According to the Use of Salisbury*, Early English Church Music EC58 (London: British Academy, forthcoming).

8 There have been a small number of unpublished doctoral dissertations on this subject, notably Adele Smaill, "Medieval Carols: Origins, forms and performance contexts." (PhD diss., University of Michigan, 2003); and Kathleen Palti, " 'Synge we now alle and sum': Three fifteenth-century collections of communal song: A study of British library, Sloane MS 2593; Bodleian Library, MS Eng. poet. e.1; and St John's College, Cambridge, MS S.54." (PhD diss., University College, London, 2008). See also Helen Deeming, "The Sources and Origin of the 'Agincourt Carol'," *Early Music* 35 (2007).

9 Louise McInnes, "The Social, Political and Religious Contexts of the Late Medieval Carol: 1360–1520." (PhD diss., University of Huddersfield, 2014).

10 Nicky Losseff, *The Best Concords: Polyphonic music in thirteenth-century Britain* (New York: Garland, 1994); Peter M. Lefferts, *The Motet in England in the Fourteenth Century* (Michigan: Ann Arbor, 1986); Julie E. Cumming, *The Motet in the Age of Du Fay* (Cambridge: Cambridge University Press, 1999).

11 On the analysis of French motets, see Sylvia Huot, *Allegorical Play in the Old French Motet* (Stanford: Stanford University Press, 1997); Lisa Colton, "The Articulation of Virginity in the Medieval *Chanson de nonne*," *Journal of the Royal Musical Association*, 133 (2008); Emma Dillon, *The Sense of Sound: Musical meanings in France, 1260–1330* (Oxford and New York: Oxford University Press, 2012).

12 Reinhard Strohm, *The Rise of European Music, 1380–1500* (Cambridge: Cambridge University Press, 1993), 80–1.

13 Peter M. Lefferts, "England." In *Cambridge Companion to Medieval Music*, edited by Mark Everist (Cambridge: Cambridge University Press, 2011), 108. Fragments of secular, popular traditions are recoverable in some ways, such as through the extraction of English-texted melodies from motet tenors. In adding some further thoughts as to evidence for popular musics from this period, Lefferts warns against seeing English-texted songs as necessarily 'popular' on account of their language; "England," 109. There is no equivalent repertoire to that of the Spanish Cantigas de Santa Maria, or the courtly love songs of the troubadours and trouvères, though the corpus of Latin-, French- and English-texted songs from medieval Britain is surprisingly substantial, as shown by recent editions by Helen Deeming and David Fallows in particular; see Helen Deeming transcr. and ed. "Songs in British Sources *c.* 1150–1300". *Musica Britannica* 95 (London: Stainer and Bell, 2013); David Fallows, ed. "Secular Polyphony 1380–1480". *Musica Britannica* 97 (London: Stainer and Bell, 2014).

14 Christopher Page, *Discarding Images: Reflections on music and culture in medieval France* (Oxford: Oxford University Press, 1993); Daniel Leech-Wilkinson, *The Modern Invention of Medieval Music: Scholarship, ideology, performance* (Cambridge: Cambridge University Press, 2002). John Haines, "The Arabic Style of Performing Medieval Music," *Early Music* 29 (2001) challenged the assumptions of performers who integrate non-Western performance practices in modern performances of European medieval music. Reception of medieval repertoire was also at the heart of his Eight Centuries of Troubadours and Trouvères: *The Changing Identity of Medieval Music* (Cambridge: Cambridge University Press, 2004).

15 Nicholas Temperley, "Review [Untitled] of *The Oxford History of English Music: Volume 1: From the Beginnings to c. 1715* by John Caldwell," *Notes* 49 (1992), 542–3.

16   The Winchester Troper comprises two collections, now Oxford, Bodleian Library MS Bodley 775 and Cambridge, Corpus Christi College, MS 473. The Old Hall Manuscript is London, British Library Additional MS 57950; I will refer to it in this book by its common name rather than its shelf mark. The most recent editions are Susan Rankin, ed. "The Winchester Troper, Introduction and Facsimile", *Early English Church Music* 50 (London: Stainer and Bell, 2007); Margaret Bent and Andrew Hughes, eds. "The Old Hall Manuscript". *Corpus Mensurabilis Musicae* 46, 3 vols (n.p.: American Institute of Musicology, 1969–73).

17   Ernest Sanders, "The Medieval Motet." In *Gattungen der Musik in Einzeldarstellung: Gedenkschrift Leo Schrade*, edited by Wulf Arlt (Berne: Francke Verlag, 1973), 538.

18   Lefferts, *The Motet in England*, 1.

19   Conference sessions at the Medieval and Renaissance Music Conference have included themed various panels on English music, often including thoughtful and provocative work by early career researchers in these areas.

20   Lefferts, "England," 107.

21   Rodney N. Swanson, *Church and Society in Late Medieval England* (Oxford: Blackwell, 1989), x.

22   Edward J. Dent, "The Relation of Music to Human Progress," *The Musical Quarterly* 14 (1928), 316; cited in Annegret Fauser, "The Scholar Behind the Medal: Edward J. Dent (1876–1957) and the Politics of Music History," *Journal of the Royal Musical Association* 139 (2014), 236.

23   Kathy Lavezzo, ed. *Imagining a Medieval English Nation* (Minneapolis, MN: University of Minnesota Press, 2003), viii.

24   Katherine J. Lewis, "'Rule of lyf alle folk to sewe': Lay Responses to the Cult of St Katherine of Alexandria in Late-Medieval England, 1300–1530" (DPhil diss., University of York, 1996), 5.

25   Roman Hankeln and James Borders, "Forward," *Plainsong and Medieval Music* 23 (2014), 1.

26   Roman Hankeln, "Reflections of War and Violence in Early and High Medieval Saints' Offices," *Plainsong and Medieval Music* 23 (2014), 5–30, at p. 6.

27   Thorlac Turville-Petre, *England the Nation: Language, literature and identity, 1290–1340* (Oxford: Clarendon Press, 1996), 71.

28   Robert R. Davies, *The First English Empire: Power and identities in the British Isles 1093–1343* (Oxford: Oxford University Press, 2000), 199–200.

29   Chronicle of Aethelweard, ed. *A Campbell* (1969), 9; cited in Davies, *The First English Empire*, 49.

30   Osbert of Clare, cited in Barlow, Frank. *The Life of King Edward Who Rests at Westminster, Attributed to a Monk of St Bertin* (London: Thomas Nelson and Sons, 1962), 71.

31   Karen A. Winstead, ed. *John Capgrave: The life of Saint Katherine* (Kalamazoo, Michigan: Medieval Institute Publications, 1999), 7.

32   *Brut*, i. 220, II. 17–23; quoted in Turville-Petre, *England the Nation*, 17, my translation.

33   Terms such as Anglo-Norman, Anglo-French or the French of England are part of on-going debates relating to historical and cultural boundaries, not only linguistic difference. The designation 'Angevin' (relating to the period between the Norman Conquest and *c.* 1225) applies to the royal line of Anjou, rather than to a country, so does not function effectively as nomenclature for musical style. See Robert Bartlett, *England Under the Norman and Angevin Kings 1075–1225* (Oxford: Clarendon Press, 2000); Mark Everist, "Anglo-French Interaction in Music *c.* 1170–*c.*1300," *Revue Belge de Musicologie* 46 (1992). An important study of English and British identities is Davies, *The First English Empire*.

34 These points have been raised by Warwick Edwards, who has examined the possibility that some of the pieces in the thirteenth-century source W1 had a Scottish rather than necessarily English origin; "Polyphony in Thirteenth-Century Scotland," In *'Our Awin Scottis Use': Music in the Scottish Church up to 1603*, edited by Sally Harper and Isobel Woods Preece (Glasgow: Universities of Glasgow and Aberdeen, 2000). Idiosyncrasies in English notations have been discussed by Peter M. Lefferts (1990a): "English Music Theory in Respect to the Dating of Polyphonic Repertories in England, 1320–1399." *Atti del XIV congresso della Società Internazionale di Musicologia, Bologna, 1987: Transmissione et recezione delle forme di cultura musicale*, 653–8. Turin: Edizioni di Torino.

35 Turville-Petre, *England the Nation*, 15.

1 'The greatest musical curiosity extant'

'Sumer is icumen in' and the canon of English music

Sumer is icumen in,
Lhude sing cuccu,
GroweÞ sed and bloweÞ med
And springÞ Þe wde nu,
Sing cuccu!
Awe bleteÞ after lomb,
LhouÞ after calue cu.
Bulluc sterteÞ, bucke verteÞ,
Murie sing cuccu!
Cuccu, cuccu, wel singes Þu cuccu;
Ne swik Þu naver nu.

Perspice Christicola
que dignacio,
celicus agricola
pro vitis vicio,
filio non parcens
exposuit mortis exicio,
qui captivos semivivos a supplicio,
vite donat et secum coronat
in celi solio.

Summer has arrived, loudly sing cuckoo. The seed grows and the meadow blossoms and the wood now sprouts [into bud]. Sing cuckoo! The ewe bleats for the lamb, the cow lows for the calf; the bullock leaps, the buck cavorts – merrily sing cuckoo! Cuckoo, cuckoo! Well do you sing, cuckoo; do not ever cease now.

Pay heed, Christian, what graciousness: the heavenly farmer, because of a fault of the vine, not sparing his son, exposed him to death's destruction; he who restores to life the captives half-living from [their] punishment, and crowns them [together] with himself in heaven's throne.

Pes I: Sing cuccu nu, sing cuccu.
Pes II: Sing cuccu. Sing cuccu nu,
Pes I and II: Sing cuckoo now, sing, cuckoo.[1]

The medieval song 'Sumer is icumen in', with its alternative Latin lyric 'Perspice Christicola', relates to the idea of canon in two ways. Most simply, it is a piece with parts written 'in canon' – a *rota* or round – whose main melody can be split into parts and sung in staggered succession over the *pedes*, which themselves alternate and overlap. But it also relates to notions of 'canon' more conceptually, in that – unusually, for a piece of medieval music – it has been treated as an important part of the history of Western music, a history traditionally taught using a 'canon' of works identified as landmarks of creativity and ingenuity.

It has long been lamented that curricula, scholarship and performing traditions that focus primarily on the standard archetypes of 'great musical works' misrepresent the creative achievements of the past. The historical landscape found in conventional textbooks has changed little since the nineteenth century, when the so-called canon of Western music became established. Books tend to focus on the major works of men (and it is usually men) considered to exemplify greatness in their time: Haydn's string quartets, Beethoven's symphonies or Wagner operas, for example, works of length and longevity, works whose quality can be demonstrated in their complexity, technical refinement and expressive power.[2]

It can be almost impossible for pieces that do not neatly fit the criteria of greatness outlined above to get noticed. Medieval music is one of a number of marginalised repertories, alongside music by women, music by non-white composers, music composed collaboratively, improvised music, pedagogical music and most forms of popular and world musics. Measured against the relatively stable criteria for entry to standard historical accounts – and thus for entry into the canon of Western music – these repertories have been found wanting. Individual pieces might be ephemeral, orally transmitted or written for amateur performance circuits; they may be intentionally entertaining rather than edifying; their structures may not seem as rigorous as those underpinned by tonality; they may have gone unnoticed in standard documents of reception such as music criticism; they may never have been published; they may be too short to be considered sufficiently substantial; they may exist in flexible versions, covers or arrangements, rather than being fixed in printed scholarly editions. As a result of these factors, a very small number of pieces of medieval or renaissance music have come to the forefront of public consciousness. Even within early music circles, there seems to be a modest number of medieval songs that are intimately familiar.[3] Indeed, many are drawn to early music by virtue of its relative obscurity, and its potential to enrich one's cultural and historical perspective on music; curiosity is a common impetus for scholars and performers working in the field.[4]

Paradoxically, a few early English pieces have become so well-known through their alignment with canonic criteria that they have reached the status of popular classic, acquiring their own mythology. Within renaissance repertoire, the iconic piece is 'Greensleeves', a song that remains readily identifiable to audiences today, even if it is probably understood by many as broadly 'old' music rather than through a detailed knowledge of its chronological context. The success of 'Greensleeves' lies primarily in its association with Henry VIII (1491–1547), erroneously identified as its composer and lyricist, who was supposed to have written it for his beloved *du jour*, Anne Boleyn. 'Greensleeves' – the first surviving evidence of which dates to the late sixteenth century – was transmitted enthusiastically by composers and performers in the centuries that followed; variations on the tune are extant for various solo and consort combinations from the seventeenth century, for example. The visual arts have also played their part in mythologising the tune. Nineteenth-century artists used 'Greensleeves' in their romantic re-imaginings of early modern culture, notably in two separate paintings entitled *My Lady Greensleeves* by Dante Gabriel Rossetti (1859 and 1863). In the earlier painting (Figure 1.1), which features the melody in the upper portion of the image, the composition suggests a late medieval or early Tudor maiden lamenting the absence of her knight, winding her green sleeves around his helmet. A label once on the back of the 1863 painting (see Figure 1.2) contained Rossetti's poetic note, conveying the romantic reimagining of the lady in relation to the original song:

> She bound her green sleeve on my helm
> Sweet pledge of love's sweet meed
> Warm was the bared arm round my neck
> As well she bade me speed;
> And her kiss clings still between my lips,
> Heart's heat and strength at need.

By the twentieth century, the tune had become symbolic of the English historical past as well as of its music. As Michael Flanders, of musical comedy duo Flanders and Swann, concluded in his satirical monologue on the history of 'Greensleeves' (1956), 'To this very day, in every period play you go to see, set in 1300 up to about 1715, I suppose, still for incidental music, Greensleeves is always played'.[5] Each recopying, rearrangement of the melody in other works, or use in diverse media contexts since its creation has re-emphasised the importance of the song in history and offered the opportunity to repeat romantic myth that an English king composed it for his mistress, a distortion of musical history that is so ingrained as to be practically irreversible. And in the early part of the twentieth century, many composers drew on the melody as part of wider interest in recovering and preserving British folk music. Gustav Holst, for example, wove 'Greensleeves' into the finale of his Second Suite for Military Band Op. 28 No. 2 (1911) and again in his St Paul's Suite Op. 29 No. 2 (1912) alongside the melody 'Dargason' from John Playford's *The English Dancing Master* (1651), creating works that entwined national and musical identities. Perhaps most famously, Ralph Vaughan Williams's *Fantasia on Greensleeves* (1934) cemented a modern association between the melody and the concepts of Englishness and nostalgia with which his music has become associated.

From the period before 'Greensleeves' was composed, the most well-known piece of English music – and the only one to rival the cult status of the sixteenth-century song – is 'Sumer is icumen in'. Although it is fair to acknowledge that its place within the popular imagination has diminished over the past century, its use on the cover of early music concert programmes for the 1951 Festival of Britain is just one example of the song's cultural resonance mid-century. Standard historical accounts of British music would seem incomplete without consideration of 'Sumer is icumen in' and its partner, 'Greensleeves'. Chappell's *Popular Music of the Olden Time* (1844), for example, included facsimiles of both pieces, calling the medieval song 'the greatest musical curiosity extant'.[6] John Haines has observed that:

> although antiquarianism on medieval song and dance was often distinct from looser medievalisms such as the ballad, the two broad strands of medievalism – antiquarian and popular – frequently overlapped. For example, the first

16 '*The greatest musical curiosity extant*'

Figure 1.1 Dante Gabriel Rossetti, *My Lady Greensleeves* (1859)

London, British Museum (Registration number 1954,0508.1). Melody and lyrics appear in the top right of the image. © Trustees of the British Museum

'The greatest musical curiosity extant' 17

volume of Chappell's *Popular Music of the Olden Time*, written for a lay audience, opened with a facsimile of 'Sumer is icumen in' and featured an historical 'Essay on English Minstrelsy'.[7]

In 1956, Flanders's monologue on 'Greensleeves' joked that in trying to find a hit song to close the first half of a new musical, the sixteenth-century writers first looked to use 'Sumer is icumen in', 'but this had got itself on the banned list;

Figure 1.2 Dante Gabriel Rossetti, *My Lady Greensleeves* (1863)
Harvard Art Museums/Fogg Museum, Bequest of Grenville L. Winthrop, 1943. 203

18 *'The greatest musical curiosity extant'*

Figure 1.3 Sumer is icumen in (1920) painted by Ernest Board (1877–1934)
Copyright Reading Museum (Reading Borough Council). All rights reserved

people had been singing "cuccu" rather too lewdly'. (The quotation from the song's tenor, 'Sing cu cu nu, sing cu cu', was perhaps associated by Flanders and Swann's audiences with the knowing nonsense lyric 'fa la la' found in saucier English madrigals.) Instead, of course, the fictitious composers of the musical were inspired to choose 'Greensleeves' by the unexpected appearance, at the back of the theatre, of Henry VIII.

As with 'Greensleeves', 'Sumer is icumen in' has been subject to various romantic re-imaginings, not least the evocative painting by Ernest Board. Displayed in Reading Museum, Board's image shows the monk composer receiving divine inspiration from a nightingale within the abbey cloister, an image that recalls St Gregory's alleged reception of liturgical chant melody from the dove representing the Holy Spirit (see Figure 1.3). The central purpose of the remainder of this chapter, then, is to consider the song from a historiographical perspective in order to reveal developments in the understanding of both the song in particular and English musical history as a whole.

'Sumer is icumen in' becomes a work

Warren Dwight Allen, comparing and evaluating various approaches to the telling of music history, called 'Sumer is icumen in' 'an indispensible beginning for every history of counterpoint.'[8] Even the editors of the very first edition of the *Grove Dictionary of Music and Musicians*, a project that claimed to track the history of music only after 1450, included an entry on 'Sumer is icumen in', making an exception to its chronological remit and placing the song at the head of the fourth volume so that the title appeared on the spine.[9] 'Sumer is icumen in' has quite literally become a monument of musical history: the unveiling of a stone tablet in the chapterhouse of Reading Abbey in 1913, decorated with a colour facsimile of the appropriate page of the manuscript source, was marked by the publication of a fifty-page book by Jamieson Boyd Hurry, a volume that summarised the current understanding of the music and its historical context.[10] The stone carving, a representation of the real monument of the book itself, remains on the cloister wall of Reading Abbey; the musical source has long been held by the British Library, where postcards of the song in facsimile are often for sale in the gift shop.

The song has dominated scholarship on medieval English music since its first description in print and has been included in musical anthologies and histories aimed at academic and popular markets throughout this time. W. S. Rockstro's article on the song in *Grove* records that the manuscript 'was first described by Mr. Wanley [. . .] who, acting in the capacity of Librarian to the Earl of Oxford, wrote an account of it in his "Catalogue of the Harleian MSS," about the year 1709'.[11] *Grove* included a transcription and a generous description of the piece in a separate article entitled 'Schools of Composition §XVI The Early English Schools (1226–1625)', which included a full-page facsimile.[12] The song has subsequently received substantial treatment in scholarship in reference to its origins, notation, poetry and stylistic context.[13]

The rota's single source, London, British Library Harley 978 (hereafter GB-Lbl 978), was described in detail by the early music historians of John Hawkins (1719–89) and Charles Burney (1726–1814), as well as various nineteenth-century writers.[14] It has also been made to represent different (sometimes contradictory) aspects of English music in its use within writing, film and in its integration in more recent musical works. We can see hints of canonicity already being claimed for the piece by Rockstro who, concurring with Charles Coussemaker's argument that the piece had been written by 1226, offered only a modest amount of caution in his boast that the date of the manuscript 'does not absolutely prove that the Art of Composition originated in England'.[15] Such a statement hinted at the weight of pressure to establish a canon in which England's musicians were prominent, not least at the end of a century when the cultural impact of English music was considered much more limited. It also demonstrates that, for Rockstro, the rota was conceptualised as art music, a *Werk* that showed creative artistry, rather than something more functional.[16] As such, two historical elements were being manipulated: the piece was being positioned at the vanguard of Western music, and the requirements of the music-historical canon were leading to the emphasis of selected aspects of the song's history over others.

It was Charles Burney's *A General History of Music* that brought 'Sumer is icumen in' to wider attention.[17] Many of Burney's observational points about the song were secure, from the transcription of the piece to his explanation of its distinctive performance practice; only the dating of the *rota*, to the fourteenth or fifteenth century, has been significantly revised by subsequent research. The most recent scholarship on 'Sumer is icumen in' locates its copying to Reading at some point between 1261 and 1265.[18] The piece was remarkable to those studying ancient music primarily by virtue of its structure since pieces built as complete musical canons do not survive until examples of the *chace* in the Ivrea Codex (Ivrea, Biblioteca Capitolare 115) and Italian *caccia* approximately a century later. 'Sumer is icumen in' contains similar pastoral imagery to such pieces. However, it lacks the hunting themes typical of these genres, and its two-chord harmonic 'ground' sets it apart.[19] It shares its consideration of human and bird-like expressions of cuckoo song with the fourteenth-century song 'Talent m'a pris', also a *chace*/canon.[20] As Elizabeth Eva Leach notes, 'Talent m'a pris' may have been used in part for pedagogical purposes, as it is found between a complex motet by Philippe de Vitry and some musical exercises.[21] The English rota is flanked in its only medieval source by a rubric describing the way in which the song should ideally be sung, instructions that indicate that the scribe viewed 'Sumer is icumen in' as a song for six performers: four on the main melody, singing in turn, and two holding the *pes* (tenor line) 'Sing cu cu', also in canon and starting with the first upper voice. The appearance of such a detailed rubric in an English manuscript of this date may also be indicative of a pedagogical role for 'Sumer is icumen in'. The tenor line singers are also instructed to sing their lines as many times as required, paying attention to the appropriate rests.

> Hanc rotam cantare possint quatuor socii; a paucioribus autem quam a tribus vel saltem duobus non debet dici, preter eos qui dicunt pedem. Canitur autem

sic: tacentibus cetertis unus inchoat cum hiis qui tenent pedem. Et cum venerit ad primam notam post crucem, inchoat alius, et sic de ceteris. Singuli vero repausent ad pausaciones scriptas et non alibi, spacio unius longe note.

This rota can be sung by four people together; however, it should not be sung by fewer than three, or at least two, not counting those who sing the 'pes'. And it is sung in this way: while the others remain silent, one person starts, together with those who are carrying the 'pedes' [tenor lines]; and when he comes to the first note after the cross, the next one begins, and so on with the others. And the individual singers should stop at the rests where they are written and not elsewhere, for the space of one long note.

For Burney, this was a 'curious composition' and a 'descriptive song'. Burney used words that bestowed the honour of a work ('composition') to a very early piece, and also related it to illustrative repertoire of his own age, perhaps to the evocations of birdsong that were known from the instrumental music of Vivaldi or in many an eighteenth-century parlour song. As one might expect, Burney judged the song against contemporary criteria for success, which were topped by the sophistication of melody and harmony that Burney valued in the music of his own age, as exemplified by Joseph Haydn:

Though this *Canon* and *Catch*, united, is very ingeniously contrived, and has not only more melody, but is in better harmony than I have hitherto found of so early a period; yet, in point of composition though its defects may not be discovered by every *Ear* during the performance, it is hardly clean and pure enough to satisfy the *Eye*, in score: as many liquors may be tolerably palatable, and yet not bear a glass.[22]

A sip of medieval song was quite enough for Burney. Chief among his complaints were the profusion of parallel perfect intervals, prohibited by more recent treatises of counterpoint. He also found it monotonous, perhaps in comparison with the canons and catches of the eighteenth century.

Over at least the past two centuries, those writing about the history of music have categorised and classified works and their creators, creating abstract 'canons' that allowed the prioritisation of particular pieces and composers in discussion, editing and performance. A preoccupation with the concept of canon also led to researchers examining pre-tonal music for precursors to modern symphonic classics. This attitude has more recently been called into question. Andrew Kirkman, for example, has criticised the dominance of the polyphonic Mass in historical writing: 'Why', he asks, 'has the Mass based on a cantus firmus been singled out as historically and artistically superior not just to songs and motets, but to Masses not based on recurring musical material?'[23]

Writers on English music focused especially on the putative Golden Age, notably the Elizabethan and Jacobean courts in which the madrigal flourished; amateur musicians performed such repertoire in madrigal, glee and catch clubs even in the nineteenth century, relishing their country's 'ancient' music in relation to the light songs of their own time. As Suzanne Cole has explained in her work on the reception of Thomas Tallis's music, nineteenth-century writers frequently sidelined works that were created for functional or liturgical contexts in their accounts, prioritising discussion of secular song.[24] The most valued repertoire was demonstrably not only skilfully composed, but was also part of a distinctive, creative process. The same attitude has prevailed to the present day: in relation to the notion of the musical work, Lydia Goehr remarks that 'We do not treat works as objects just made or put together, like tables and chairs, but as original, unique products of a special, creative activity'.[25] The central problem that faces medieval music, in terms of its canonic value, has been this very simile. So often in discussions of pre-Reformation English music, one comes across the 'justification' of composer anonymity in terms of the musicians seeing themselves not as individual artists, seeking fame and glory, but in the same bracket as those craftsmen and women who provided stained glass windows, church furniture or decorations.[26]

We can see the difficulties for scholars attempting to view the song as a work in the traditional sense through their discussions of the lack of fixity in the notation in GB-Lbl 978. The revised form of the melody was first identified by Wooldridge in 1901.[27] In one of the fullest explorations of the genesis of the song in written form, Wolfgang Obst argued that there were six stages in the making of the *rota*: the Latin poem was pre-existent; the poem was set to a rota; an English text was created; the piece was copied into GB-Lbl 978; and lastly changes were made to the musical notation for clarification, and finally for modernisation.[28] The most recent edition, by Deeming, presents the 'earlier' version of the melody before it had been adjusted by later scribal intervention; although the differences are relatively few, they reveal something of the challenges of dealing with notions of textual fixity – as modern editors have to – in medieval song.

'Sumer is icumen in' and English music history

English music history has been formed by diverse traditions of writing over the ages. In the Middle Ages, annals, chronicles, treatises and legends – though not purporting to be accurate historical accounts – alluded to the shaping of musical practices, sometimes highlighting the input of individuals or nations.[29] Musicians of the sixteenth and seventeenth centuries cited English music as influential but did not concern themselves with writing historical descriptions of repertoire or stylistic development.[30] Eighteenth-century writers examined manuscripts with the intention of reflecting the progress made in notational and contrapuntal practice, while always holding up examples of medieval music as primitive forms of the tonal repertoire of their present. This was also an age of taxonomies, studies that sought to categorise and document the arts in a scientific, objective manner, forging them into what has become known as the musical canon. As long-forgotten music manuscripts were rediscovered and evaluated in the nineteenth and twentieth centuries, new information was embedded into what was, by at least 1900, a standardised narrative of English music.

Burney helped to establish the commonly held perception of a lack of significant music produced in the early medieval period in England, commenting for example that during the pre-Conquest period in Britain, 'no works of taste or genius, in the polite arts, appear to have been produced at this time in any part of it'.[31] Burney had been keen to attribute any sign of musical accomplishment to the influence of Roman or Greek models, from the knowledge of instruments to the ability to sing in harmony. This was in keeping with Enlightenment ideals of their own cultural achievements. However, the story was in opposition to that told by Gerald of Wales (c. 1146–c. 1223), who described what he saw as a peculiarly northern-English skill of singing in two parts, and claimed that it had been achieved through Norwegian and Danish conquest:

> In their musical concerts [the Welsh] do not sing in unison like the inhabitants of other countries, but in many different parts; so that in a company of singers, which one very frequently meets with in Wales, you will hear as many different parts and voices as there are performers, who all at length unite, with organic melody, in one consonance and the soft sweetness of B flat. In the northern district of Britain, beyond the Humber, and on the borders of Yorkshire, the inhabitants make use of the same kind of symphonious harmony, but with less variety; singing only in two parts, one murmuring in the base [sic], the other warbling in the acute or treble. Neither of the two nations has acquired this peculiarity by art, but by long habit, which has rendered it natural and familiar; and the practice is now so firmly rooted in them, that it is unusual to hear a simple and single melody well sung; and, what is still more wonderful, the children, even from their infancy, sing in the same manner. As the English in general do not adopt this mode of singing, but only those of the northern countries, I believe that it was from the Danes and Norwegians, by whom these parts of the island were more frequently invaded, and held longer under their dominion, that the natives contracted their mode of singing as well as speaking.[32]

However, Burney, who reflected on Gerald of Wales's discussion, reassigned these same vocal practices to the influence of the ancient Romans, 'who may probably have first brought over the art of *discant,* or *double singing*'.[33] The musicological writing of the nineteenth century continued to seek the origins of musical talent in the distant past, though not always finding it in the same place as had Burney or Gerald of Wales. Frederick Crowest's *The Story of British Music*, for example, promoted a view that the Druids had been responsible, influenced by men from the East, arguing that the Romans occupied Britain with no lasting impact on the country's musical traditions. 'Indeed,' as Bennett Zon has reflected, in Frederick Crowest's eyes, 'British music retained its "warmth and sympathetic character, untainted by any influence of the conquerors"'.[34] In these three accounts by Gerald, Burney and Crowest, we can see the making of music history according to the social context of their own time. Whereas it served Burney to identify with Classical civilisation, a more isolationist perspective allowed Crowest to champion British achievements as strongly independent of its Roman conquerors' culture.

In relation to the later medieval era, music historians continued to seek major figures (or Schools) in the composition of sacred, or (preferably) secular, vocal polyphony, as this type of music was seen as most individual, artistic, sophisticated and personalised in comparison with monophonic or instrumental music. Inextricably bound within the values of the Western canon developed over the past three hundred years, English repertoire was seemingly deficient in terms of 'great works', whose pre-eminence would have been attested by their copying into luxuriously illuminated manuscripts, with firm composer attributions, a wide dissemination and contemporary discussions of their significance.

The favouring of 'Sumer is icumen in' within musical discourse can be accounted for not only because of its unique musical structure, but primarily because commentators have approached it as a significant moment in English musical history.[35] It has appeared in numerous publications, from scholarly editions to materials designed for use in the school curriculum. In 1944, Manfred Bukofzer was able to remark that 'so much has been written about the Summer-canon that further discussion may seem all but superfluous'.[36] Almost as a response to this concern, the edition of the song in the 1946 *Historical Anthology of Music* was accompanied by the commentary: 'This composition is too well-known to require explanatory remarks'.[37] As Ross Duffin reflected in 1988, 'Since that time, the tide of writings has not been stemmed, and popular enthusiasm for this most famous of medieval compositions has not diminished', a comment that might do just as well to describe the decades since his own article on the subject.[38] In order to understand the common tropes of English music, it is therefore crucial to question how 'Sumer is icumen in' has achieved a position in musicological scholarship awarded to no other piece from the repertory.

'Sumer is icumen in' has been subjected to scrupulous musical and textual analysis. Within the history of Middle English lyric, it has featured prominently in texts analysing its poetic structure. Musically, the piece has been approached using methods usually reserved for tonal repertoire, aligning it by implication with the instrumental works of the Classical and Romantic periods that were the focus of primarily pitch-based analytical systems. Indeed, Sanders argued that 'the Summer Canon is the earliest extant secular composition that must be called a tonal organism, both harmonically and melodically'.[39] Peter Marr broke the melodic aspect into short figures (see Figure 1.4), speculating an earlier, now lost, simple version of the song, which may have incorporated instrumental lines; he also analysed the earlier and revised versions of the melody as found in GB-Lbl 978.[40] Shai Burstyn identified melodic 'formulae' with 'Sumer is icumen in', arguing for an interrelationship with other insular repertoire through the use of common phrases, as well as producing a quasi-Schenkerian reductive melodic framework, complete with descending *Ersatz*.[41]

Criticism of these types of approach predated the above analyses by some time: as early as 1949, Jacques Handschin made the reasonable assessment that:

Figure 1.4 Speculative earlier version of 'Sumer is icumen in'

Peter Marr, 'The Melody of "Sumer is icumen in"', *The Musical Times*, 108 (1967), 1105; by permission of The Musical Times Publications Ltd

Modern musicians have perhaps been too impressed by the use of the canonic device in our composition, but this device is not in itself a sign of art; they have also been impressed by the 'natural sweetness' of the harmony, but that only because it anticipates their cherished 'perfect chord' habits.[42]

Handschin's criticism of Bukofzer here was equally directed at writers who used features such as indications of binary rhythm and sonority to force 'Sumer is icumen in' into a fourteenth-century copying context, when such elements were described in French theoretical treatises. As Busse Berger has explained, Handschin was 'deeply opposed to an evolutionary interpretation of music history', as exemplified by Friedrich Ludwig who preferred to consider musical expression and technique within its own cultural context, in part as a result of his experience of folk music traditions and his overall empathy with ethnomusicology as it was understood at that time.[43]

The employment, by some writers, of nicknames for the piece such as the 'Reading rota', 'the Summer canon', or simply 'Sumer' has helped to situate the piece in the popular imagination in a similar manner to the 'Moonlight' sonata or 'Jupiter' symphony, and has reflected that 'the song's rustic theme and quaint spelling has come to represent the very essence of 'Merrie England'.[44] The definite article, *the* Summer Canon – with an unspoken *the* [*one and only*] – crops into many accounts, serving to monumentalise the song: Paul Henry Lang's *Music in Western Civilization*, for example, referred to it as 'the famous Summer canon', a piece that represented 'a unique monument of medieval polyphony'.[45] Poetic titles have also provided a hook for a piece whose authorship is unknown, and which may have originated as collective improvisation rather than formal, 'single-authored' composition. 'Sumer is icumen in' is contained in a manuscript compilation that contains a wide range of sacred and secular material, including the *Lais* of Marie de France, Marian lyrics in Latin, instrumental items, a copy of *Ysope*, a tantalising list of (since largely lost) pieces of liturgical polyphony, and a liturgical calendar; though its contents are of great interest, it is one of about thirty miscellanies containing music that have survived from the twelfth and thirteenth centuries.[46] Having studied its codicology in detail, Deeming views the manuscript GB-Lbl 978 as follows: 'far from being the work of a single scribe, consciously intended as a collection, the various contents of Harley 978 may have ended up together through the more random choices of several compilers'.[47] It seems dangerously anachronistic to describe the rota as being 'found in a collection of art-music', and thus suggestive of it 'being the product of a learned composer', as Burstyn once did, though such views are not untypical.[48] Deeming's examination of the manuscript has revealed evidence that it was likely to be 'the product of a small group of educated enthusiasts, with interests in collecting and preserving literature and in recording and cultivating music', and cautioned against overemphasising the sequence of items and quires as any sort of pre-determined collection by a single author.[49]

If 'Sumer is icumen in' has been depicted as part of a collection whose internal coherence has been overstated, it is no surprise that the piece has been described as a 'work' in the modern sense, particularly in view of the technical aspects of the *rota*. Nineteenth-century writer Rockstro argued that 'the "Reading Rota" is no rude attempt at Vocal Harmony. It is a regular Composition', distinguishing the song from associations with music devised through collaborative performance practices of the age.[50] A similar attitude can be found several decades later in Harrison's remarks that 'it is a measure of the composer's artistry that he succeeded in realizing these technical requirements in a piece of such enduring charm and attractiveness'.[51] Harrison's words recall critics of Bach, squaring the 'mere' technical mastery of complex fugal writing against the *artistic* value of the work itself, a result always ascribed to the composer's particular genius.

The use of criteria that form the foundation of writing on works of the musical canon can also be detected in scholars' eagerness to show either the innovative nature of the work (usually located in its structure) or in its influence on other repertories, despite our lack of evidence that the piece was ever found outside of its single surviving source. Sanders, in particular, sought to articulate the piece as indicative of more general English influence on the Parisian repertoire of the thirteenth century:

> Owing to freakish luck it has been preserved through the centuries and indicates the prior existence of a highly developed musical culture that evidently exerted a vital influence on the specifically English evolution of the conductus and the motet in 13th-century England as well as on the second generation of Notre Dame composers.[52]

With only a single copy of the song – ironically, one of its many points of interest – and no further contemporary references to it, such claims must remain speculative. The link between the anthologising of 'Sumer is icumen in' and perceptions of the piece's influence is subtle but important. As Marcia Citron has written, in relation to later repertoire:

> The 'great pieces' paradigm, underlying the notion of anthologized works, exerts tremendous power. A tacit assumption is that anthologized works embody high quality and exemplify the important stylistic and historical points that students should know. In varying proportions, each composition is deemed significant in its own right and representative of other works of like-minded values. [. . .] It suggests that the work and composer exemplify a style that influenced others; for works after 1800 add innovative and original.[53]

The collision of sacred and secular worlds

The categorisation of works as 'liturgical' has historically emphasised their functionality, their purpose in an additional context to the absolute or purely musical. By extension, the designation of a piece as secular has brought with it an assumption of intrinsic musical value. Cole has argued that the early music movement has been 'a campaign to bring an increasingly wide range of music under the concept of the autonomous musical work, and the secularisation and aestheticisation of early sacred music are a direct consequence of this'.[54] 'Sumer is icumen in' is a song easily neutralised of religious context by ignoring its alternative Latin lyric, *Perspice Christicola*. The song is one of several contrafacta known from the thirteenth century, some of which probably originated as loose translations of Latin originals, others that may have acquired a Latin text to make use of a secular song as part of religious devotion. There is no direct link between the English and Latin texts in terms of their specific meaning, and there are no passages that suggest that one originated as a translation or paraphrase of the other.

It is possible to detect two camps in the reception of the song: one pushing its monastic, Latin, liturgical heritage, the other viewing it as a fortuitous remnant of an otherwise largely lost secular repertoire of English lyric song. This bifurcated reception can be seen not only in the British musicological writings of the nineteenth century, but right through the twentieth and beyond. The conflict between the liturgical and artistic view of 'Sumer is icumen in' was already fully established by the time that Ernest Board came to depict its inspiration in 1920 (Figure 1.3). In Board's painting, the sacred aspect of the piece is necessarily shown because of the purpose of the artist, who wished to link the song with its origin at Reading Abbey. His monk is flanked by church furniture, in an area for writing and reflection within the cloister. In contrast, the small organ resting to the right of the composition alludes to practical musicianship and the secular world, as well as implying the man's familiarity with music beyond plainchant. Surrounded by the rays beaming into the cloister, the monk appears dually inspired by the light of God and by the cuckoo who signals the coming of spring (or, for this song, summer). Indeed, the cloister is a convenient metaphor, representing both the interior and exterior worlds that Benedictine monks inhabited. The monastic setting establishes the location for the genesis of the song, but also suggests its performance context. Board perhaps speculates in his image the extent to which the song stemmed from sacred or secular aspects of the monk's experience; was it used in the liturgy? Was it an escape from prayer? Did the cuckoo and the blossoming tree remind the monk of the association between nature, awakening sexuality and the warmer months? Of course, Board's composition represented only the received view of 'Sumer is icumen in', one learned from the canonic wrangles that had already befallen it in the nineteenth century, and that chimed with his own career as an artist involved in ecclesiastical projects, including stained glass and historical subjects. Yet, his painting also continued to be representative of the difficulties facing writers through the decades that followed.

The primacy of the English or Latin melodic song text has been contested because assigning the piece to sacred or liturgical repertory might put at risk its 'canonic' status.[55] Bukofzer placed the song within the context of items in the Red Book of Ossory, because he believed that the original, secular song was made more appropriate for performance by religious men through the creation of a more suitable Latin text, perhaps as a result of Franciscan influence.[56] Handschin wondered if the scribe himself 'engaged in spiritualizing by providing the canon with a Latin text'.[57] Writers are often drawn to the English lyric for pastoral, national poetic tradition, linking it to other early vernacular verse and, in many accounts, making little mention of the second text. In some cases, the fresh and simple qualities of the English words have become subject to rather overblown analytical remarks. In his own analysis, Gregory H. Roscow reflected that: 'The characterization of the piece as a song of welcome to the spring seems difficult to expand without treating it as the effusion of a thirteenth-century Wordsworth'.[58] To do so was a tradition stretching back into medievalism of the nineteenth century. William Chappell, ignoring the sacred lyrics, argued that:

> The chief merit of this song is the airy and pastoral correspondence between the words and music, and I believe its superiority to be owing to its having been a national song and tune, selected according to the custom of the time, as a basis for harmony, and that it is not entirely a scholastic composition. The fact of its having a natural drone base would rather to confirm this view than otherwise.[59]

The evocation of spring or summer has been one of the many appeals of the song, and has also led to discussions as to whether there is any birdsong imitation in the melodic line – whether it is intended as such, and whether it is successful in portraying a cuckoo – and finally whether or not this might prove the earlier provenance of the English lyric; after all, the *pedes* are provided only with one, secular text.

For those who have seen the Latin text as being a pre-existent, formal argument usually approaches the question musically, such as in seeking quotation or paraphrase of liturgical chant in the lower voices. Harrison, noting a melodic match between the first five notes of the *pes* ('Sing cu cu nu') and the opening of the Easter Marian antiphon *Regina caeli*, suggested that the piece might 'properly be described as the rota-rondellus-motet *Perspice Christicola* – Pes duplex *Regina caeli*'; indeed, he and Dobson listed it by the Latin title in their edition. This alternative title has not found much favour in standard literature on the piece, perhaps because it draws the *rota* back firmly into the realm of liturgical polyphony, or simply because it lacks the poetic charm of the English.[60] Marr, although accepting that the composer may have had *Regina caeli* in mind, rejected the strength of Harrison's claim, because although the *pes* resembled the chant, 'with almost as much conviction one can relate it elsewhere'.[61] David Wulstan regarded the melodic match as 'sheer coincidence'.[62] When the Hilliard Ensemble recorded the canon for their CD based around English music, they sang the Latin version of the words against the *pes* with lyrics 'Resurrexit Dominus' – a chant whose first three pitches match the rising and falling tone of the *pes* – in place of the secular 'Sing cu cu'.[63]

Sanders argued that Harrison's identification of liturgical music in the *pes* was unnecessary because 'taken by themselves, these notes form a quite faceless pentad; their all-purpose neutrality becomes more obvious when the Summer Canon is compared with the other English *Stimmtausch* motets in F'.[64] Why would it be important to emphasise the neutrality or facelessness of the tenor line? While Sanders's comment appears on the surface to be a reasonable and cautious warning against reading too far into the significance of small-scale melodic resemblances, his words also reveal his desire to keep the 'Summer canon' in the secular world, and even to treat the *pes* as a form of absolute music, akin to a fugal subject. Similar comments were made by Bukofzer about the fourteenth-century St Edmund motet *Ave miles celestis curie*.[65] Bukofzer's view was that in *Ave miles celestis curie*, 'even a person well acquainted with the plainsong will not be able to follow it in actual performance. Its melodic line is obscured if not obliterated'.[66] The arguments for and against certain types of 'audibility' in the motet, distinguished as a genre by its polytextuality, are well-known.[67] What Bukofzer was arguing was not really about the problem of discerning the meaning of motets texts in performance, but about the extent to which they might reasonably be understood as liturgical music if their liturgical tenor is so distorted that the melodic properties of the pre-existent chant are destroyed:

> These observations will leave no doubt that it is not the presentation of the chant as an audible and continuous entity that the composer was striving for. The tones of the borrowed melody are no more than pegs to hang the tenor on, or mere raw material for its structure [. . .]. With its mechanical divisions and non-liturgical repeats the chant almost loses its identity and becomes a rational, if not mechanical means of structure. To the medieval composer it does not matter that it cannot be heard from without [the context of performance . . .]. The main point is that the chant exists in the music. It provides the sacred ground on which the human mind can erect its rational artifices.[68]

Bukofzer was keen to point out that such an obscuring of the original plainchant melody was not a compositional weakness, but a strength. By emphasising its 'obliteration', Bukofzer was able to build an argument that would not have been out of place in Burney's writings, identifying aspects of the musical language as predictors of later musical techniques.

Handschin's influential reports on the contents of GB-Lbl 978, in a pair of articles published across *Musica Disciplina* in 1949 and 1951 and part of a burgeoning of interest in English medieval music after World War II, were peppered with comments that downplayed the 'devotional' and emphasised the secular elements of the music, grouping the musical items into 'compositions in which the secular affinities are more apparent' (including 'Sumer is icumen in') and compositions 'more markedly spiritual, although not intended as liturgical sequences'.[69] It was a categorisation that did not disrupt the prevailing understanding of the song.

'Sumer is icumen in' in the popular imagination

Whether understood as an ancient piece of English classical music or a remnant of a lost folksong tradition, 'Sumer is icumen in' has been found in many re-workings and has been used within new compositions. The appearance of 'Sumer is icumen in' in more recent music and films is testified by its listing of 'Renditions and Recordings' as a major part of its Wikipedia article.[70] The ubiquitous online encyclopedia informs the reader of places where 'Sumer is icumen in' has been spotted outside of its expected context of academic text books, concert performances or recordings. Although it is tempting to see the 'Renditions and Recordings' listing as simple trivia, it is in fact helpful in tracing the way in which the song has been appropriated in other cultural contexts, and can act as a point of reference in understanding the changing value of the song to creative artists and their audiences over the past century.

The use of pre-existent musical fragments in the creation of new music or multimedia has been a hallmark of diverse musical genres, especially since World War II, from knowingly postmodern classical repertoire to the practice of sampling that lies at the heart of hip-hop. The integration of 'old' pieces of music, audibly, such as in Berio's *Sinfonia*, or in subtle re-workings, as in Peter Maxwell Davies's *Worldes Blis*, carries strong connotations and invites imaginative interpretative strategies. In the early and middle decades of the twentieth century, 'Sumer is icumen in' was a standard part of the cultural knowledge of the educated elite in the English-speaking West. This was a period in which there was also a great academic interest in the song, especially as an icon of what might have been a since-lost national song repertory, of the scale found in France (the music and poetry of troubadours and trouvères) or Spain (the Cantigas de Santa Maria). Poetically informed parodies illustrate the cultural currency of the song at various times. Ezra Pound's 'Ancient Music' ('Winter is icumen in, Lhude sing Goddamm', 1913–15) and P. D. Q. Bach's 'Summer is a cumin seed' as part of the baroque parody *The Seasonings* (1966) made full sense only to audiences who knew the original and could understand the rhythmic, musical as well as lyrical jokes. The Fugs's 'Carpe Diem' drew on the song for left-wing political purposes in the 1960s, performing their five-minute meditation with lyrics such as 'Sing cuckoo/young girl/soldier sing, death is icumen in'.[71] In this example, the band drew on the repetitious structural properties of the *rota*, subverting its announcement of spring with lyrics that heralded death over the insistent two-chord ostinato; it is an interpretation whose power is strengthened by knowledge of the original song and awareness of the song's original positive and optimistic message. Here and elsewhere, the use of 'Sumer is icumen in' in film, television and as borrowed material emphasised the popular and folk heritage, rather than a seeing it as a piece of structural complexity stemming from a learned monastic context.

The use of 'Sumer is icumen in' in film and as a melody incorporated into contemporary classical music shows composers and directors engaging with the song in relation to an assumed secular origin, based upon the song's depiction of Merrie England. In most examples, the song loses its underpinning *pes*, and often its canonic structure, entirely. For example, the melody is whistled by Little John in *The Adventures of Robin Hood* (dir. Michael Curtiz and William Keighley, 1938) as he approaches the eponymous hero (played by Errol Flynn) for the first time.[72] Although it appears only this once, in that fleeting moment the tune serves to introduce the character through performance: the melody was presumably sufficiently recognisable to be representative of medieval English music, but perhaps, more importantly, the fact that Little John is whistling the song emphasises his peasant status. Whistling has long been associated with working-class vernacular contexts, and whistling outdoors evokes freedom and a carefree attitude. Whistling has also been more acceptable for men than women, perhaps because of the associations between outdoor whistling, the public sphere and physical labour, as well as because of the facial distortions necessary to produce a note. Contemporary cinematic contexts for whistling were most often rooted in precisely these situations, featuring women or men marginalised from the dominant culture.[73] In *Robin Hood*, Little John's performance of 'Sumer is icumen in' locates him socially as a contented, lower-class male, a symbol of the romanticised ideal of the medieval peasant. By implication, of course, the song itself further absorbed that same cultural meaning.

If the use of 'Sumer is icumen in' in *Robin Hood* is illustrative of character and period, its use in *The Wicker Man* (dir. Robin Hardy, 1973), can be seen as radically different, tapping into an alternative reception of the song in which its relationship with folk culture is emphasised. In *Robin Hood*, and similar contexts, 'Sumer is icumen in' was chosen for its evergreen Englishness, its rose-tinted image of a rural idyll. By contrast, the piece appears in *The Wicker Man* as part of the terrifying climax in which Scottish pagans perform the song, motet-like, in visual and sonic counterpoint with the final Christian hymns and prayers of the policeman victim. Depictions such as these, in popular contexts, might appear independent of formal scholarship, but in fact they result from historical perceptions of certain types of English music – from which 'Sumer is icumen in' is the main exemplar – that have been articulated over hundreds of years, especially since the first flourishing of music-historical writing in the eighteenth century. Many performances of 'Sumer is icumen in' present the song as a secular piece aligned with an imagined context that might be best described as maypole dancing on the village green. A good example of such an approach is the charming and quite lengthy performance by the Dufay Collective, in which the song is accompanied by a variety of plucked, bowed and drone stringed instruments. On the CD version, the track fades out in a manner suggestive of rustic minstrelsy, echoing its textual sentiment that the singing of 'cucu' should never stop.[74] Other groups have employed instrumentation, performance styles, or production techniques that emphasise the connection with folk music or with musical traditions associated with primitive or amateur, rather than professional, musical skills. Although there is insufficient space here to present a detailed comparative analysis of performances of 'Sumer is icumen in', it is fair to make the general comment that most fall into the portrayal of the song as secular rather than sacred, with the Hilliard Ensemble representing an exception.[75]

The folk-based performance tradition sometimes seems to draw on the tone and information found in important and widely disseminated music history books written in the middle of the twentieth century. Gustave Reese associated 'Sumer is icumen in' with secular instrumental music, the link being made explicitly through the 'obvious' use of 'dance rhythms' in this and similar vocal music, as well as through the diverse contents of the rest of GB-Lbl 978.[76] Donald J. Grout's discussion of the well-known polyphonic song *Alle psallite cum luya/Alleluya* likened its 'fresh, folklike' melody line and its 'harmoniously blended' parts to features he also identified in 'Sumer is icumen in', though he stood back from saying that either song was folk music *per se*.[77] Richard Hoppin's consideration of 'Sumer is icumen in' as evidence of a tradition of 'popular or even folk polyphony' that might have inspired it belongs to the same imaginative frame.[78] Even in recent British pedagogical resources, advice to teachers is that the song is 'A bright and sunny 13th-century folk melody. Keep it simple or try it as a round, building in some instrumental accompaniment to bring out the folk style'; not only the piece but also its twentieth-century reception as folk music are being perpetuated here.[79]

Twentieth-century British composers and music critics, perhaps informed by the sorts of standard reference books mentioned above, have also tended also to emphasise the relationship between 'Sumer is icumen in' and folk music. This can be seen very clearly in discourse relating to Benjamin Britten's *Spring Symphony*, the finale of which closes with a boisterous climax in which 'Sumer is icumen in' features prominently. Perhaps surprisingly, Britten had not initially planned to use the song: rather, he had originally intended to draw on medieval Latin verse, and had already made a selection of suitable lyrics. Significantly, Britten does not seem to have viewed 'Sumer is icumen in' as a religious or medieval song: he specifically referred to it as 'the great 13th Century traditional song "Sumer is i-cumen in," sung or rather shouted by the boys', thereby eliding it with folksong repertory.[80] Britten's use of *this* medieval English song (even *the* medieval English song) comes as little surprise, for it would have been instantly recognisable to amateur and professional musicians in 1949, to a significantly greater degree than some of the other poetry used in the *Symphony*. The immediacy of the tune was also suited to young voices, a timbre that the composer enjoyed working with for specific effect.[81] In *Spring Symphony*, rather than quote the medieval song in its intended form – as a four-part canon in the equivalent of modern compound time, with an underlying *pes* ostinato – Britten set it as a simple melodic line in unison, in 2/4 rather than 6/8, and transposed into C major (his traditional 'key of transcendent purity').[82] The effect is akin to a nursery rhyme, heightening its sense of innocence and disguising its original performance context. One anonymous commentator for *The Times*, probably William Mann, picked up on this in a review that detected 'a kind of expressive genuineness, even innocence, about the music'.[83] The rota's appearance was picked up by also by Frank Howes in the same publication:

> The finale is a rollicking Moto Perpetuo from Beaumont and Fletcher with the oldest and freshest of English tunes, 'Sumer is icumen in', suddenly irradiating it with a crystalline ray.[84]

> The joyous canonic finale, which by the double suggestion of 'Oranges and Lemons' and 'Sumer is icumen in' translates Beaumont and Fletcher's 'London to thee I do present the merry month of May' into a paean of that gusto of living that once we had but seem to have lost awhile.[85]

Britten's inclusion of 'Sumer is icumen in' effectively grafted *Spring Symphony* onto the tree of British music, whose deep roots could be traced to a song that Britten exploited simultaneously as the first piece of 'art music' in the English canon, and more spuriously as representative of ancient English folk music.

Conclusions

When 'Sumer is icumen in' captured the imagination of scholars and those interested in early music more generally in the late nineteenth century, it did so against a backdrop of scholarly interest driven by patriotism as much as musicological interest. Elsewhere in scholarship, studies of Arthurian legend or of Robin Hood were dominated by similar forces, contributing to 'the construction of a "Merrie England" imagined to rescue late Victorian England from the dangers of industrialism'.[86] The general enthusiasm for the song within scholarly debate has been generated by a nationalist discourse in search of its own Holy Grail – a medieval English masterwork – coupled with long-standing English pride in the compositional craft of the piece itself and compounded by its frequent recurrence in various types of artistic discourse. The song has been anthologised like no other before 1500. It is no coincidence that the debates relating to the origin and function of the song were especially heated in the decade following World War II, marked elsewhere by such nationalist cultural statements as the Festival of Britain and the revival of the York Mystery Plays.

Within the standard histories of English music, there are two recurrent negative themes. The first derives from the fact that the vast majority of music produced in medieval England remains without a firm authorial attribution. A second concerns the fragmentary nature of many of the remaining sources. Author attributions, corroborated by the survival of details of biography and career history of a composer, give musicologists the confidence to discuss the purpose of the music, even the intentions of the composer, as can be evidenced by the greater proportion of scholarship related to attributed pieces. In the twenty-first century, one might challenge the validity of seeking definite answers to questions of artistic intention within medieval repertoire. Against these concerns, the admittedly remarkable survival of 'Sumer is icumen in' has overshadowed efforts to explore other music from the same period. After all: it too is found only in a single source; we know little of its purpose within the manuscript miscellany; we know nothing of its composer(s), and as such its place in the history of English music remains largely speculative. Yet, writers continue to return to it, hanging their views on aspects of the song that might link with notions of greatness in art music. The ubiquity of 'Sumer is icumen in' in musicological and wider discourse offers us a rare glimpse at changing understandings of English musical history in general, and the song's role as barometer of this process may be added to its many fascinating characteristics.

Notes

1 The texts are taken from Helen Deeming, transcr. and ed. *Songs in British Sources c. 1150–1300*. Musica Britannica 95 (London: Stainer and Bell, 2013), 125–8.
2 The concept of a canon in music has been treated extensively in a number of publications, the majority focusing on post-medieval repertoire. See in particular Katherine Bergeron and Philip V. Bohlman, eds., *Disciplining Music: Musicology and its canons* (Chicago and London, 1992); Lydia Goehr, *The Imaginary Museum of Musical Works* (Oxford: Oxford University Press, 1992); Marcia Citron, *Gender and the Musical Canon* (Urbana and Chicago: University of Illinois Press, 1993); William Weber, "The History of Musical Canon." In *Rethinking Music*, edited by Mark Everist and Nicholas Cook (London and New York: Oxford University Press, 1999), 336–55; Suzanne Cole, *Thomas Tallis and his Music in Victorian England* (Woodbridge: Boydell and Brewer, 2008).
3 The term 'early music' is used here its broadest sense, acknowledging its complex, changing and contested definitions over the past century. For a full exploration of 'early music', see Thomas Forrest Kelly, *Early Music: A very short introduction* (Oxford: Oxford University Press, 2011).
4 Forrest Kelly, *Early Music*, 1.
5 Michael Flanders, 'Greensleeves', accompanied by Donald Swann at the piano, a monologue premiered on 31 December 1956 at the New Lindsay Club, London, as part of the review *At the Drop of a Hat*, and subsequently released in the United Kingdom as Flanders and Swann, *At the Drop of a Hat* (Parlophone PCS 3001, 1960).
6 William Chappell, *Popular Music of the Olden Time* (London: Cramer, Beale & Chappell, 1844), xiii.
7 Chappell, *Popular Music of the Olden Time*, vol. 1, frontispiece and 1–47; cited in John Haines, "Medievalist Music and Dance." In *The Oxford Handbook of Victorian Medievalism*, edited by Corinna Wagner and J. Parker (Oxford: Oxford University Press, 2016).

8   Warren Dwight Allen, *Philosophies of Music History: A study of general histories of music 1600–1960*, 2nd edn (New York: Dover Publications, 1962), 161. The broader context of his remarks is explored in Chapter 5.
9   W. S. Rockstro, "Sumer is icumen in," *A Dictionary of Music and Musicians*, edited by George Grove (London, 1890), 4 vols, volume 3, 765–8.
10 Jamieson Boyd Hurry, *Sumer is icumen in* (London: Novello, 1913; 2nd edn 1914). The book included an extensive set of quotations from the literature on the song from sources dating from the eighteenth to the early part of the twentieth century.
11 Rockstro, "Sumer is icumen in," 765.
12 W. S. Rockstro, "Schools of Composition §XVI The Early English Schools (1226–1625)," *A Dictionary of Music and Musicians*, 4 vols. Edited by George Grove, III (London: Macmillan, 1890), 268.
13 Early articles on the subject that were particularly influential included Bertram Schofield, "The Provenance and Date of 'Sumer is icumen in'," *Music Review* 9 (1948); Nino Pirrotta, "On the Problem of 'Sumer is icumen in'," *Musica Disciplina* 2 (1948); Jacques Handschin, "The Summer Canon and its Background: I," *Musica Disciplina* 3 (1949); Jacques Handschin, "The Summer Canon and its Background: II," *Musica Disciplina* 5 (1951).
14 Hawkins cites Mr Wanley's catalogue of Harleian manuscripts as the source of his own discussions: John Hawkins, *A General History of the Science and Practice of Music*, 4 volumes (1776); edited and reprinted with additional introduction by Charles Cudworth (New York, Dover Publications, 1963), 201–4, at 202. A summary of the various eighteenth- and nineteenth-century descriptions of 'Sumer is icumen in' can be found in Rockstro, "Sumer is icumen in," at 765 and 768 (pages 766–7 are taken up with an edition of the piece, with both English and Latin texts underlaid).
15 Coussemaker's dating of the manuscript was expressed in *L'Art Harmonique aux xii et xiii siècles* (Paris: A. Durand and Didron, 1865), 144 and 150.
16 On the relationship between medieval English music and the concept of musical works see Chapter 3.
17 Charles Burney, *A General History of Music from the Earliest Ages to the Present Period* (London: 1776–89), edited by Frank Mercer in 2 vols (London: G. T. Foulis, 1935. Reprinted New York: Dover, 1957), II, 680–5.
18 Andrew Taylor and A. E. Coates, "The Dates of the Reading Calendar and the Summer Canon," *Notes and Queries* 243 (1998).
19 Richard Hoppin, *Medieval Music, Medieval Music* (New York: Norton, 1978), 370.
20 See the discussion of 'Talent m'a pris' in Elizabeth Eva Leach, *Sung Birds: Music, Nature, and Poetry in the Later Middle Ages* (Ithaca: Cornell University Press, 2007), 156–60, in which she notes the inherent humour of the song, juxtaposing the natural call of the bird with the complexity of learned polyphony.
21 Leach, *Sung Birds*, 160. Leach draws here from Anna Maria Busse Berger, *Medieval Music and the Art of Memory* (Berkeley and Los Angeles: University of California Press, 2005), Chapter 6 "Visualization and the Composition of Popular Music," 198–252.
22 Burney, *A General History of Western Music*, 682.
23 Andrew Kirkman, *The Cultural Life of the Early Polyphonic Mass: Medieval context to modern revival* (Cambridge: Cambridge University Press, 2010), 4.
24 Cole, *Thomas Tallis and his Music*, 6.
25 Goehr, *The Imaginary Museum of Musical Works*, 2.
26 See the discussion of the relationship between author attribution and value in Chapter 3.
27 Harry Ellis Wooldridge, *The Oxford History of Music* 1 (Oxford: Clarendon Press, 1901), 177–84.
28 Wolfgang Obst, '"Svmer is icumen in" – A contrafactum?' *Music and Letters* 64 (1983), 151–61 at p. 161.

36 '*The greatest musical curiosity extant*'

29 See Justin Lake, "Authorial Intention in Medieval Historiography," *History Compass* 12 (2014), 345.
30 Thomas Morley's *Plain and Easy Introduction to Practical Music* (1597) listed a number of important musicians as influential on his text, divided into 'Authors whose authorities be either cited or used in this book' (including theorists working in England such as Robertus de Handlo), 'Practioners' (none of whom are English) and 'Englishmen' (including Leonel Power and John Dunstable). See R. Alec Harman, ed., *Thomas Morley: A plain and easy guide to practical music* (New York: Norton, 1952), 319–22.
31 Burney, *A General History of Music*, 455.
32 Gerald of Wales, *Descriptio Cambriae* (1194); see Thomas Wright, ed. *The Historical Works of Giraldus Cambrensis* (London: George Bell & Sons, 1863), 498.
33 Burney, *A General History of Music*, 484; his discussion of Gerald of Wales's comments is at pp. 482–4. On the reception of Gerald of Wales's music-related comments, see Shai Burstyn, "Gerald of Wales and the *Sumer* Canon," *The Journal of Musicology* 2 (1983); Shai Burstyn, "Is Gerald of Wales a Credible Musical Witness?" *The Musical Quarterly* 70 (1986).
34 Bennett Zon, *Music and Metaphor in Nineteenth-Century British Musicology* (Aldershot: Ashgate, 2000), 189; citing Frederick Crowest, *The Story of British Music (From the Earliest Times to the Tudor Period)* (London: Richard Bentley, 1896), 12–13.
35 On canon formation, see especially Goehr, *The Imaginary Museum of Musical Works*; Mark Everist, "Reception Theories, Canonic Discourses, and Musical Value." In *Rethinking Music*, edited by Nicholas Cook and Mark Everist (Oxford, Oxford University Press, 1999).
36 Manfred Bukofzer, "'Sumer is icumen in': A Revision," *University of California Publications in Music*, 2 (1944), iii; cited in Ross W. Duffin, "The *Sumer* Canon: A New Revision," *Speculum* 63 (1988), 1.
37 Archibald T. Davison and Willi Apel, eds, *Historical Anthology of Music. Oriental, medieval and renaissance music* (Cambridge, MA, Harvard University Press, 1946), 220.
38 Duffin, "The *Sumer* Canon: A New Revision," 1.
39 Ernest Sanders, "Sumer is icumen in," *Grove Music Online. Oxford Music Online.* Oxford University Press. Accessed 21 December 2015. Stable URL to the current entry "Sumer is icumen in" provides a link to Sanders's previous version www.oxfordmusiconline.com/subscriber/article/grove/music/27110.
40 Peter Marr, "The Melody of 'Sumer is icumen in'," *The Musical Times* 108/1498 (1967), 1104–06.
41 Burstyn, "Gerald of Wales and the *Sumer* Canon," 148.
42 Handschin, "The Summer Canon and its Background: I," 79.
43 Busse Berger, *Medieval Music and the Art of Memory*, 32–3.
44 Helen Deeming, "An English Monastic Miscellany: The Reading Manuscript of *Sumer is icumen in*." In *Manuscripts and Medieval Song: Inscription: Performance, context*, edited by Helen Deeming and Elizabeth Eva Leach (Cambridge: Cambridge University Press, 2015), 116.
45 Paul Henry Lang, *Music in Western Civilization* (London: J. M. Dent: 1942), 128, 142–3.
46 Losseff, *The Best Concords*, 25, had about a dozen, but only included thirteenth-century sources that contained polyphony. The higher number is from Deeming's research.
47 Deeming, "An English Monastic Miscellany," 139.
48 The citation is from Burstyn, "Gerald of Wales and the *Sumer* Canon," 139, but it is important to note that the historical acceptance of *Sumer is icumen in* as the first piece in a medieval English canon extends back over 200 years.

49 Deeming, "An English Monastic Miscellany," 139. Andrew Taylor, *Textual Situations: Three medieval manuscripts and their readers* (Philadelphia: University of Pennsylvania Press, 2002) focuses on four manuscripts including GB-Lbl 978, but his account is undermined by its pursuit of a single owner or author for this book.
50 Rockstro, "Schools of Composition §XVI The Early English Schools (1226–1625)," 268.
51 Frank Ll. Harrison, *Music in Medieval Britain* (London: Routledge and Kegan Paul, 1958), 142.
52 Sanders, "Sumer is icumen in."
53 Citron, *Gender and the Musical Canon*, 201.
54 Cole, *Thomas Tallis and his Music in Victorian England*, 195.
55 Gregory H. Roscow, "What is 'Sumer is icumen in'?" *The Review of English Studies*, New Series, 50 (1999), 188. Studies that argue that the piece originated with a Latin text include Eric J. Dobson and Frank Ll. Harrison eds. *Medieval English Songs* (New York: Cambridge University Press, 1979), especially pages 95 and 144; and Wolfgang Obst, ' "Svmer is icumen in" – A contrafactum?' *Music and Letters* 64 (1983), 151–61.
56 Manfred Bukofzer, "Popular and Secular Music in England." In *The New Oxford History of Music 3: Ars Nova and the Renaissance, 1300–1540*, edited by Anselm Hughes and Gerald Abraham (London: Oxford University Press, 1960), 118. See also Ernest Sanders, "Tonal Aspects of 13th-century English Polyphony," *Acta Musicologica* 37 (1965), 20–21, fn 14.
57 Handschin, "The Summer Canon and its Background: I," 68.
58 Roscow, "What is 'Sumer is icumen in'?" 188.
59 Chappell, *Popular Music of the Olden Time*, 23.
60 Harrison, *Music in Medieval Britain*, 142.
61 Marr, "The Melody of "Sumer is icumen in'." Obst accepted the possibility that the composer of the *pes* had the plainchant antiphon in mind; " 'Svmer is icumen in" – A Contrafactum?" 161.
62 David Wulstan, "Sumer is icumen in: A Perpetual Puzzle Canon?" *Plainsong and Medieval Music* 9 (2000), 3.
63 Hilliard Ensemble, *Sumer is icumen in: Medieval English Songs* (Harmonia Mundi, HMU 1951154, 2002), track 11.
64 Sanders, "Tonal Aspects of 13th-century English Polyphony," 21, where *stimmtausch* is synonymous with a round, musically speaking.
65 Manfred Bukofzer, "Two Fourteenth-century Motets on St Edmund," *Studies in Medieval and Renaissance Music* (New York: Norton and Company, 1950), 27. Subsequent studies of the motet by Harrison and Lefferts argued that the arrangement of the cantus firmus was 'arbitrary'; Lefferts, *The Motet in England*, 35; Frank Ll. Harrison, "Ars Nova in England: A New Source," *Musica Disciplina* 21 (1967), 75. My own study of the motet contests that viewpoint; "Music, Text and Structure in Fourteenth-century English Polyphony: The case of *Ave miles celestis curie*," *Early Music* 45 (forthcoming for 2017).
66 Bukofzer, "Two Fourteenth-century Motets on St Edmund," 27.
67 For a full exploration of this aspect of motets see Emma Dillon, *The Sense of Sound: Musical meanings in France, 1260–1330* (Oxford and New York: Oxford University Press, 2012).
68 Bukofzer, "Two Fourteenth-century Motets on St Edmund," 28–29.
69 Handschin, "The Summer Canon and its Background: I," 68.
70 "Sumer is icumen in," *Wikipedia*. Accessed 27 November 2014, en.wikipedia.org/wiki/Sumer_Is_Icumen_In.
71 'Carpe Diem' was released on *The Fugs' First Album* (1965, track 7). Album originally released as Broadside Records 304, later reissued as ESP Disk 1018;

38 *'The greatest musical curiosity extant'*

re-released by Fantasy Records, Berkeley, CA, 1994. Lyrics by Tuli Kupferberg; produced by Ed Sanders and Harry Smith.

72   The original film music for *The Adventures of Robin Hood* was provided by Erich Korngold, who won an Academy Award for his score. See Ben Winters, *Erich Wolfgang Korngold's* The Adventures of Robin Hood: *A Film Score Guide* (Lanham, MD: Scarecrow Press, 2007).

73   It is difficult to imagine a better example here than 'Whistle while you work', from Walt Disney's *Snow White and the Seven Dwarfs* (1937), in which the heroine outcast, a princess in hiding, whistles as a distraction from the domestic tasks in which she currently engages.

74   BBC1, *Dawn At Snape* (May 2000) Accessed 15 August 2014, www.youtube.com/watch?v=kuo9Utynyuc; recorded version found on The Dufay Collective, *Miri It Is: Songs and instrumental music from medieval England* (Chandos, CHAN9396, 1995). It is also possible that the production elements relate the performance to the fade-out on popular music tracks; my thanks to John Bryan for this suggestion.

75   A further example of the Latin lyric on recording is the LP recording directed by Frank Ll. Harrison and Eric J. Dobson, *Medieval English Lyrics: Recorded in association with the British Council* (Argo, ZRG5443, 1965).

76   Gustave Reese, *Music in the Middle Ages* (London: J. M Dent, 1940), 406.

77   Donald J. Grout, *A History of Western Music* (New York: W. W. Norton, 1960), 131.

78   Hoppin, *Medieval Music*, 503.

79   See the Song Bank, a resource forming part of the Sing Up national singing initiative in the United Kingdom; accessed 13 August 2014, www.singup.org/songbank/song-bank/song-detail/view/239-sumer-is-icumen-in. Comments from users indicate that teachers received the song warmly as useful for their projects on Tudor England and on Henry VIII in particular.

80   Benjamin Britten, "A Note on the Spring Symphony," *Music Survey* 2 (1950), 237.

81   Children's voices were employed on several occasions by Britten in combination with materials either inspired by or designed to evoke the past: *A Ceremony of Carols*, and the 1958 work *Noye's Fludde*, for example, both set medieval English lyrics for performance by young people.

82   Arved Ashby, "Britten as Symphonist." In *The Cambridge Companion to Benjamin Britten*, edited by Mervyn Cooke (Cambridge: Cambridge University Press, 1999), 227.

83   [William Mann], "Reviews. Joyful Spring Symphony," *The Times* 55713 (29 May 1963), column A, 13.

84   Our Music Critic [Frank Howes], "Britten's Spring Symphony: Form and Content," *The Times* 51440, column D (22 July 1949), 7.

85   Our Music Critic [Frank Howes], "The 'Spring Symphony', Britten's New Work" (Reviews), *The Times* 51636, col. B (10 March, 1950), 10.

86   Kathy Lavezzo, "Introduction." In *Imagining a Medieval English Nation*, edited by Kathy Lavezzo (Minneapolis, MN: University of Minnesota Press, 2003), ix.

2 *Anglicus angelicus*
Was English music political?

A music book, such as a handsome Gradual, an ornate collection of polyphony or a marginal jotting, is a powerful document, whether one considers it in its historical context or as a modern symbol of past cultures. It can be experienced in a multisensory way: seeing the notation, text and decoration; feeling and smelling the parchment; and perhaps above all realising its notation as sounding text, and hearing its effects. Intellectually, one can also engage with a book by meditating upon the text, analysing musico-textual relationships or by marvelling at the beauty of illuminated scripts and imagery.

One might expect that medieval English writers would reflect this viewpoint, and indeed writers on the senses rank the sonic experience highly. However, at the top of the tree, the sense most commonly prioritised was that of sight, of visual witness to actions, nature or physical beauty. In one early fifteenth-century manual, a character reflects in dialogue that 'often man is more steryd by syghte than be heryng or redyngge'.[1] Above all, sight was considered more capable of stirring the passions of the human heart and mind. In the modern day, it is no surprise that the appetite for colour facsimiles of ornate historical sources such as the Lindisfarne Gospels extends far beyond academia, with a market appeal that extends to larger audiences than might, for example, attend a concert of medieval music. It seems that in many cases, the care with which certain texts are presented, through bold colour and decoration – often involving complex heraldic schemes or liturgical referencing – matched the value and significance of those texts for their makers, owners and users.

What of musical sources of the later Middle Ages? From Italy, the fourteenth-century Squarcialupi Codex boasts the importance of the composers and repertoire represented within it; the visual display matches the value of the sonic. Machaut's music, preserved across a number of carefully presented and corrected copies and depicting the arms of owners and even a likeness of the composer himself, is clearly of a similar level of value.[2] The richness of detail found in sources of the Cantigas de Santa Maria, full of images of musicians with their instruments, hints at the significance of the collection as music, not merely lyric, and reveals something of the performance culture of the time.

Pre-1500 English music sources, by contrast, rarely give much beyond the musical notation, some coloured initials and some light pen work. There are no composer portraits, no joyful instrumental players, no pseudo-musical grotesques lurking in the margins. Plain, simple and restrained, they do not wear their heart on their sleeve in terms of the value of their contents, or the intentions of their authors and scribes. They barely hint at the broader cultural significance of their songs. Even the arrangement of items in collections shows little of the creative force at work in luxurious and highly planned books such as the *Roman de Fauvel*.[3] Quite simply, it is no surprise that scholars of English music have responded with a history that emphasises the functional, the structural, the practical or the theoretical above questions of ideology or identity.

In this chapter, I address questions that relate to the politics of musical expression. In some ways, I will place the historical tendency to be stirred by sight more than by sound to one side in order to reveal ways in which the musical presentation of ideas was often of the highest significance to its originators. On the other hand, the music on which I have chosen to focus was designed with physical performance in mind, so also had important visual components: ceremony, liturgical ritual and movement or sound within particular architectural environments. Although musical language in the Middle Ages was not programmatic or emotive in ways found in tonal repertories of later centuries, in combination with text it was capable of being used subtly and persuasively, not least to write and rewrite elements of national history. Monasteries and major cathedrals were places whose personnel were regularly at the heart of politics, whether as ambassadors, chroniclers or spiritual advisors. Royal foundations, such as the Abbey of Bury St Edmunds, maintained a close relationship with the Crown. Noble families frequently sent their daughters to reside at wealthy nunneries until marriage or more permanently, and monastic establishments regularly received widows. A religious life was one potentially filled with diplomatic mission and the hosting of diverse visitors; depending on the level of enclosure specified by the rule governing an individual house, a monk or nun was sometimes free to travel locally or abroad for purposes such as pilgrimage. It is therefore to the votive music of institutions that I turn most frequently in this chapter, places that acted as the locus for some of the most important forms of writing: from saints' lives (or *vitae*) to chronicles, and from liturgical chant to motets.

Kingship and liturgical ceremony

One area in which matters of historical and musical discourse come into a dynamic relationship with one another is in the production of song in praise of saints who were also kings or members of the English nobility. English history is replete with figures whose earthly lives had been marked out as also spiritual, through their pious works, their use of political power to uphold Christian ideals or as a result of martyrdom. The transferral of a king or queen from governor to saint was not as difficult as for the general population, as it was widely believed that royalty occupied a divine right to rule and were, by their genealogy, closer to God. Such notions were reinforced by the gradual accretion of additional saintly figures into English history, and by the creation of detailed chronological surveys of the country and its rulers during the Middle Ages. Hagiographical materials, along with historical accounts of monastic or ecclesiastical foundations, were important parts of medieval political discourse.[4] Music, too, played its part in the liturgical rituals that validated the cults and their feast days, from plainchant used in the Divine Office to polyphonic motets and cantilenae, all potentially powerful vehicles for composers to promote political agendas.[5] Men and women already received as royal saints were not the only beneficiaries of musical discourse; it was standard practice for the noble elite to use elements of the past to legitimise their own social position, not least in new claims to the throne. This interplay between historical reality, mythology and the arts acts as the central theme of this chapter, which demonstrates late medieval English music's close engagement with historical and political contexts.

The ruling elite have always offered patronage to art and literature for political purposes, in order to cast its members in a good light. By associating themselves with historical characters, especially saints, the medieval nobility presented an image that people could admire and were afraid to challenge. Unlike France or other countries in mainland Europe, the English monarchy never appointed an official chronicler; thus surviving historical and political texts offer diverse perspectives on key events. The political power of song stemmed from its fundamental connection with acts of memory: textual ideas woven together in music as part of a performance were tools for sharing and remembering, as well as for projecting and image-making – all activities attractive to the ruling elite.[6] Conceptually, medieval kingship had absorbed elements from the Christian and pagan past, frequently drawing on figures from the Old Testament for its models.[7] The preferred male primogeniture followed by medieval kings mirrored the rod of Jesse, which linked King David to Christ. In a musical form, this textual heritage – notably the practice of Biblical quotation and broader devotional texts, as well as more historical ones – was then typically combined with textual or rhetorical gestures such as rhyme, repetition, alliteration or the use of refrain such that an individual song acted as a subtle container for political thought.

Several studies of the construction of kingship in the reigns of Henry III to Henry VI have highlighted the importance of image manipulation in England, a country governed by a frequently contested lineage that was entangled by marriage with France and other European countries.[8] The cultural patronage of magnates directly influenced the arts and religious artistic expression, which served as a vehicle for fashioning positively themed messages of power, strength and legitimacy.[9] The undisputed position of head of state relied on the maintenance of a perceived status in between that of mankind and God: an unquestionable, quasi-divine image in the eyes of the populace. By the fifteenth century, the king 'stood at the apex of human society, looking to God immediately above and to his subjects below him'.[10] It was, arguably, the narrowing of the gap between monarch and God that was of prime concern in most royalist propaganda, including propaganda devised or performed in song. Consider, by way of a well-known example, the Agincourt Carol, written in celebration of the English victory over the French in 1415. King Henry V of England had fought under the banner of St George, and the subsequent elevation of St George's feast day served as opportunity for people to worship the saint while simultaneously considering the image of Henry himself as *miles Christi*, soldier of Christ.[11]

Royalty also drew on imagery directly from the cult of the Blessed Virgin Mary, and this created opportunities for mutual reverence of holy and earthly figures in song. The portrayal of Mary in royal apparel from about the fourth century – and the subsequent adoption of such symbols as the sword, rod, orb, ring and sceptre into earthly regalia – gained significant popularity in England during the Anglo-Saxon period. Paintings and sculptures of *Maria Regina* were compounded by the language used to describe her in liturgical texts, such as Alcuin's *De laude Dei*, which praised Mary in distinctively regal terms.[12] Marian antiphons appeared in the liturgy from about the end of the tenth century. The *Salve Regina* was composed at Cluny in the twelfth century and its earliest notated source is a Cistercian antiphonary dating to 1140.[13] It quickly became popular as a daily devotional chant, not only within Cistercian houses. Over time, and especially from this period, the traditions of secular/royal and religious became entwined: soon the worship of a regal Mary was an act of allegiance to one's ruler on earth. In this way, newly written items of Marian chant and polyphony also served to venerate secular rulers.

The image of the coronation of the Virgin, generated from the twelfth century, does not appear to have been adopted into common exemplars until the end of the fourteenth century in England, though elements of the same symbolism, used for both male and female saints and in royal coronation ceremonies, are found much earlier. Frank Barlow described the significance of the regalia in relation to the coronation of Edward the Confessor:

> The ring was the 'seal of holy faith' and with its help the king was to drive back his foes with triumphal power, destroy heresies, unite his subjects and bind them firmly in the catholic [*sic*] faith. The sword was for the protection of the kingdom and the camp of God. [. . .] The crown was 'the crown of glory and justice', the sceptre 'the rod of the kingdom and of virtue' [. . .]. Finally, the king was given the rod 'of virtue and equity'.[14]

It is clear from this passage how closely enmeshed were the two ideas of earthly ruler and Christ-like majesty in the coronation ritual. Warner has put it more simply: 'when kings and queens wore the sceptre and the crown they acquired an aura of divinity'.[15] In the twelfth century, John of Salisbury – a writer known to musicology through his anxieties about the effeminising and corrupting powers of vocal and instrumental music on impressionable men and women, as expressed in his *Policraticus* – explained that princes were subject to God and to those in religious orders who carried out God's work on earth. In England, as with many other countries, this position of authority was pushed further and kings considered themselves to be inferior to God alone.[16]

The rituals associated with coronation show this transition, as well as demonstrating the elements that, increasingly, became associated with sanctity and nationhood, such as symbolic allusions to English saints.[17] Since the tenth century, the coronation ceremony had become more elaborate. Its three sections – the election by the people, the promise of the king, and finally his anointment and reception of the regalia – were followed by a Mass and a banquet.[18] That the ceremony traditionally took place at Westminster, with the Archbishop of Canterbury presiding, demonstrated the nation's ecclesiastical support for the king at the highest level; Westminster was most strongly associated with St Edward the Confessor who founded its Abbey Church and was the last English king before the Norman Conquest, whereas St Thomas of Canterbury was the most ubiquitous and politically charged English martyr. The Abbey of Bury St Edmunds, a royal foundation, cast its own shadow on proceedings, since from 1308 a plainchant from St Edmund's Office was adapted for use in anointing the new ruler, and the enthronement took place in the Chair of St Edmund.[19] At his coronation on 16 July 1377, Richard II wore both the slippers of St Edmund and the coat of St Edward the Confessor, reflecting the interest in these figures within the piety of the Plantagenet dynasty as a whole as well as providing an illusion of direct descent.[20]

From the eleventh century, there are detailed accounts of how the coronation *laudes* were incorporated into the coronation ceremony in England, including textual acclamations and liturgical directions. The version found in the Worcester Antiphonal is expanded slightly in the Gradual of the same provenance by the addition of St Edward the Confessor's name to those invoked on the king's behalf.[21] It is possible that the special coronation plainchant *Christus vincit* was augmented by polyphony but, at the very least, the specialist skills of solo singers were remunerated from as early as the end of the twelfth century. At Richard I's second coronation at Winchester (17 April 1194), 'three cantors sang the *Christus vincit* after the first collect'.[22] Henry III's payment of 100 shillings to Walter de Lenches and his assistants for the singing of the *Christus vincit* at the coronation of his queen, Eleanor (1236), and at his own crown-wearing ceremony in 1237 reflects the importance of this chant. *Christus vincit* was of crucial importance to the monarch in forging a link between himself and God. It is notable, for example, that the sixteen or more occasions on which Henry III heard the *Christus vincit* between Epiphany 1239 and the same feast the following year included the main feast day of St Edward the Confessor, the feast celebrating the translation of Edward's relics and the feast of St Edmund, in addition to major liturgical feasts, the queen's Purification and the birthday of Prince Edward (later Edward I). It served, essentially, as a public acclamation of Henry's divine rule.

Kantorowicz has asserted that 'we should assume that from the increase of laudes days we can read off, as from a fever-curve, the progress of this king's religious zeal', but I would suggest instead that Henry became more aware of the symbolic effect of *Christus vincit* performances on feast days linked to his saintly forebears.[23] These occasions emphasised the divine empowerment of the coronation ceremony, and embodied ideas seen as representative of the nation and the faithful within in it, promoting a Christian and typically masculine agenda. From 1189, women and Jews were banned from admission to coronation ceremonies 'because of the magic arts which Jews and some women notoriously exercise at royal coronation', according to the St Albans chronicler Matthew Paris.[24] Coronation was one of the most vulnerable points in the rule of a king – unless the ceremony had occurred in full, the monarch had no legal or spiritual authority – and only features acceptable to the image of English nationhood were included.

At times of political upheaval, and especially when lineage was a factor in such struggles, it became imperative for a ruler to present his or her genealogy in as many locations and through as many different media as possible. Genealogical imagery can still be seen in wall painting, stained glass, decorated ceiling bosses and manuscript illumination. Edward III's genealogical displays meant that 'by the middle years of his reign Edward was already commonly seen as the divinely inspired instrument of English salvation, the epitome of Old Testament kingship, and an exemplar to Christian princes'.[25] The celebration of his dynasty was a fundamental part of Edward's personal piety but, more importantly, it was a crucial element of the claim to legitimacy that lay at the heart of dynastic struggles during the Hundred Years War.[26] Although there are no narrative song texts discussing royal lineage from England, votive music in honour of royal and saintly forebears was arguably a strong contributor to this type of political writing.

Two fourteenth-century cantilenae can help us to explore this point more fully: *Singularis laudis digna* and *Regem regum collaudemus*, both of which are found in New York, Pierpont Morgan Library, MS 978 (US-NYpm 978, items 1 and 3), the latter also in Oxford, Corpus Christi College MS 144 (GB-Occc 144). Additionally, a motet written unambiguously in honour of Edward the Confessor, *Civitas nusquam conditur*/T. *Cibus esurientum*/*Cives celestis curie* (Oxford, New College, MS 362, collection item XXVI, ff. 86v–87r, hereafter GB-Onc 362), can be used to show the security of associating *Regem regum* with the same Edward. Both cantilenae make reference to figures including an Edward, and both have a devotional character. A close examination of these three songs shows the benefits of situating song into this sort of political and devotional discourse. I will also show the way in which *Singularis laudis digna* has been scrutinised for datable political references in a way familiar from fourteenth-century political motets, such as those in the *Roman de Fauvel*, and explain why placing it in a literary context can shed light on its meaning.

Music for Edward the Confessor

The text of *Regem regum collaudemus* is only partially preserved because its scribe failed to enter the second half of each double versicle, and then the manuscript has subsequently been trimmed, cutting off line endings.[27] The Latin text has been translated by Bowers as follows:

> Let us together praise the king of kings in whom let us sing the praises of Edward the king . . .
>
> He is a being dear to God, the whole manner of whose life shone with sanctity . . .

And therefore, O citizen of heaven, from this exile [lead] us up to the certain abode of your soul to venerate [you as] worthy in all respects to be exalted with praise.[28]

Who is the King Edward mentioned in the text? There are five main candidates: Edward King and Martyr (murdered in 978), Edward the Confessor (d. 1066, canonised in 1161), Edward I, Edward II (murdered in 1327) and Edward III. Harrison and Sanders identified the dedicatee as Edward III, pairing its sentiments with those of *Singularis laudis digna*, which explicitly praises a King victorious in the Hundred Years War.[29] Bowers refuted the identification of *Regem regum*'s text with Edward III, noting that:

> The overall character of the terminology of this text makes it plain that it is addressed not to a recently deceased King Edward III (ruled 1327–77) but to a canonised King Edward, already a saint. In particular, the (apparent) reference to its addressee as a 'citizen of heaven', able to guide others thither – that is, as one not awaiting the Day of Judgement but already admitted to the company of saints in heaven – rules out any identification with Edward III, to whom in any event the terms of the second stanza ('the whole manner of whose life shone with sanctity') were conspicuously inapplicable.[30]

Equally, Edward I acquired no cult following after his death in 1307 and can thus be discounted. Nothing in the text or music seems directly relevant to the life of Edward, King and Martyr, to whose cult little attention seems to have been paid during this period. Edward II did attract some claims of sanctity as a result of his murder (reframed by some chroniclers as a martyrdom), but the chronology does not work since his main supporter for ultimately unsuccessful canonisation was Richard II (ruled 1377–99). Before Richard lent his support to Edward II's cult, there was limited enthusiasm for it; contemporaries did not consider Edward II's life to have 'shone with sanctity' in the manner described in the lyric. Like many medieval chroniclers, historian May McKisack summarised Edward II's character as 'feeble, incompetent and irresponsible'.[31]

The relatively generic terms of praise in *Regem regum* are typical of the depiction of the Confessor saint in contemporary literature, but the reference that stands out most fully as indicative of the Confessor's cult is that his life shone with sanctity. Edward the Confessor's holiness was depicted primarily through emphasis on his peacefulness, his charity and his virginity. These were exceptional qualities of a king, whose perceived power was often constructed through narratives of military success and of fertility, leading to legitimate male heirs. The anonymous eleventh-century *Vita Aedwardi Regis* highlighted the examples of Edward's character that might be praised in musical form:

Aedwardi regis carmine primus eris.
Hunc dic Anglorum regem, forma speciosum,

corporis arque animi nobilate bonum,
eius ut adventu depresso secula luctu
aurea mox Anglis enituere suis.

You shall be the first to sing King Edward's song.
Describe him thus, this English king, so fair
In form, so nobly fine in limb and mind;
How at his coming, with all grief repressed,
A golden age shone for his English race. [32]

In the 1230s or early 1240s, Matthew Paris wrote the *Estoire de Seint Aedward*, under the patronage of Henry III.[33] In this text, Paris praised Edward's charity, and drew on Biblical imagery taken from Matthew 25: 35–46:

Ki fist les bens fors rois Aedward?
Ki vesti les poveres nuz,/Fors Aedward li seint, li duz?
Ki pesseit les fameillus,/Fors Aedward li glorius?

Who did these good things but King Edward? Who clothed the naked in poverty, but Edward the holy, the gentle? Who fed the hungry, but Edward the glorious?[34]

The same Biblical passage was used in the motet *Civitas nusquam conditor*, which likewise praised Edward for his charity. The tenor text, 'Cibus esurientum, salus languentum, solamen dolentum' (Sustenance of the hungry ones, salvation of the feeble ones, consolation of the suffering ones), recalls the intercessory powers of Edward for those in need found in his *vita*.

The author of *Civitas nusquam conditur* drew on Gospel accounts of Jesus's teachings by the shore in Luke 11: 33, Matthew 5: 14–15 and Mark 4:21. These specific verses were traditionally associated with the translation ceremonies of saints:

No man lighteth a candle, and putteth it in a hidden place, nor under a bushel; but upon a candlestick, that they that come in, may see the light.[35]

You are the light of the world. A city seated on a mountain cannot be hid. Neither do men light a candle, and put it under a bushel, but upon a candlestick, that it may shine to all that are in the house.[36]

And he said to them: Doth a candle come in to be put under a bushel, or under a bed? and not to be set on a candlestick?[37]

The motet's triplum text makes particular reference to these passages, which are used to highlight Edward's own virtues; the duplum is more general, but does refer to the idea of being exalted, or raised up towards heaven, as a main theme (for the Latin texts see Ex. 2.1):

Triplum

Nowhere is a city founded which is placed on top of a high mountain, nor is a shining lamp enkindled and concealed beneath a measure of corn; rather it is set in a lofty candelabrum to shed light on a darkened populace. For whoever lacks light knows not the direction of his journey, nor whether he progresses usefully or deviates wretchedly. And likewise the conduct and very many doctrines of Edward's life are visible and shine, and they are not kept from plain view [Matthew 5]. To the common people lacking the true light of salvation he held forth the light of wisdom and clemency [Matthew 25]. And to the talents entrusted him by the Lord, he responded a hundred-fold, just as the good servant [Matthew 13]. Therefore glory is accorded him, for whom joy will never be absent for ages without end.

Duplum

The citizens of the heavenly court are made joyful today awaiting the presence of Edward, who is about to receive joy with the saints, because the court better resounds and is sweetened, deservedly, by the gathering together of good men, now and in all the years to come. Sweet is the reunion, just as sweet the dwelling together in the exalted palace before the king of the heavens, where Edward today is exalted to joy. By his prayers may we be guided to the company of those who will live forever.[38]

The textual troping of passages from the Gospel of St Matthew relates *Civitas nusquam conditur* to the liturgical basis of translation ceremonies. Aelred of Rievaulx (1110–67) was requested to compose a new *vita* for the first such occasion, which was presented to Westminster at the translation ceremony on 13 October 1163. Aelred would also have delivered a homily, probably one on Luke 11:33 *Nemo accendit lucernam*, since Walter Daniel, who wrote a *vita* of Aelred himself, mentioned the Abbot's production of both a life and a homily.[39] Matthew Paris's *Estoire de Seint Aedward* similarly drew on *Nemo accendit lucernam* when relating the miracles performed at Edward's tomb:

> Ne puet virtu tapir en umbre;/Einz se multiplie e numbre
> De miracles e vertuz,/Ke Deus pur li feseit a muz.
> Le cors puet hum ensevelir,/Mais sa vertu ne puet tapir.

> Virtue cannot be hidden in shade; on the contrary it multiplies itself and numbers miracles and healing powers that God did to many through Edward. Man may bury the corpse, but Edward's virtue cannot be hidden.[40]

Biblical passages about charity and shining virtue were associated with the writings about Edward's life, miracles and particularly materials to celebrate the translation of his relics to Westminster, where the tomb was literally elevated from its original grave in front of the high altar to one raised up behind it in 1269. In 1220, Henry III had witnessed the translation of St Thomas's relics from his grave to a new shrine in the Trinity Chapel at the east end of Canterbury cathedral, and he was physically involved in moving the Confessor's relics to their new shrine at Westminster Abbey. Chronicler Thomas Wykes (1222–93) was an important contemporary witness to Edward's new tomb, describing the relics as 'not hidden under a bushel, but raised on high like a candle, so that they might shed light on all who entered the building'.[41]

The use of source texts from Matthew, so regularly used in relation to the translation of relics, reminds us that the motet *Civitas nusquam* was composed within living memory of Edward's new shrine being constructed; the phrase about his positive qualities being in plain sight may even suggest that the motet was initially written for performance at the celebration of Edward's translation (13 October), rather than his feast day (4 or 5 January), at Westminster Abbey. The only surviving copy of *Civitas nusquam* contains a marginal note that it is a piece about St Edward ('de Sancto Edwardo', GB-Onc 362, f. 86v), but does not link it specifically to a liturgical feast. Similarly, the lack of surviving office chants for St Edward – presumably the source for the tenor melody, though its distinctive poetic features may indicate a non-liturgical origin – means that there is no assistance here from liturgical sources. The general rise in the significance of Edward the Confessor's cult during the later Middle Ages can be demonstrated by the addition of one or other of Edward's feast days to the limited occasions of royal almsgiving. These rose from four in 1323 to six by the middle of the fifteenth century, having added these days to Christmas, Epiphany, All Saints and Whitsun.[42]

The motet *Civitas nusquam conditur*, on the surface only drawing on Edward's reputation as generally saintly, can be read more closely as emphasising Edward's hagiographical image as peacemaker, wise and divine ruler, and virgin. Having established that the textual references in *Civitas nusquam conditur* are both subtle and refined in affirming the traditional, or at least approved, Westminster view of Edward, we should pause to consider the musical setting, which is also a strong contributor to the overall message of the motet (see Ex. 2.1). The opening phrase of the tenor, whose melody has not been identified in any other surviving sources, is repeated intact to finish the piece as a coda, using a fairly standard dedicatory formula in which both duplum and triplum emphasise the endlessness of Edward's place in heaven. When the opening phrase of the tenor repeats, so too do the harmonies of the upper two parts, completing the symmetry. Harrison showed that by interpreting the vertical stroke – visually resembling a bar line, found simultaneously in all vocal parts – as a *longa* rest, the tenor proves to be isorhythmic.[43] The tenor is arranged into a distinctive pattern of sound and silence, represented below by the number of longs before each rest: 3 — 5 — 3 — 5 — 8 — 3 — 5 — 3 — 5.

This arrangement features the number eight through the patterns of three and five, but also through the central placement of the eight, uninterrupted longs. The Confessor's full name (appearing as Edwardus and Edwardi) appears three times in total: twice in the duplum (bars 7 and 35) and once in the triplum (bar 25), amidst the set of eight long tenor notes. The second main section of the motet (bar 24), immediately preceding Edward's name, contains the only moment in

Extract 2.1 Civitas nusquam conditur/T. *Cibus esurientum*/*Cives celestis curie*
After the edition in Frank Ll. Harrison and Peter M. Lefferts eds. *Motets of English Provenance. Polyphonic Music of the Fourteenth Century 15* (Monaco: Editions L'Oiseau-Lyre, 1980), 13–15

50 *Anglicus angelicus*

Extract 2.1 Continued

Extract 2.1 Continued

which the lower voice ('Sweet is the reunion') rises above the triplum, and is the central section of the piece, highlighting the dedicatee and his rising up through the transference of his name to a higher part of the texture. The 'sweetness' of the duplum text may be deliberately reflected in the use of imperfect sonorities, which are used most densely in this part of the motet. The two structures, musical and textual, were thus designed in a complementary manner.

Edward the Confessor is the only viable candidate for the dedication of *Regem regum*, and I would offer the possibility that it too was written for the translation feast rather than for his standard feast day, based on the prominence of the translation at Westminster, the internal textual references of the surviving lyrics and the relative importance of the translation feast over Edward's main feast day in general. The Confessor's cult regularly benefitted from royal patronage, not least in Westminster, and became central to the personal piety of Richard II (ruled 1377–99). Richard empathised with the Confessor's peacefulness, and, like Henry III, was a generous patron of the Abbey at Westminster. There is much evidence to suggest that Richard considered Westminster his personal church, visiting it at key moments in his reign. In 1386, following his tour of the north of England, Richard attended the shrine before finally turning home.[44] The Westminster Chronicle provides evidence that Richard visited Westminster Abbey for the translation feast of Edward the Confessor in both 1390 and 1392, during which he sat in the choir wearing his crown, a political act in itself.[45] Even though Edward III had relatively little time for the Confessor's cult (concentrating instead on the mythical St George in the same way that his grandfather had identified with King Arthur), a song like *Regem regum* was, in performance, an act of support for his Plantagenet dynasty, publically reaffirming what could otherwise have been seen to be a rather unstable lineage.[46] Whether sung during the reign of Edward III or Richard II, a performance of *Regem regum* would be been effective in confirming the complex political and religious heritage of England's kings and the institutions to which they lent their patronage.

Singularis laudis digna

The cantilena *Singularis laudis digna* is an altogether different style of song, and has been attractive to writers for its apparent reflection of specific political events in a manner more common on the continent. Taking as their starting point the appearance of Edward III's name at the end of the text, writers have understood the song as an unusual example of a cantilena in honour of the earthly King rather than the Blessed Virgin Mary. I would argue, however, that this piece – although containing fascinating and unusual examples of political commentary – is no exception to that particular rule: the cantilena is expressly Marian, and relies on Marian imagery to frame its more contemporary references. It seems to me that previous accounts have underplayed this aspect of the song in order to give greater weight to the possibility of English musicians having written something more akin to the political motets found in France and Italy during the fourteenth and fifteenth centuries. I would further suggest that the cantilena text is much more closely related to other political texts of the fourteenth century than has previously been understood. A more detailed consideration of the linguistic imagery positively assists in locating the song as part of a broader body of political and Marian writings, in which the exceptional nature of *Singularis laudis digna* lies in the presentation of that tradition in polyphony.

Let us start with the Marian aspects of the cantilena (see the text and translation below). The song is built from three pairs of versicles, all employing a common metre. The name of Mary – and allegorical or metaphorical representations of that name – appears in various forms. She is called 'sweet and kind mother' and 'star of the sea' (maris stella), both common epithets. The opening word 'Singularis' occurs frequently in Marian poetry, emphasising the Virgin's unique quality of chaste mother, and occurs within the popular medieval text 'Ave maris stella', a hymn to which the cantilena also alludes. Although previous writers have been keen to identify the cantilena's 'queen' 'governing Edward' with specific fourteenth-century women, no queen but Mary could have been celebrated for 'governing our king'. The 'peril of the sea' in lines 10–12 may, as Bowers has suggested, contain a double meaning, relating specifically to the warfare across the Channel in 1369; it also continues the 'stella maris' trope. It is Mary's spiritual guidance of the English that allows military success for 'Edward, worthy king in battle' in the final lines. The victorious tone is echoed in the musical setting; Christopher Page's notes to Gothic Voices's powerful performance notes that 'where the composer names the English ('fit Anglorum') and then their King, Edward III ('sit Edwardo'),' he does so 'with a blaze of parallel writing'.[47]

Text of *Singularis laudis digna*

Singularis laudis digna
Mater dulcis et benigna,
Sumas 'ave' gracie.
Stella maris apellaris
Deum paris expers maris
Loco sedens glorie.

Hester flectit Assuerum
Judith plectit ducem ferum
Precis in oraculo.
Tu, regina, regis regem
Er conserva tuum gregem
Maris in periculo.

Cesset guerra iam Francorum
Quorum terra fit Anglorum
Cum decore lilii,
Et sit concors leopardo
Per quem honor sit Edwardo
Regi probo prelii.

Sweet and kind mother, worthy of unique praise, please accept this thankful greeting. You are called 'star of the sea', you gave birth to the Lord and, equalled by none, you sit in the place of glory.

Esther is winning Ahasuerus over, Judith manipulates a fierce general [Holofernes] through the divine power of prayer. You, O Queen, rule our king; and preserve your flock in peril of the sea.

Let the warfare of the French now cease; may their land become that of the English, with the adornment of the lily. And may it [the lily] accord with the leopard, through which let there be honour to Edward, worthy king of battle.[48]

What of the other Biblical women mentioned in the cantilena? Marian lyrics spanning the thirteenth to the fifteenth century incude the common trope of addressing the Virgin by means of allusion to female Old Testament figures (Judith, Esther, Sara, etc.). Esther was commonly invoked for her persuasive intercessory manner, and Judith for her militaristic strength, but these qualities were also part of Mary's reputation, since she embodied the positive qualities of all women. The poet uses allusion here to complement Mary: just as Esther and Judith did these things, so too may Mary rule through guiding our king.

The substantial repertory of carols from fifteenth-century England gives a number of particularly appropriate, if later, examples. *Sancta Virgo Maria*, copied in the late fifteenth-century into a book owned by Cambridge Franciscan James Ryman (Cambridge University Library, Ee.I.12, f. 16), reads:

O stronge Judith
O Hester meke,
Tha the serpentes hede did streke
At nede of the conforte we seke,
Dei genitrix pia.[49]

Here one can see the juxtaposition of a plea for Mary's intervention with the use of the same characters as found in *Singularis laudis digna*. *O virgin marie, quene of blis* is found in the same source as *Sancta Virgo Maria* and reflects similar concerns when it addresses Mary as, 'O quene Hester moost meke of myende', and, 'O stronge Judith that Holoferne decapitate' (GB-Cu Ee.I.12, f.15–16). The idea of the regal Mary, *virgo regia*, embodying both the meekness and persuasive powers of Esther and the 'masculinised femininity' of Judith is a powerful combination.[50]

The reference to Anglo-French warfare in *Singularis laudis digna* is an unambiguous contemporary allusion to the Hundred Years War. The first element of the text that is linked specifically to the reign of Edward III is the linking of the arms of England and France, described here as the lilies (or fleurs-de-lis) of the French bowing to the leopard of the English flag. Edward III officially joined the two coats of arms in 1340, adopting the fleurs-de-lis upon declaring his title as King of England and France; he thereby made his claim to the throne of France official after three years of animosity.[51] The allegorical reference to this moment in the literature of Edward's reign was relatively common. Edward III was described in one lyric as 'Ad bona non tardus, audax veluti leopardus' (not slow to do good, bold as a leopard), but it is where the two symbols of leopard and lily are used together that the imagery is more powerful.[52] This type of allegorical lyric is typical of the period of English victory in the wake of the battles at Crécy (August 1346) and Calais (1347). Lesley Coote is keen to point out that these successes were followed 'by the catastrophe of the bubonic plague', so the positive note to lyrics with a political sentiment fell out of favour for a time.[53] By the early 1350s, however, reference to the joining of arms was enjoying a revival. Laurence Minot's poetry collection (London, British Library, Galba E. IX) included a song written in the wake of the English victory of 1352, *How gentill Sir Edward, with his grete engines/Wan with his wight the castell of Gynes*:

> That somer suld shew him
> In schawes [woods] ful schene;
> Both the lely and the lipard
> Suld geder on a grene.[54]

The nature of this 'gathering' is deliberately obscure, in that it could refer to the English and French joining physically on a battlefield or symbolically on the English coat of arms.[55] From the same song collection, an anonymous invective against France, written in Autumn 1346, includes these lines (from which the title of this chapter derives):

> Rex leopardinus est juste rex Parisinus . . .
> Alia rubescunt, leopardis lilia crescunt;
> Per se vanescunt, leopardis victa quiescunt.
> Alia miscentur, leopardis regna tremiscunt . . .
> Anglicus angelicus Edwardus.

> The leopard-king is rightly the Parisian king . . . [The lilies of the French] grow red [with blood], the lilies increase for the leopards; through them [the French] vanish, the vanquished are quiet for the leopards. [The lilies of the French] are thrown into confusion, their kingdoms tremble for the leopards . . . Edward the English Angel.[56]

As is evident from the examples above, the leopard was a powerful symbol because it exceeded the possible strength of the French lily. The same symbolism was emphasised in the Bridlington Prophecies in the same period, a text variously ascribed to St John of Bridlington (who was not its author), to Robert of Bridlington and to John Erghome, a canon at York, who provided it with a lengthy and complex gloss *c.* 1361–63.[57] The role of a gloss was to comment in whatever manner on a pre-existent text, often expanding upon its central ideas. The historical focus of Erghome's gloss is the rule of Kings Edward II and III, up to the early 1360s, and he dwells on the Battle of Crécy (October 1346) in particular:

> Iam crescit bella, crescunt ter trina duella,
> Alma maris stella, fre nunc vexilla, puella.
> Bis dux vix feriet cum trecentis sociatis
> Phi. falsus fugiet, non succerret nece stratis.

> Now battles increase, thrice three duels increase,
> Bear now the standard, kind star of the sea, maiden.
> Twice the leader will strike with 300 companions.
> The false Philip [IV] will flee, nor will he succour those overthrown by slaughter.[58]

Notable in this passage is the combination of historical battles with the plea to the 'kind star of the sea', the Blessed Virgin Mary, just as in the cantilena, *Singularis laudis digna*. Erghome's gloss states that 'Bridlington':

> In primo dicto ostendit auctor multitudinem bellorum futurorum implorando auxilium Marie virginis pro rege Edwardo, dicens, *Iam crescunt bella* ... auctor invocat auxilium beatae Virginis sicut prius solebat, dicens, *Alma maris stella*, scilicet virgo Maria, *puella Christi* ... regis Edwardi contra inimicos suos.
>
> Begins by showing many future battles, imploring the aid of the Blessed Virgin Mary for King Edward, saying *Now battles increase* ... the author invokes the help of the blessed Virgin as before, saying *Hail star of the sea*, namely the virgin Mary, *daughter of Christ* ... to aid Edward against his enemies.[59]

As is clear from these passages, Erghome uses the symbolism of a contrived prophecy text, combined with his own gloss, in order to present a plausible historical explanation for events. His text is comparable to the cantilena *Singularis laudis digna* in several ways. The use of the leopards and lilies in order to represent, as he states, the joining of the arms of England and France symbolises not only Edward III's physical joining of the heraldry, but also the coming together in battle of the knights of these nations for many years. The nature of Erghome's text enables this allegory to be just as powerful in the 1360s as it would have been in the 1340s when Edward adopted the French arms. Perhaps the most striking similarity is the use of the intervention of the Virgin Mary as *stella maris*, invoked on the side of the English.

Both Sanders and Bowers placed some importance on identifying the Biblical characters named in *Singularis laudis digna* with historical figures and particular events. Sanders saw the queen who was governing the king in the second double versicle as Queen Philippa of Hainaut, since in 1346–7 she negotiated the pardon of six citizens of Calais against the death sentence issued by her husband. He therefore concluded that 'Esther and Ahasuerus could hardly stand for anyone other than the queen and king; and the poem could only have been written in 1347, presumably October of that year, when Edward returned to England'.[60] Sanders's dating of the poem rested on his belief that it was designed for performance in front of King Edward. Bowers criticised Sanders's interpretation, perceiving the need to find a candidate who is 'a woman of *our* race deflecting an enemy from his hostile purposes' to match the reference to Judith.[61] He also argued that this woman need not be a queen as such, and offered Princess Isabella, Edward III's eldest daughter, as the solution to this allegorical puzzle. Bowers related the text of *Singularis laudis digna* to 'certain important transactions of the year 1369, Esther/Judith representing Princess Isabella [...] and Ahasuerus her husband Enguerrand VII, lord of Coucy and Count of Soissons in the Kingdom of France'.[62] Their marriage was a useful tool in maintaining the neutrality of the French soil governed by Enguerrand VII in the context of an English attack on France. As a result of this analysis, Bowers concluded that the composition of the music and text of *Singularis laudis digna*:

> may thus be ascribed to the year 1369, and particularly to the months of August and September, as Enguerrand set off for foreign parts to distance himself from the fighting, and as a military expedition left England under John, Duke of Lancaster, to brave the perils of the sea (cf. line 12) and cross the Channel to Calais. The text would have lost its impact after 1375, when the resumption of the Hundred Years War that had begun in 1369 was concluded by the Truce of Bruges.[63]

Bowers's dating of the cantilena would situate it in 1369, having greatest resonance in autumn of that year and for the few years that followed. His conclusions are the most convincing of those that link *Singularis laudis digna* to a particular event and its aftermath, but it is also possible to read the cantilena as politically relevant to a broader chronological and devotional context. The lyric would not have been out of place among those non-musical texts discussed above, and has arguably most in common with Erghome's gloss of the early 1360s. A compositional date in the 1360s would not, of course, prevent *Singularis laudis digna* from having particular impact on its audiences from 1369–75 in the way that Bowers suggests.

Erghome's commentary to the prophetic verses of 'Bridlington' exists in three copies: one has no fixed provenance, one is from the London area and one is from Bury St Edmunds.[64] GB-Onc 362 has been linked with Canterbury on account of the dedication of some of its contents. *Singularis laudis digna* is found in manuscripts that have been linked to a royal chapel and to the great chronicle-producing Abbey at St Albans. Wherever the surviving sources of polyphony praising Edward the Confessor and Edward III originated, the motet and cantilenae discussed here must surely have circulated in the southeast of England and formed part of important royal and liturgical ceremonies at Westminster and Canterbury.

Conclusions

Current affairs featured less explicitly in the texts of English polyphonic compositions than in those written on the continent, and I have argued that even the cantilena *Singularis laudis digna* is as much part of Marian devotion as political commentary on a specific set of events. In the thirteenth century, the conductus genre had been used to explore political ideas and events in England and France. Janet Knapp sums up the subjects typically covered in the texts of conductus as follows:

Songs dedicated to feasts of the Lord, particularly the Nativity, have preference [. . .]. Among the saints, however, it is not only the companions of Christ who are honoured, but also more modern witnesses to the faith: Martin, Germanus of Paris, William of Bourges and Thomas à Becket. There are laments [. . .] on the deaths of temporal and ecclesiastical princes, and more joyful songs associated, also by tradition, with coronations, elevations and homecomings. Outraged protests against corruption in the clergy have a significant place in the repertory; pious in intent, they can hardly be considered sacred.[65]

In France, the conductus and the motet both continued to act as vehicles for a broad range of topics, with the motet favoured for amorous and other secular subjects.

Similar to Knapp's description of the intentionally pious but 'not sacred' conductus on clerical behaviour, the fourteenth-century French motet (whether texted in Latin or the vernacular) is usually depicted as having been cultivated at arm's length from the daily liturgy. Peter Lefferts, for example, has portrayed it as 'a sort of aristocratic chamber music for an educated elite at court, among the clergy, friars, and monks, and at the university'.[66] In contrast, Lefferts argued that 'the [English] motet texts offer virtually no opportunity for the kinds of interpretive analysis that musicology has seen so successfully applied to the rich, figurative language of 14th-century isorhythmic motets and *grandes ballades*, whose political, often polemical texts can usually be associated to definite historical circumstances'.[67]

Supporting perceptions of the separation of French and English musical traditions, Bowers states that fourteenth-century English music 'appears to be devoid of items commemorating recently deceased politicians and saints' in comparison to thirteenth-century repertoire, from which four such pieces survive.[68] Lefferts further contrasted English with continental practice:

In the later fourteenth century the motet in both France and Italy became a vehicle for propaganda and political ceremony, honoring the kings of France, the doges of Venice, popes and antipopes [. . .]. With regard to the themes treated in its texts, then, the English motet may be sharply distinguished from the Latin motets written within the French or Italian traditions in the thirteenth and fourteenth centuries [. . .]. An important distinction remains there as well, in the relative preponderance of texts on saints and feasts in England over those on homiletic topics.[69]

Julie Cumming has agreed that, generally speaking, 'English motets . . . had multipurpose sacred texts, with no political or social allusions'.[70] Cumming also contrasted such pieces with the specific events related or alluded to in many continental motets, ranging from general political concerns and successful battles to a significant number of pieces about papal schism.

This kind of comparison does a disservice to English pieces, which are subsequently perceived as lacking localised colour in their supposedly neutral texts, simply because they were not written with the same kind of overt references to current affairs as their continental counterparts.[71] Most of all, the perception that English motets were not political relies on a specific understanding of what political music might be in the Middle Ages, one in which living or recently deceased nobles are named and battles or other events celebrated unambiguously.

As I have shown with the pieces discussed in this chapter, English composers worked within a different type of artistic climate in which engagement with the political was undertaken through the generation of particular repertories in honour of English saints, themselves strongly political figures from various perspectives. Put simply, a motet in honour of St Edward the Confessor, performed in late fourteenth-century Westminster, would honour not only the historical Edward who founded the Abbey, but also by association Henry III who rebuilt it and Richard II as ruling monarch, underpinning the legitimacy of Plantagenet rule and thus serving a distinctly political end. English composers do not appear to have engaged in hermeneutics, disguising references to contemporary events, dates or individuals that might be uncovered through acrostics, or numerological analysis; however, political canonisation through more broadly based musical and textual associations was of itself a powerful instrument.

Devotional music in honour of a saint who had at some point ruled as monarch measured its subject against intertwined models of kingship and sanctity, and this image was also much more powerfully compared to that of Christ. Paul Strohm has argued that texts constructed for political ends can be 'powerful without being true'.[72] English music reflected this type of fictionality when it promoted the cult of royal and noble saints. At times of political tension, the features of holy historical figures could be reconstructed for political ends. Hankeln has applied this rationale to his examination of liturgical plainchant, which he argues should be 'taken seriously, as a reflection of and point of reference for the political thought of the Middle Ages', since the repertory 'was clearly involved in communicating messages of considerable political relevance to those capable of understanding the liturgical texts'.[73] English motet texts that relate not only to saintly figures but also to saints who were also members of the royal dynasty have been largely overlooked for their power to tell us about the social and political climate in which they were produced.

It was through music and other artistic and literary statements that the king, his ancestry and his piety came to symbolise the English nation.[74] The arts were particularly adept for this purpose, since allegory, quotation, allusion and symbolism could be used to construct an image of a ruler that was not, by definition, necessarily lifelike. It was far more important that the image in these products referred to qualities of strength and authority, regardless of the actual strength of a king's claim to the throne. As at the coronation ceremony, references to national saints or associations made between divine power and the ruler's power on earth were particularly favoured.[75] From approximately the end of the fourteenth century, the image of the Virgin Mary being crowned by the Trinity gained a substantial popularity.[76] It is impossible to see the interest in the coronation of the

60 *Anglicus angelicus*

Virgin as separate from the increased importance of the sacred elements of kingship that dominated during the same period.

Although England was not alone as a country in which the historical record was entwined with perceptions of the nation's special favour with God, so many of the country's rulers and noble elite had been canonised – officially or through localised popular cults – that there existed an especially rich fabric of historical material ready to be crafted into symbolic narrative and lyric.[77] Furthermore, the pervasive mythology that the English people – and kings of England in particular – were especially close to God continued to inform medieval writing and later accounts, and it is clear that some composers used their skills to stir listeners as much by what was heard as by what could be seen in devotional environments.

Notes

1   Priscilla Heath Barnum, ed. *Dives and Pauper*, Volume 1, Part 1. Early English Text Society, original series, 275 (New York: Oxford University Press, 1976), 82; cited in Richard Marks, *Image and Devotion in Late Medieval England* (Stroud: Sutton Publishing, 2004), 1.
2   See Elizabeth Eva Leach, *Guillaume de Machaut: Secretary, poet, musician* (Ithaca: Cornell University Press, 2011).
3   Emma Dillon, *Medieval Music-Making and the* Roman de Fauvel (Cambridge: Cambridge University Press, 2002).
4   Justin Lake reminds us not to exclude hagiography from scholarship relating to medieval history; "Authorial Intention in Medieval Historiography," *History Compass* 12 (2014), 347.
5   There are many excellent accounts of medieval liturgy, but see in particular John Harper, *The Forms and Orders of Western Liturgy from the Tenth to the Eighteenth Century* (Oxford: Clarendon Press, 1991).
6   See Patrick J. Geary, *Phantoms of Remembrance: Memory and oblivion at the end of the first millennium* (Princeton, NJ: Princeton University Press, 1994).
7   Joel T. Rosenthal. "Edward the Confessor and Robert the Pious: 11th Century Kingship and Biography," *Mediaeval Studies* 33 (1971), 7.
8   On medieval kingship, see Fritz Kern, *Kingship and Law in the Middle Ages*, translated by S. B. Chrimes (Oxford: Greenwood Press, 1957); Ernst H. Kantorowicz, *The King's Two Bodies* (Princeton: Princeton University Press, 1957); Anne J. Duggan, ed. *Kings and Kingship in Medieval Europe.* King's College London Medieval Studies 10 (Exeter: Short Run Press, 1993); Elizabeth M. Hallam, "Royal Burial and the Cult of Kingship in France and England, 1060–1330," *Journal of Medieval History* 8 (1982); Gerald L. Harriss, ed. *Henry V: The Practice of Kingship* (Oxford: Oxford University Press, 1985); John Watts, *Henry VI and the Politics of Kingship* (Cambridge: Cambridge University Press, 1996).
9   See especially Paul Binski, *Westminster Abbey and the Plantagenets: Kingship and the representation of power 1200–1400* (New Haven and London: Yale University Press, 1995).
10 Harriss, *Henry V: The practice of kingship*, 10.
11 Helen Deeming, "The Sources and Origin of the 'Agincourt Carol'," *Early Music* 35 (2007).
12 Mary Clayton, *The Cult of the Virgin Mary in Anglo-Saxon England* (Cambridge: Cambridge University Press, 1990), 107–8; Nigel Morgan, "The Coronation of the Virgin by the Trinity and other Texts and Images of the Glorification of Mary in

Fifteenth-Century England." In *England in the Fifteenth Century*, edited by Nicholas Rogers, Harlaxton Medieval Studies 4 (Stamford: Paul Watkins, 1994).

13 Marina Warner, *Alone of All Her Sex: The myth and the cult of the Virgin Mary* (New York: Vintage Books, 1976), especially Chapter 7, "Maria Regina," 103–17.
14 Frank Barlow, *Edward the Confessor* (London: Eyre and Spottiswoode, 1970), 63.
15 Warner, *Alone of All Her Sex*, 111.
16 Ralph A. Griffiths, "Monarchy and Kingship." In *Medieval England: An Encyclopaedia*, edited by Paul E. Szarmach, M. Teresa Tavormina, and Joel T. Rosenthal. New York and London: Garland, 1998, 520.
17 Previous studies of music and coronation include Ernst H. Kantorowicz, *Laudes Regiae: A study in liturgical acclamations and mediaeval ruler worship, with a study of the music of the laudes and musical transcriptions by Manfred F. Bukofzer* (Berkeley and Los Angeles: University of California Press, 1946); Andrew Hughes, "Antiphons and Acclamations: The Politics of Music in the Coronation Service of Edward II, 1308," *Journal of Musicology* 6 (1988).
18 Janet L. Nelson and Peter W. Hammond, "Coronation." In *Medieval England, An Encyclopaedia*, edited by Paul E. Szarmach, M. Teresa Tavormina and Joel T. Rosenthal (New York and London: Garland, 1998), 208.
19 Andrew Hughes, "Coronation Ceremony, Music and Ritual of." In *Medieval England*, edited by Paul E. Szarmach, M. Teresa Tavormina, and Joel T. Rosenthal, 209–10.
20 Samantha J. E. Riches, *St George: Hero, Martyr and Myth* (Stroud: Sutton, 2000), 102.
21 Kantorowicz, *Laudes Regiae*, 171–2. The Worcester Antiphonal is Worcester Cathedral Cod. F. 160, at f. 201; [n.a.] (1997): *Le Codex F.160 de la Bibliothèque de la Cathédrale de Worcester, Antiphonaire Monastique (XIIIe siècle)*. Paléographie Musicale 12. Solemnes: Monks of Solemnes. (first published, Tournai: Desclée, 1922; repr. Berne: Lang, 1972).
22 Kantorowicz, *Laudes Regiae*, 175. The fullest discussion of performances of *Christus vincit* is Ian Bent, "The English Chapel Royal Before 1300," *Proceedings of the Royal Musical Association* 90 (1963).
23 Kantorowicz, *Laudes Regiae*, 176.
24 Matthew Paris, cited in Cecil Roth, *A History of the Jews in England*, 3rd edn (Oxford: Clarendon Press, 1978), 19.
25 Mark Ormrod, "The Personal Religion of Edward III," *Speculum* 64 (1989), 849.
26 Ormrod, "The Personal Religion of Edward II," 876.
27 Roger Bowers, "Fixed Points in the Chronology of English Fourteenth-Century Polyphony," *Music and Letters* 71 (1990), 314.
28 Bowers, "Fixed Points", 314.
29 Frank Ll. Harrison, "Polyphonic Music at the Chapel of Edward III," *Music and Letters* 59 (1978), 421; Ernest H. Sanders "English polyphony in the Morgan Library Manuscript," *Music and Letters* 61 (1980), 173.
30 Bowers, "Fixed Points," 315.
31 May McKisack, *The Fourteenth Century, 1307–1399* (Oxford: Clarendon Press, 1959), 103.
32 Frank Barlow, *The Life of King Edward who Rests at Westminster, Attributed to a Monk of St Bertin* (London: Thomas Nelson and Sons, 1962), 3.
33 Cambridge, University Library MS Ee.3.59 is the only surviving copy of Matthew Paris's Anglo-Norman text, and probably dates to about twenty years later; fuller details and a digital facsimile of the manuscript may be found at http://cudl.lib.cam.ac.uk/view/MS-EE-00003–00059/1.
34 Henry Richard Luard, ed. and transl. *Lives of Edward the Confessor, I: La Estoire de Seint Aedward Le Rei; II: Vita Beati Edvardi Regis et Confessoris; III: Vita Aeduuardi Regis Qui Apud Westmonasterium Requiescit* (London: Longman, 1858), 78–9, lines 1894–8, my translation.

62   Anglicus angelicus

35 'Nemo lucernam accendit, et in abscondito point, neque sub modio: sed supra candelabrum, ut qui ingrediuntur, lumen videant' (Luke 11: 33).
36 'Vos estis lux mundi. Non potest civitas abscondi supra montem posita; Neque accendunt lucernam, et ponunt eam sub modio, sed super candelabrum, ut luceat omnibus qui in domo sunt' (Matthew 5: 14–15).
37 'Et dicebat illis: Numquid venit lucerna ub sub modio ponatur, aut sub lecto? nonne ut super candelabrum ponatur?' (Mark 4: 21).
38 Translation by Peter M. Lefferts in Frank Ll. Harrison, and Peter M. Lefferts eds. *Motets of English Provenance. Polyphonic music of the fourteenth century 15* (Monaco: Editions L'Oiseau-Lyre, 1980), 175–76. The opening of the duplum reads 'Tu es', but for reasons of sense and alliteration was amended in Lefferts's and Harrison's edition to 'Cives', and I have accepted their alternative reading here.
39 Frederick M. Powicke, ed. *The Life of Ailred Abbot of Rievaulx by Walter Daniel* (London: Thomas Nelson and Sons, 1950), xlvii–xlviii.
40 Luard, *Lives of Edward the Confessor*, 137, lines 3975–81; my translation.
41 Henry Richard Luard, ed. *The Chronicle of Thomas Wykes*. Annales Monastici 4. Rolls Series 36 (London: Longman, 1869; repr. New York: Kraus Reprint, 1964), 226; John Crook, *The Architectural Setting of the Cult of Saints in the Early Christian West c. 300–1200* (Oxford: Clarendon Press, 2000), 34.
42 Bent, "The English Chapel Royal", 83–4.
43 Harrison, in Harrison and Lefferts, eds, *Motets of English Provenance*, 159.
44 Michael J. Bennett, "Richard II and the Wider Realm." In *Richard II: The art of kingship*, edited by Anthony Goodman and James L. Gillespie (Oxford: Clarendon Press, 1999), 191.
45 Eleanor L. Scheifele, "Richard II and the Visual Arts." In *Richard II: The art of kingship*, 265.
46 The fullest description of the various ways in which Richard II showed his affection for Edward the Confessor at Westminster Abbey is Nigel Saul, "Richard II and Westminster Abbey." In *Cloister and the World: Essays in medieval history in honour of Barbara Harvey*, edited by John Blair and Brian Golding (Oxford: Clarendon Press, 1996).
47 Christopher Page, CD liner notes to Christopher Page, dir. *Masters of the Rolls: Music by English composers of the fourteenth century* (Hyperion, CDA67098, 1999), 3.
48 This translation draws on Ernest Sanders, Frank Harrison, and Peter M. Lefferts, eds. *English Music for Mass and Office. Polyphonic music of the fourteenth century 17* (Monaco: Editions L'Oiseau-Lyre, 1986), 215; Bowers, "Fixed Points," 315; and Page, *Masters of the Rolls*, 10.
49 Edited carol texts from Richard L. Greene, ed. *The Early English Carols*, 2nd edn (Oxford: Clarendon Press, 1977), 127–8.
50 *Salve Regina glorie* (GB-Cu Ee.I.12, f.88), opens with these two verses: 'O stronge Judith so full of myght / By thy vertu we be made fre / For thou hast putte oure foo to flyght / *Mater misericordie;* O meke Hestere so fayre of face / Kyng Assuere for love of the / Hath take mankynd until his grace; *Mater misericordie*'; Greene, *The Early English Carols*, 136. There are numerous other examples. The phrase 'masculinised femininity' is Paul Strohm's; see Paul Strohm, ed. *Hochon's Arrow: The social imagination of fourteenth-century texts* (Princeton: Princeton University Press, 1992), 110.
51 Lesley A. Coote, *Prophecy and Public Affairs in Later Medieval England* (Woodbridge: Boydell and Brewer, 2000), 121.
52 Thomas Wright, *Political Poems and Songs Relating to English History, Composed During the Period from The Accession of Edward III to that of Richard III, 2 vols.* Rolls Series 14 (London: Longman, 1859–61), 137.
53 Coote, *Prophecy and Public Affairs*, 121.

54 Wright, *Political Poems and Songs*, 89.
55 Basil Cottle, *The Triumph of English 1350–1400* (London: Blandford Press, 1969), 66.
56 Wright, *Political Poems and Songs*, 31; translation by Anne Walters Robertson, *Guillaume de Machaut and Reims: Context and meaning in his musical works* (Cambridge: Cambridge University Press, 2002), 203.
57 The contested authorship of these texts is discussed in Paul Meyvaert, "John Erghome and the *Vaticinium Roberti Bridlington*," *Speculum* 41 (1966).
58 Cited in Paul Strohm, *England's Empty Throne: Usurpation and the language of legitimation, 1399–1422* (New Haven and London: Yale University Press, 1998), 10–11.
59 Text from Wright, *Political Poems and Songs*, 156–57, my translation.
60 Sanders, "English polyphony," 173.
61 Bowers, "Fixed Points," 316.
62 Bowers, "Fixed Points," 316.
63 Bowers, "Fixed Points," 317.
64 Coote, *Prophecy and Public Affairs*, 144.
65 Janet Knapp, "Conductus," *Grove Music Online. Oxford Music Online*. Oxford University Press. Accessed 16 November 2015, www.oxfordmusiconline.com/subscriber/article/grove/music/06268.
66 Lefferts, *The Motet in England*, 9.
67 Peter M. Lefferts, "Text and Context in the Fourteenth-Century English Motet," *L'ars nova italiana del trecento* 6 (1984), 171.
68 *O decus predicancium* in honour of Peter of Verona (canonised in 1254), *Miles Christi gloriose* and *Salve Symon Montisfortis* for Simon de Montfort (d.1265) (two motets), and *Thomas gemma/Thomas cesus*, celebrating both Thomas of Canterbury (d. 1170) and Thomas of Dover (d.1295). *Thomas gemma Cantuarie* must belong to the very end of the thirteenth century at the earliest, and circulated in the fourteenth century, so its chronological placement is not quite as straightforward as the other examples; Bowers, "Fixed Points," 313–14.
69 Lefferts, *The Motet in England*, 186–7.
70 Julie E. Cumming, *The Motet in the Age of Du Fay* (Cambridge: Cambridge University Press, 1999), 22.
71 Cumming has pointed out how the vague information available regarding the function of motets cannot be used as part of the definition of the motet as a genre; *The Motet in the Age of Du Fay*, 60–2. Similarly, Lefferts acknowledged 'the function of the motet' in England as 'the most unsettling gap' in current understanding; *The Motet in England*, 9.
72 Strohm, *Hochon's Arrow*, 5.
73 Roman Hankeln, "Reflections of War and Violence in Early and High Medieval Saints' Offices," *Plainsong and Medieval Music* 23 (2014), 27.
74 Griffiths, "Monarchy and Kingship," 520.
75 For the liturgies of king saints developed during the Middle Ages, see Andrew Hughes, "The Monarch as the Object of Liturgical Veneration." In *Kings and Kingship in Medieval Europe*, edited by Anne J. Duggan (Exeter: Short Run Press, 1993).
76 Morgan, "The Coronation of the Virgin," 223.
77 For the relationship between music and fourteenth-century French kingship, see Walters Robertson, *Guillaume de Machaut and Reims*, 224–56. The Capetians developed a similar allegiance to royal saints, as exemplified by Louis IX's canonisation in 1297; see Gabrielle M. Spiegel, "The Cult of St Denis and Capetian Kingship." In *Saints and their Cults: Studies in religious sociology, folklore and history*, edited by Stephen Wilson (Cambridge: Cambridge University Press, 1983).

3 Authorship, musicianship and value in medieval English history

Traditional historical writing is typically structured around key figures, events in which they participated and the texts that they produced. The prevailing anonymity of English music before 1400 – even after which attribution remains patchy – makes the task of writing its history more than a little difficult. This chapter seeks to understand the effect of a lack of known authors on the writing of English musical history, especially the history of polyphonic music. I explore what happens when pieces of music *are* attributed, taking the case of 'St' Richard Scrope and St Edburga, whose musicianship was discussed by medieval chroniclers. An examination of notions of musicianship in the biographies of Scrope and St Edburga will be used to revisit what authorship meant at that time, inviting us to reconsider early and more recent perceptions of individuality and value.

Scribal practice in the attribution of music, poetry and broader literature during the later Middle Ages is still insufficiently understood. Authorial attribution can add weight to the perceived significance of music, and invites us to reflect on questions of genesis, reception, personal style, influence and value. In short, it has helped writers to view pieces as worthy of modern scholarly activities such as edition, public performance, critical contemplation and recording, often at the expense of anonymous repertoire. Before the scribes working on the Old Hall Manuscript named an array of its contributors, there is very little English music that survives with reference to its composer, or that can be linked securely with such a person, especially in relation to polyphony.[1] This can be contrasted with a slightly higher survival rate for authored musical treatises in England, a healthy record of named singers working in institutional contexts and even the presence, if very limited, of the names of scribes.[2]

Music manuscripts convey their contents in a similar manner to the architectural settings that housed them, betraying evidence of a flourishing and sophisticated profession of craftsmen and women for whom the addition of a name to such things as stained glass windows, grotesques, bells or devotional images was – for various reasons – usually superfluous. English song remains a history of discrete and reproducible but 'unclaimed' works; it is useful to use Michael Talbot's term here, which reminds us that music was authored even if we do not know its composers' names from the surviving sources.[3]

The number of concordant sources for English music suggests its value beyond the immediate sphere of the composer: motets such as *Thomas gemma Cantuarie* and *Rota versatilis* were evidently known in more than one location. Concordances with items in the Old Hall Manuscript show that some of the codex was compiled from pieces that had circulated for some time as well as items that went on to be copied elsewhere.[4] On the other hand, William Summers argues that 'though the number of concordances is significant, it is clear that many institutions apparently produced quite a bit of unique music', suggesting sophisticated, creative activity in numerous different locations.[5] Copying practices become clearer in the late fifteenth and especially the sixteenth century. There survives a larger number of references in the records to payments for the copying of plainsong, or of polyphony (often identified as 'pricksong') from this time in or for places like York, Beverley and Durham where interest in new music for the liturgy flourished with the rise of interest in votive Masses such as those in honour of the Holy Name of Jesus.[6] The foundation of collegiate institutions like Tattershall and Eton broadened the range of places where polyphony was generated beyond the probable dominance of monasteries before 1400. The large-scale loss of so much polyphony in the religious reforms of the sixteenth century makes it difficult to estimate the balance that would have existed at different institutions between the pressure to produce new, or innovative, music against the availability of music copied elsewhere or used over several decades. In this way, it is nearly impossible to answer the question of what was most highly prized by singers and copyists or what their priorities might have been: did they value some songs more highly than others? Did they race to acquire new music by a particular composer? What caused scribes to change their copying practices or to travel for new music, beyond feasts added to the liturgical calendar?

The problem of English music's relative neglect in scholarship (as outlined in the first two chapters of this book) cannot only be a lack of known authors. For example, there still remains very limited engagement with individual pieces of music – whether monophonic or polyphonic – using analytical methods similar to those applied to thirteenth-century French motets, a corpus also lacking composer attributions.[7] A contributory factor has been the relatively recent awareness of the substantial repertory of song in medieval England before 1300, bolstered in no small part by the work of Deeming.[8] Unclaimed repertoire discourages critical appraisal of individual pieces. The emergence of attributed music at the close of the Middle Ages has offered scholars opportunities to use a range of evidence – stylistic and contextual – to reclaim anonymous pieces as belonging to the work of known composers. This strategy has been evident in particular in relation to securing (or uncoupling) attributions to composers such as John Dunstaple, John Bedyngham and Walter Frye, for whom a sufficiently large quantity of polyphony has survived as to make meaningful comparisons of form, mensural arrangement, melodic style, text-setting, contrapuntal approach and manuscript context.[9]

Writing history through genre and liturgical function

Scholars working on unclaimed polyphony before the Old Hall Manuscript must tell its stories using frameworks that go beyond the composer-focused approaches common to accounts of the tonal period; such methods might employ themes of notational development, musical style, manuscript sources or genre. These can be liberating, avoiding reliance on stories of the great composers and their works that continue to bolster the traditional canon, but they also bring their own pitfalls. A brief consideration of one genre, the motet, can illustrate some of the problems.

Harrison viewed liturgical function as the chief manner by which genre could be determined. His influential book, *Music in Medieval Britain* (1958), prioritised institutional history and genre. In his introduction to a facsimile volume of manuscripts of fourteenth-century English music, published over twenty years later, Harrison developed his view further, clarifying that classification of liturgical function and musical structure could together elucidate the reasons for particular manuscript layouts.[10] His approach affected his portrayal of the surviving repertoire, as can be seen from a brief exploration of contrasting his own definition of the motet and that of other writers.

Harrison was willing to classify pieces as 'motets' only if their cantus firmus was identified, or if they consisted of two or more texted parts. This narrow acceptance of pieces into the motet genre was challenged by Bent, who noted that English composers considered the choice of a liturgically appropriate tenor as only one of many possible starting points for the construction of polyphonic works.[11] Bent's more inclusive definition – 'a piece of music in several parts with words' – might, on the one hand, lead to a large number of hitherto separate genres being included under the motet umbrella (the cantilena, for example), but it usefully moved away from the tendency to measure English genres against the conventions of continental compositions.[12] Lefferts defined the motet corpus via the continental model of the late thirteenth century: 'a composition a3 with two upper voices, each having its own text, over a tenor cantus firmus', adding the categories of English motets based on a *pes*, or over a pair of voices with tenor function. He further considered pieces written using rondellus techniques to be types of conductus and identified troped chant settings as a separate genre, albeit one that became intertwined with motets in the early part of the fourteenth century.[13] Lefferts's study of motets distinguished them from conductus and rondellus items, but did not apply or accept Harrison's categories of free and cantus firmus settings as separate genres, observing that distinctions between genres were blurred.[14] Bent's opinion, that 'evidence suggests that genre boundaries were broader than we have allowed them to become', echoed Lefferts's conclusions, leaving the reader with the realisation that genre can be a more difficult point of departure for tracing the history of English music than might be expected.[15] The motet certainly does not offer as clearly delineated a corpus of material as later genres, such as the string quartet or symphony (not to say that later genre classifications are not problematic in their own ways).

Harrison offered a model by which sacred music could be understood by identifying its specific religious ritual context.[16] Yet his liturgical bias was restricted in many ways by his view of polyphony as an 'additional element in ceremonial, and as a further means of festive adornment and elaboration of the ritual'.[17] For Harrison, polyphonic music was typical of pre-Reformation Catholic largesse, which sought always to decorate the 'authentic' religious ritual with a gold trim. The idea that polyphony had been created as little more than an accretion to the basic chant was as typical of its time as it was influential. The model distinguishes between 'established plainsong', viewed as a timeless monument, and polyphony which, rather than being an 'integral part of the Christian liturgies from the beginning of history', functioned only to 'lend ceremonial distinction to the performance of the established plainsong'.[18] Sanders expressed similar opinions. His detailed examination of the European motet through its early history considered voices added to Gregorian chant from the twelfth century onward as 'embellishments'.[19] Embellishment is a useful word, for example in describing musical and textual materials that go beyond the strict requirements of earlier liturgical custom.[20] Much polyphonic music functions as trope in that it may use pre-existent text or musical material as a basis for new parts or lyrics. The difficulty arises with the cultural baggage associated with embellishment in relation to what has gone before: the implication of timeless, static, permanent, authentic liturgical practice is, in the end, a fantasy.

Whose music was valued in England?

Bowers has highlighted the ephemeral nature of composed, polyphonic settings in the fifteenth century:

> There were no classics, no established repertory pieces [...]. As a creative artist contributing to the worship of God [the composer's] offering was on a level comparable with that of the parish ladies who arrange flowers on Christmas Eve – a genuine contribution to the overall effect, pretty while it lasts, but not destined for more than immediate use, and therefore of only limited value and esteem.[21]

Bowers contrasted this with the artistic contributions made by painters, architects, poets and book illuminators, whose works he considered as major art forms because of their permanence or because their producers were engaged in creating them full time, in comparison to the 'staple fare' of plainsong.[22] In a reprint of Bowers's article, he explained that the original's:

> somewhat negative tone arises from the fact that I was endeavouring to show that whatever may have been the function of the church as patron (strictly interpreted) on the Western European mainland, in England its role was not at all strong.[23]

Bowers was right to dissuade us from looking for what might be termed professional composers in England before 1500, and there is certainly no evidence of a 'canon' of works in the nineteenth-century sense. On the other hand, the evidence of recopying many pieces between manuscripts and locations argues that there was a repertory of music used in England that was of more than temporary or local significance.[24] This is a different issue to the fact that improvised music, and performances themselves, were ephemeral in that they were not part of written tradition.

The permanence of music collections was adversely affected by notational developments. Whereas changing fashions in artistic symbolism, for example, would not have prevented the contemplative imagery on a high-status item such as the Wilton Diptych having a resonance for owners or viewers for many centuries after its production *c*. 1395–99, the interpretation of fourteenth-century music sources was far more challenging for those examining them in later periods. Visual artistic 'language' and style may have greater longevity of meaning, but there is evidence that scribes wished pieces of music to remain current in that some pieces can be found in notation updated or clarified by later scribes. Some repertoire certainly survived more significant notational changes, as shown through works found in both black full and white mensural notation in different sources circa 1400.

The turn of the fourteenth century is sometimes understood as a watershed in the relationship between music and authorial presence or value. Specifically, the attribution of works in the Old Hall Manuscript has given writers greater confidence in working on specific pieces and the relationships between them in contrast to earlier music. Compare, for example, Caldwell's discussion of fourteenth-century English repertoire with Strohm's characterisation of Old Hall pieces:

> It would be idle to claim, for English fourteenth-century music, a status comparable with that enjoyed by the great literary masterpieces of Chaucer, Langland, and their contemporaries, or indeed a humanity approaching that of such devotional writers as the Lady Julian of Norwich, Richard Rolle, or Walter Hilton. On the whole it *quietly fulfilled its function* as an adjunct to the liturgy, as an expression of princely or magnatial dignity, or as pure entertainment (or any combination of these). England produced no *individualist* comparable to Machaut or Landini, and while we might like to know the names of its composers, the *very anonymity* of virtually all this music seems appropriate to its *humble function* [emphasis added].[25]

Here, Caldwell contrasted the lack of authorial presence in fourteenth-century music with the composers and authors who worked within vernacular culture in England and abroad. He emphasised the relationship between artistry, cultural status and the author him/herself, in both secular and devotional contexts. There is an important difference between musical and literary history underlying these remarks, in that even during their lifetimes, the authorial reputations of Chaucer, Machaut, Hilton and others were more fully endorsed in literary and artistic media than were their musical contemporaries. Put simply, the reason we often know more about continental music authorship is because its composers were also poets,

70 *Authorship, musicianship and value*

in which a tradition of attribution had been common in various genres, from troubadour and trouvère song to the poetic oeuvre of Philippe de Vitry, for example. The reason we know comparatively less of English musicians is, in part, because the acceptance of English as a suitably high-status vernacular was comparatively slow; once the social position of the language changed, through the works of Chaucer and his contemporaries, the number of attributed pieces of music rose accordingly.

Composer portraits do exist in various forms in continental sources of the fourteenth and fifteenth centuries. For example, there are exceptional depictions of Machaut in manuscript Paris, Bibliothèque Nationale, fr.1584 (known within Machaut scholarship as MS A), and the images of Italian musicians in the Squarcialupi Codex are also well-known.[26] Dufay and Binchois's pairing in the manuscript copy of Martin Le Franc's *Le Champion des Dames* (Arras, 1451), and the sculpture of Dufay on his funeral monument (*c*. 1474) are particularly fine examples from the fifteenth century. Within English devotional literature, the closest exemplar is probably the depiction of English hermit Richard Rolle (d. 1349), whose Latin and vernacular literary output frequently drew on his special relationship with liturgical and musical contexts.[27] In Cambridge, St John's College, MS 23 B.1, in a fifteenth-century collection of his writings, Rolle is portrayed displaying the contents of his book using standard symbolism used to show literacy, piety and authority (see Figure 3.1).[28] Manuscript images found in psalters or similar books sometimes illustrate the status, identity or musical skills of groups of individuals (typically clerics or nuns), such as the monks and nuns shown praying and singing in the Psalter of Henry VI (London, British Library, Cotton MS Domitian A XVII, ff. 74v, 177v, 150v). A lively tradition of illustrating Psalm 97 with an image of three clerics singing together, in one case performing an extant English motet *Zelo tui langueo*, shows that miniaturists were capable of depicting polyphonic singing and even repertoire as early as the beginning of the fourteenth century.[29] There remains, however, no composer portrait of an English musician comparable to those from elsewhere before the Reformation.

So were musicians known individuals? Did people recognise their names beyond their local context? Was individuality a desirable concept within medieval English musical culture, and how might that have been expressed? Once the Old Hall Manuscript adds to our knowledge of musicians' names, scholars discuss individuality as if it were something that had become a more dominant concept than previously. For example, in relation to the repertoire of Old Hall itself, Strohm identified an 'appreciation of *individual* achievement', and a 'deliberately *individual* style of many of its works' [emphasis added].[30] For Strohm, this feature marked a departure from the repertoire of the previous century, which 'for all its worth had not yet found such heralds and ambassadors: a corollary of its collective, *functional* orientation perhaps' [emphasis added].[31] Both Caldwell and Strohm distinguish between the functional and the individual, between creative humility and artistic ego, with Strohm finding individuality in music from a collection that names a good number of its contributors. From Strohm's description, it is easy to forget that aside from a handful of motets – which may have been written for

Figure 3.1 Richard Rolle as depicted in a fifteenth-century collection of his works, Cambridge, St John's College, MS 23 B.1, f. 41r. By permission of the Master and Fellows of St John's College, Cambridge

performance at important ceremonial occasions – the contents of Old Hall are primarily settings of movements of the Ordinary of the Mass, functioning as liturgical music, some of which were conceived pre-1400.[32]

Of course, many of the pieces in Old Hall display innovative stylistic features, such as five-part writing and the use of double canon; in this sense, particular pieces within the collection are unusual and ambitious, though that does not necessarily equate with being more 'individual' (a word that might imply personal?) than other works, which is a matter of judgement in relation to cultural context. Many anonymous pieces of music from thirteenth- and fourteenth-century England contain unusual approaches to structure or style. Perhaps the most obvious example is the St Katherine motet *Rota versatilis*, which Sanders called 'one of the most magnificent English compositions', and whose appearance in several manuscript locations at least testifies to its more widespread transmission than some items similarly praised but surviving in only one source.[33] But does this mean that we should construct our history around them, or should we view them as cultural outliers and seek more common exemplars to tell our historical story? As with 'Sumer is icumen in', Strohm, Sanders, and others have continued to seek idiosyncrasy as justification for ranking some items above others in terms of their cultural significance. An unusual and challenging technical or structural approach, even in settings of the Gloria or Credo, is seen as a marker of artistry, of prioritising purely musical decisions over functional constraints, of pursuing and expressing a personal aesthetic agenda.

What happens when musical works *are* claimed in contemporary records, but in ways that make little historical sense, or for which we have insufficient evidence to judge the reliability of medieval witnesses? Chroniclers, authors of saints' lives and other writers of the Middle Ages referred to musical practices regularly, but they did not intend to produce what we might recognise as a history of music, an undertaking that began only in the eighteenth century.[34] Sometimes writers were vague, speaking only of an individual's particular aptitude for song, or inspiring devotional singing in others; on other occasions writers suggested that historical and holy figures wrote specific musical items, sufficiently well-known from the liturgy to be plausible candidates for such attribution.[35] Arguably, a consideration of how we might respond to what are, at best, questionable attributions in plainchant can have a useful and cautionary bearing on how we might handle dealing with attribution in polyphony. Medieval exemplars of writing in which the performance and composition of liturgical song are linked to individuals in diverse ways, can be used as a lens through which to reconsider contemporary evidence for the biography of early English composers of polyphonic music.

The case studies below relate to two historical, holy English figures: St Edburga and Richard Scrope. Each one attracted biographical discussion by contemporaries and later medieval writers that linked them with musical ability. Such historical discourse seems, at face value, to offer records of musical biography; however, the claims made in these texts are revealed to be quite complex in their intention, and in their factual reliability. Although we may wish to discover new texts that name men or women as composers of polyphony, the examples below serve to remind us of the pitfalls of treating early accounts of musicianship with anything other than the greatest of care.

Music, sanctity and identity in the cult of St Edburga

Within medieval texts that relate the lives of popes, abbots, bishops and saints, it was not unusual to represent the central figure as a composer of sequences, antiphons or other liturgical songs. Such attributions are frequently fanciful, leading to the withdrawal of some of the most well-known examples – such as the hymn *Dies irae*, once attributed to Franciscan friar Thomas of Celano (*c.* 1200–65) – reverting these songs to anonymity.[36] The reasons for false attributions varied, but typically stemmed from an author's wish to emphasise the erudite and chaste life of their central character, especially when the saint themselves lived at least partly in the outside world or was of noble origin. Similarly, individuals were sometimes credited with particular musicality, in ways that may or may not be evidenced as true. Simply removing the composer attribution for liturgical song in our history, or dismissing accounts of exceptional musical skill, misses an important opportunity to consider the meanings of such associations. Furthermore, it would be unwise to assume that composer attributions for liturgical song (i.e. those typically made in saintly *historiae*) function in an entirely separate conceptual space to those made about polyphonic song and its composers.

Consideration of the authenticity of musical biography can be highlighted through a brief survey of the hagiographical materials for St Edburga of Pershore (d. 960, canonised 972). Edburga's saintly biography, her *vita*, is problematic at the outset and it is perfectly possible that there was more than one St Edburga in Anglo-Saxon England, including one or two minor figures whose stories were combined in accounts by writers who knew of only one historical figure of that name. Most writings about Edburga have seen her through the biographical lens of Osbert of Clare, whose account, written around 1140, justified why Edburga's relics might be found in different places (Winchester, Pershore near Worcester and Bicester near Oxford) and consolidated the legend to clarify that at least some of her bones were – at one point – moved from Winchester to Pershore. Certainly, the monks of Pershore believed that they possessed St Edburga's relics, and her cult was therefore of particular importance there.[37]

According to legend, St Edburga was a granddaughter of Alfred the Great, and entered the Nunnaminster in Winchester at the age of four. Evidence of St Edburga's musicianship is suggested by an anonymous Latin legend of the mid-fourteenth century stating that St Edburga sang seven times a day, and that the effect of constant prayer and devotion had an impact on her physicality:

> Macerabat namque corpus suum vigiliis et orationibus, psalmos assidue canens nocte ac die: *Septies in die laudem dixi tibi* (*Ps.* 118, 164). Studebat per septenarium numerum ymnorum cotidie perficere.[38]
>
> For her own body was wasted with vigils and prayers, singing the psalms assiduously night and day [. . .]: *Seven times a day I have given praise to Thee*

74 *Authorship, musicianship and value*

(Ps. 118, 164). She studied the seven numbered hymns daily in order to perfect them (my translation).

Laurel Braswell notes the textual gloss of Psalm 118 (119) 'Septies in die laudem dixi tibi super iudicia iustitiae tuae' ('Seven times a day I have given praise to thee, for the judgements of thy justice');[39] the 'seven numbered hymns' are the Seven Penitential Psalms. Jocelyn Wogan-Browne believes that the account 'partly encodes the ability of a house to carry out its liturgical duties', confirming the importance of key religious texts to private and institutional worship.[40] The relationship between Edburga's focus on singing and prayer and her emaciated body reflects a particular, gender-inflected aspect of constructions of female religious devotional activity through acts that could be perceived as masochistic but that also had the potential to demonstrate spiritual power and control, especially one's control over weakness of the flesh that might threaten chastity.[41] A sanctorale from Hyde Abbey describes a further example of a distinctly feminine-inflected musical experience. Lessons 5–6 of Edburga's Office recount a story in which the young princess is coaxed into singing Psalm 58 (59): 2 'Eripe me de inimicis meis Deus et ab insurgentibus in me libera me' ('Deliver me from my enemies, O my God; and defend me from them that rise up against me'). This psalm, with its prayer for relief from political conflicts, may have been cited on account of a particular resonance with the events of her family at the time, but the fact that Edburga was invited to sing it reflects the modesty appropriate to her sex and noble status. Other medieval accounts are less precise about the nature of Edburga's musical ability. Osbert of Clare, for example, noted only her general ability to sing.[42]

Reports of Edburga's musicality are not simple acts of documentation: they are interpretative, reflective and complex references to elements of her combined identity as young woman, nun, virgin, princess and saint. The single polyphonic work in her honour, the three-part motet *Virgo regalis fidei* (in the Worcester Fragments, now Oxford, Bodleian Library, Latin liturgical d. 20, Worc xxviii, f. 1vlxxiv verso) is a contrafact of an item initially conceived for St Katherine of Alexandria, a saint popular in medieval England whose cult combined nobility and chastity with holy martyrdom, mention of which in the motet text clarifies the relationship between the original and adapted versions of the piece.[43] *Virgo regalis fidei* is constructed as four sections of voice exchange and a short coda.

It has not previously been noted that the text of the motet tropes the Matins antiphon to St Katherine, *Virgo regalis fidei merito specialis ut jubar in tenebris mundo Katharina refulsit*, found in diverse European sources from the twelfth century.[44] It is likely that the motet was employed as part of liturgical celebration on the feast days of St Katherine and St Edburga. Lefferts singled this motet out as an 'unequivocal example' of a piece whose text was 'so general in reference that it was suitable for any number of institutions', since the majority of the lyric is 'more or less appropriate for any virgin-martyr with a four-syllable name' (E-ad-bur-ga).[45] While this may be broadly correct, the liturgical origin of the motet as an item for praising St Katherine can be conclusively established through its tropic relationship with the antiphon. Additionally, as Christopher Hohler has pointed out, St Edburga was not a martyr, despite her relatively short life; her death was, we can assume, relatively unremarkable.[46] In this way, the marginal scribal invitation in the Worcester Fragments to sing this piece on her feast day reflects a culture of fairly crude adaptation. The text draws initially, verbatim, on the Matins antiphon, before concluding with original text that reflects the poetic elements of the opening:

> Virgo regalis/fidei merito specialis
> ut iubar in tenebris/Katerina refulsit in arvis
> hind animo forti/pro Christo subdita morti
> celorum castis/glomerata choruscat in astris.

> The regal virgin Katherine [or Edburga], outstanding in the merit of her faith, has shone throughout the lands like a heavenly light in darkness. Strong in soul she was delivered to death for Christ; therefore she was formed into a sphere in the castles of heaven and glitters among the stars.

The motet dates from a period in which St Edburga's life featured in three of the surviving copies of the *South English Legendary*, one of which was written in 1280, the remaining copies being roughly contemporary.[47] A contributory factor has been the relatively recent awareness of theWhat we can infer of the authorial intentions of the motet's later copyist, adapting the St Katherine piece for the celebration of St Edburga in the late thirteenth century, is that they most likely saw the expressive potential of venerating a reportedly musical female saint with polyphony. The role of liturgical song in Edburga's *vita* was tropic – taking passages from the psalms to make broader points about sanctity, gender and political history. Similarly, the motet's tropic origin offers a particular window into the overlapping traditions of borrowing, homage, adaptation and musical expression found in medieval England before the cult of musical authorship was more fully developed.

Richard Scrope's personal piety and his impact on York liturgy

As has been shown from the materials relating to St Edburga, establishing the purpose of reference to musicality in medieval texts is far from straightforward. Musicianship might be related to contemporary perceptions of an individual's identity, especially for someone whose life and career were experienced primarily through the Church. It is within this context that it is instructive to examine an attribution of specific liturgical materials to Richard Scrope, Archbishop of York. The personal piety of Scrope (*c*. 1350–1405) was reflected in his support of a number of English saints, including John of Beverley and John of Bridlington. It has not previously been noticed by musicologists that one of the authors of the anonymous *Chronica Pontificum Ecclesiae Eboracensis* claimed that Scrope composed two liturgical items himself, namely the sequences 'Scrupulosa' (an item in honour of the Eleven Thousand Virgins) and 'Spe mercedis' (for the Mass

76 *Authorship, musicianship and value*

of St Thomas of Canterbury). The attributions of both these songs raise some interesting questions, even though they hold little water as secure claims of authorship. They can also shed light on the relationship between high-status figures, their piety and their representation as 'composers', going further than the discussion of St Edburga because of their ostensible insight into surviving songs.

Scrope's family had connections in North Yorkshire; his father was first Baron Scrope of Masham (d. 1392). Studies in Oxford and Cambridge, various clerical appointments and travel to Rome were followed by election as Bishop of Chichester (1385), then as Bishop of Coventry and Lichfield (1386). Scrope was confirmed as Archbishop of York on 15 March 1398. His perceived role in the rebellion against the Lancastrian Crown led to his execution as a traitor in 1405. Scrope was decapitated on Clementhorpe, outside York's city walls, by five blows – suggestive of the five wounds of Christ – and his body was then moved to the Minster for burial, where it remains today in the Scrope Chapel. A cult developed almost immediately, as a result of rumours that Henry IV's orders had resulted in the king contracting leprosy and that there had been miracles performed at Scrope's tomb. In 1406, the tomb was walled off in an attempt to curtail the cult's development. The Pope ordered the excommunication of everyone involved in Scrope's death. In the 1450s, Richard, Duke of York encouraged the cult in order to strengthen his claim to the English throne, and formal (though ultimately unsuccessful) claims were made for Scrope's canonisation in 1462.[48]

Following Scrope's death, historical records and the materials that formed part of his personal cult drew obvious parallels between his martyrdom at the command of Henry IV and the execution of Thomas of Canterbury by Henry II's knights in the twelfth century. The attempt to align Scrope's nascent cult with the Canterbury saint comes as little surprise and was found in several accounts such as those by the Clement of Maidstone (*c.* 1413), Thomas Gascoigne and a further chronicler from York, who 'emphasised Scrope's similarity to Thomas à Becket [St Thomas of Canterbury] both in the manner of their deaths and in their defence of ecclesiastical liberties'.[49] Scrope's own cult maintained its popularity through the fifteenth century, and surviving materials include a liturgical office, a carol and saintly images in manuscript and glass.

Around the turn of the sixteenth century, the author of the third part of the *Chronica Pontificum Ecclesiae Eboracensis* wrote that, as representative of his sanctity and strong moral character, Scrope produced:

> plurimas Sequentias, quae in Missis canuntur in usu Eboracensi, ad laudem Dei et Sanctorum formoso stylo compilavit, scilicet de Sancto Thoma Martyre, *Spe mercedis et coronae*; Undecim milibus Virginum, *Scrupulosa*, cum diversis aliis. Multas etiam prosas et orations devotas compilavit de hoc nomine Jesu, et illud quam totiens devotionis gratia oretenus exprimere solebat, sic, *Jhesu mercy*, sic vulgariter fando.[50]

> A very great number of sequences, that were sung at Masses in the Use of York, to the praise of God and the Saints, compiled in the formal style, namely of St Thomas the Martyr, *Spe mercedis et coronae*; of the Eleven Thousand

Virgins, *Scrupulosa*, with diverse others. Many prosas [sequences] and devoted prayers were compiled in the name of Jesus, and that all the devoted expressed their thanks saying thus, *Jhesu mercy*, thus in the vernacular.

The chronicler was evidently familiar with the liturgical interests of Scrope during his lifetime and was also interested in producing an account that emphasised and exaggerated the Archbishop's genesis of liturgical materials. The mention, for example, of Scrope's commitment to the Holy Name of Jesus – a cult that took root in England during the fifteenth century and became widespread by 1500[51] –reflects the fact that Scrope had established a chantry by the altar in Lichfield dedicated to the Holy Name in 1396.[52] The fifteenth-century York Gradual that survives as Oxford, Bodleian Library, Latin Liturgical b. 5 includes both 'Spe mercedis' and 'Scrupulosa', bearing witness that the sequences were in use in the northern province.[53] The sequence for St Thomas is also found in sources from elsewhere in England and from the continent; it does not form part of the standard Sarum rite, which prescribes the sequence *Solemne canticum hodie resonet in terra* for the Mass on St Thomas's feast day.[54] 'Spe mercedis' dates at least as far back as the thirteenth century. Its melody may be French or English – Hiley considers it to be of possible Canterbury origin – and it occurs in England both with the text to Thomas and as 'In hoc mundo', a sequence in honour of St Edmund King and Martyr.[55] Although the chronicler's attribution of 'Spe mercedis' was false, his motivation was presumably intended to draw a parallel between the martyrdom of both Archbishops, Thomas and Richard, not least since the text focuses directly on the suffering of Thomas at the moment of his martyrdom: 'In the hope of the reward and the [martyr's] crown Thomas [and by implication, Richard] stood in agony, obedient unto death'.[56]

The second item claimed for Scrope's authorship is the sequence 'Scrupulosa', with its obvious wordplay on the Archbishop's noble family name. It is possible that the writer of the chronicle was likewise trying to make some broader point about Scrope's clerical identity, even though on the surface such an association – with the cult of the Eleven Thousand Virgins – seems rather obscure. 'Scrupulosa' is one of eighteen sequences found in the surviving York Gradual that are peculiar to its Use, many of them with regional significance. Hiley has commented that 'there is evidence of a good deal more composition [in the sequences] than among the ordinary of mass chants', predominantly limited to textual composition, writing new lyrics to well-established melodies.[57] Indeed, 'Scrupulosa' is a contrafactum, a standard way of creating new devotional materials.[58] The melody is perhaps most readily known from *Rex omnipotens*, the Sequence for Ascension Day in the Sarum Use.[59] 'Scrupulosa' survives in ten liturgical sources, all of which were copied or printed for use in the province of York after 1400.[60] Given the provenance of extant sources, it is reasonable to speculate that the text of 'Scrupulosa' was written in or around York.[61] The local composition of 'Scrupulosa' is suggested by details that go beyond the incipit. The English nationality of St Ursula, who led the Eleven Thousand Virgins in pilgrimage, is referenced in verse 5. Verse 4 opens 'Velut ebur' ('Like ivory'), a simile implying the whiteness representative of virginity; in addition, it also puns on the Latin name for York, Eboracum, giving the line the double meaning, 'Just like [at/in] York, ancient red coming out of the bodies of the saints'. As such, it is possible that the text was intended to reflect, on a fairly subtle level, the piety of Scrope himself as well as the bloodiness of his martyrdom.

Although the appeal of St Ursula and her companions' cult to a male cleric might seem unlikely, elements of the hagiography offered relevant models of chastity, obedience and political power. The cult of St Ursula and the Eleven Thousand Virgins (21 October) was reinvigorated following the discovery of human remains near Cologne in 1106. Ursula was believed to have been a Christian British princess, initially betrothed to a non-Christian prince. She avoided marriage by way of pilgrimage with her companions before their eventual martyrdom near Cologne. The legend became widely known throughout Europe after 1100, and was disseminated to various countries via the visions of Elisabeth of Schönau as collected by Roger of Forde, the first English copies of which date to the twelfth century.[62] Elisabeth's visions drew on materials including liturgical texts and the *Regnante domino* (Passion of St Ursula, *c.* 1100), written for the convent of Saint Ursula in Cologne.[63] Ursula's legend later formed part of devotional materials that were circulated in England, such as Jacobus de Voragine's *Legenda Aurea*, as well as in subsequent redactions and translations of this text, including the *South English Legendary*, Caxton's *Golden Legende* and Osbern Bokenham's *Legendys of hooly wummen*, which further disseminated knowledge of Ursula's cult in the later medieval period in England.[64] Following a lull in the popularity of the cult in England during the fourteenth century, mention of Elisabeth of Schönau's work by Dominican writer Nicholas Trevet (1257/65–1334) in two texts of political history – his *Annals of the Angevin Kings* (*Annales sex regnum Angliae*), and his Anglo-Norman *Cronycles*, the latter of which were written for the nun Mary of Woodstock, sister of Edward II – revived interest once more.[65] Reflecting this trend, on 12 September 1401, Scrope established the feast of the Eleven Thousand Virgins across the York province, indicating that it should be celebrated with nine Lessons, and that anyone participating in the celebrations on the feast day would receive a papal indulgence of forty days.[66] As Cullum, who considered the attribution of the sequence to Scrope reliable, remarks:

> The choice of Eleven Thousand Virgins, rather than the cult of one specific virgin martyr, suggests an interest in the cult of virginity itself. The one defining feature of these women was their deaths as virgins. They had no names or individual stories other than as the companions of St Ursula, whom, perhaps surprisingly, the archbishop did not mention. Generally the virgins appear as the companions of St Ursula rather than in their own right. Virginity, unadulterated by any contextual issues, is the sole focus of Scrope's interest here.[67]

The sequence text 'Scrupulosa' is likely to have been composed as an acknowledgement of Scrope's patronage of the cult and perhaps as an act of devotion to

Scrope himself; if written after 1405 it may also have functioned as a memorial. Here, the attribution of liturgical materials to the Archbishop was not about him as a composer in a musicological sense – it seems unlikely to me that he personally created the lyrics for the pre-existent melody. Rather, the attribution of 'Spe mercedis' and 'Scrupulosa' contributed to the mythology of the man, already considered saintly through his rapid rise to popular cult status. The attribution offered a rich and multi-layered symbolism: through his liturgical patronage and supposed 'creation' of musical materials, Scrope was seen as a figure worthy of veneration in his own right. In gaining greater familiarity with the musical items listed by the writer of the *Chronica Pontificum Ecclesiae Eboracensis*, the reader was invited to engage in veneration of Scrope through the underlying associations found in materials actually intended for St Thomas and the virgins martyred in Cologne.

Conclusion

Through the attribution of specific musical items to a holy figure, chroniclers and writers of liturgical materials were able to build a nuanced, idealised picture of their subject. There is little need for Scrope to have actually *written* the items attributed to him in order for them to play a meaningful role in cultivating a sense that the Archbishop was key to local and national spiritual life, with the province of York as significant as its sister province of Canterbury. English history is replete with holy historical figures: men and women whose lives were characterised by nobility and chastity, and whose roles were both spiritual and political. References to musicianship – as seen in the cases of St Edburga and Scrope – were acts of homage, showing an understanding of deeper political and social climates and were part of demonstrating the wider contextual impact of each person. They were not intentionally deceptive, rather they formed part of a broader, more subtle notion of authority and authorship.

How can this context inform our understanding of musical attributions in the polyphony of the later Middle Ages? In contrast to vernacular English poetry (and to some extent, music theory), English music lagged behind in terms of how regularly it was attributed to named individuals in manuscript sources. Even during the fifteenth century, when the notion of those whose profession was essentially 'musicus' was emerging, attribution remained inconsistent and unreliable. We can learn from the sorts of references that we have in relation to monophony and devotional musicianship in order to better understand the attributions that occur in English polyphony.

Attributions found in prose or poetic accounts, chronicles, treatises and other works were not legally binding; they had nothing to do with modern notions of intellectual property. Musicianship was a sign of an individual's literacy and piety, since it allowed a person to praise God fully and properly. A choice of song attributed could reflect spiritual and political concerns, casting alleged authors or performers in a favourable light. The development of the cult of authorship within English music occurred in parallel with the rise of humanism, leading to a pseudo-mythological expression of composers' skills and abilities in some

80 *Authorship, musicianship and value*

fifteenth-century accounts. These issues will be considered most fully in Chapter 6, in which I will focus on one of the most thorny and opaque attributions of the period, *contenance angloise*. They should also be borne in mind in Chapter 4, which seeks to reposition John Dunstaple's biography in the light of evidence that his life was as typical of a well-connected member of the English gentry than it was as a composer in the more recent sense of the word.

Notes

1 The one composer of the period before the Old Hall Manuscript with whom a specific composition can be associated is J. Alanus, who may in any case have worked on the continent (see Chapter 5).
2 On medieval English music theory, see in particular Peter M. Lefferts, "English Music Theory in Respect to the Dating of Polyphonic Repertoire in England, 1320–1399," *Atti del XIV congresso della Società Internazionale di Musicologia, Bologna, 1987: Transmissione et recezione delle forme di cultura musicale*, 3 vols (Turin: Edizioni di Torino, 1990); Peter M. Lefferts, *Robertus de Handlo Regulae and Johannes Hanboys Summa. A new critical text and translation* (Lincoln, Nebraska, and London: University of Nebraska Press, 1991); Elina Hamilton, "Walter of Evesham's *De speculatione musicae*: Authority of Music Theory in Medieval England," *Musica Disciplina* 58 (2014). On records of singers in institutional contexts, the standard point of reference remains Roger Bowers, "Choral Institutions within the English Church: Their Constitution and Development 1340–1500" (DPhil diss., University of East Anglia, 1975). See also Roger Bowers, *English Church Polyphony: Singers and sources from the 14th to the 17th Century* (Aldershot: Ashgate, 1999).
3 Michael Talbot, "Introduction." In *The Musical Work: Reality or invention?* edited by Michael Talbot (Liverpool: Liverpool University Press, 2000), 4.
4 Concordances for the Old Hall Manuscript were listed in Andrew Hughes and Margaret Bent eds, *The Old Hall Manuscript. Corpus Mensurabilis Musicae* 46. 3 vols ([Rome]: American Institute of Musicology, 1969–73); subsequently discovered concordances are updated to the relevant source page on DIAMM.
5 William John Summers, "The Effect of Monasticism on Fourteenth-Century Polyphony," *La Musique et Le Rite Sacre et Profane* (Strasbourg: University of Strasbourg, 1986), 137.
6 Lisa Colton, "Music in Pre-Reformation York: A New Source and Some Thoughts on the York Masses," *Plainsong and Medieval Music* 12 (2003): 86–87. On the rise of the votive liturgy of the Holy Name see Judith Aveling, "The Late Medieval Mass and Office of the Holy Name of Jesus in England: Sources, Development and Practice." (PhD diss., Bangor University, 2015).
7 Emma Dillon, *The Sense of Sound: Musical Meaning in France, 1260–1330* (Oxford: Oxford University Press, 2012) provides a recent example of critical engagement with the French motet corpus *c*. 1300.
8 Helen Deeming, transcr. and ed., *Songs in British Sources c. 1150–1300*. Musica Britannica 95 (London: Stainer and Bell, 2013). See also Deeming's detailed engagement with the monophonic 'Dulcis Jesu memoria'; "Music and Contemplation in the Twelfth-Century *Dulcis Jesu memoria*," *Journal of the Royal Musical Association* 139 (2014).
9 On attributions to Walter Frye see in particular Andrew Kirkman, "The Style of Walter Frye and an Anonymous Mass," *Early Music History* 15 (1992) and James Cook, "The Style of Walter Frye and an Anonymous Mass in the Lucca Choirbook," *Music and Letters* 96 (2015). On the attribution of 'O Rosa Bella' to Bedyngham, see David

Fallows, 'Dunstable, Bedyngham and *O rosa bella*', *The Journal of Musicology* 12 (1994), pp. 287–305; Fallows reminds readers that French repertory shares some of these problems because so many works are attributed in only one source.
10   Frank Harrison and Roger Wibberley, eds. *English Polyphonic Music of the Late Thirteenth and Early Fourteenth Centuries*. Early English Church Music 26 (London: Stainer and Bell, 1981), xvii.
11   Margaret Bent, "The Late-Medieval Motet." In *Companion to Medieval and Renaissance Music*, edited by Tess Knighton and David Fallows (London: Dent and Sons, 1992), 117.
12   Bent, "The Late-Medieval Motet," 114.
13   Lefferts, *The Motet in England*, 3–4.
14   Lefferts, *The Motet in England*, 12–13 and 4–8 respectively.
15   Bent, "The Late-Medieval Motet," 118.
16   This view was strengthened for the author by his research regarding Aosta, Seminary Library, MS 9-E-19 (olim MS 4), as described in Frank Ll. Harrison, "Benedicamus, Conductus, Carol: A Newly-Discovered Source," *Acta Musicologica* 37 (1965).
17   Harrison, *Music in Medieval Britain*, 104.
18   Harrison, *Music in Medieval Britain*, 104.
19   Ernest Sanders, "The Medieval Motet." In *Gattungen der Musik in Einzeldarstellung: Gedenkschrift Leo Schrade*, edited by Wulf Arlt (Berne: Franke Verlag, 1973), 497.
20   On the relationship between old and new materials in liturgical repertory before 1200, see Alejandro Enrique Planchart, ed. *Embellishing the Liturgy: Tropes and polyphony* (Aldershot: Ashgate, 2009), a compendium of previously published essays in which the contributors explore some of the complex
21   Roger Bowers, "Obligation, Agency, and *Laissez-faire:* The Promotion of Polyphonic Composition for the Church in Fifteenth-Century England." In *Music in Medieval and Early Modern Europe*, edited by Iain Fenlon (Cambridge: Cambridge University Press, 1981), 13.
22   Bowers, "Obligation, Agency, and *Laissez-faire*," 11 and 13–14.
23   Bowers, *English Church Polyphony*, 11.
24   Some of the earliest contract arrangements for the employment of musicians date to the middle of the fifteenth century, when it became increasingly common to instruct boys to improvise, read and perform polyphonic music. See for example the records of Lincoln Cathedral that list organists of the quire (after 1446) and the Lady Chapel (after 1477), and the instructor of the choristers (after 1437), which were duties sometimes separately identified and sometimes combined; Margaret Bent and Roger Bowers, "The Saxilby Fragment," *Early Music History* 1 (1981).
25   John Caldwell, *The Oxford History of English Music: From the Beginnings to c. 1715*, 2 vols (Oxford: Oxford University Press, 1991), I, 107.
26   On identifying individuals in this manuscript, see Elizabeth Eva Leach, "Seeing *Sens*: Guillaume de Machaut and de Melun" (2012) http://users.ox.ac.uk/~musf0058/MachautMelun.html (Accessed 10 August 2015). The Squarcialupi Codex is Florence, Biblioteca Medicea Laurenziana, Med. Pal. 87.
27   On Rolle, Julian of Norwich, Hilton, Kempe and other writers engaging with sound in the later Middle Ages, see Lisa Colton, "'Sowndys and Melodiis': Perceptions of Sound and Music in the Later Middle Ages." In *Cultural Histories of Noise, Sound and Listening in Europe, 1300–1918*, edited by Ian Biddle and Kirsten Gibson, 19–30 (Abingdon: Routledge, 2016).
28   The rosary in Rolle's right hand suggests he is at prayer, perhaps reciting the *Ave Maria*, a text that would not have required the verbal prompt of the book; books were also used as a devotional tool in the contemplation of word and image. The host source, GB-Cjc 23 B.1, includes unrelated musical flyleaves dating to the early fourteenth century; Peter M. Lefferts and Margaret Bent (compilers), "New Sources of English

82 *Authorship, musicianship and value*

Thirteenth- and Fourteenth-Century Polyphony," *Early Music History* 2 (1982), 306–14.
29 On the appearance of *Zelo tui langueo* in iconographical sources, see especially Christopher Page, "An English Motet of the Fourteenth Century in Performance," *Early Music* 25 (1997); Lisa Colton, "Languishing for Provenance: *Zelo tui langueo* and the Search for Women's Polyphony in England," *Early Music* 39 (2011).
30 Reinhard Strohm, *The Rise of European Music 1380–1500* (Cambridge: Cambridge University Press, 1993), 198.
31 Strohm, *The Rise of European Music*, 197.
32 On the ceremonial function of motets see Robert Nosow, *Ritual Meanings in the Fifteenth-Century Motet* (Cambridge: Cambridge University Press, 2012).
33 Ernest Sanders, Review of *Répertoire International des Sources Musicales, B IV2: Manuscripts of Polyphonic Music (c. 1320–1400)*, by Gilbert Reaney. *Music and Letters*, 51/4 (1970), 458. On this motet and references to it from the Middle Ages, see Margaret Bent, "Rota Versatilis – Towards a Reconstruction." In *Source Materials and the Interpretation of Music, A Memorial Volume to Thurston Dart*, edited by Ian Bent (London: Stainer and Bell, 1981).
34 Some pre-1700 texts – for example, Thomas Morley's *A Plain and Easy Introduction to Practical Music* (1597), or even the treatise by Anonymous IV – do give what can be seen as historical perspectives on music and refer to past composers, but these are exceptional and usually tied into treatises on notation or other theoretical matters. On the problems of using such accounts as histories, see Hendrik Van der Werf, "Anonymous IV as Chronicler." *Musicology Australia* 15 (1992): 3–13.
35 This recalls similar questions in relation to the authorship of Parisian song in the late twelfth century, as most famously discussed in the treatise of Anonymous IV. The theorist's comments can either be seen as a highly unusual example of composer biography, or another example of questionable attribution. Many writers take the historicity of his account as the starting point for their work; for a more cautious consideration, see Van der Werf, "Anonymous IV as Chronicler".
36 Wolfgang Bretschneider, "Bewundert-verstoßen-wiederentdeckt: Die Sequenz 'Dies irae'. Ein musiktheologischer Beitrag," *Bibel und Kirche* 63 (2008).
37 Susan Janet Ridyard, "St Edburga at Pershore: A Case of Mistaken Identity?" In *The Royal Saints of Anglo-Saxon England: A Study of West Saxon and East Anglian Cults* (Cambridge, Cambridge University Press: 1988).
38 Anonymous, *De vita sanctae Edburgae virginis* (London, British Library, MS Lansdowne 436, ff. 41^{va}32 – 43^{va}34), Chapter 1, f. 41^v. The legend is most fully outlined in Laurel Braswell, "Saint Edburga of Winchester: A Study of her Cult, AD 950–1500, with an Edition of the Fourteenth-Century Middle English and Latin Lives," *Mediaeval Studies* 33 (1971), where the passage cited is found on page 300.
39 Braswell, "Saint Edburga of Winchester," 303.
40 Jocelyn Wogan-Browne, *Saints' Lives and Women's Literary Culture c. 1150–1300: Virginity and its Authorizations* (Oxford: Oxford University Press 2001), 199.
41 On the relationship between female spirituality and eating, see Caroline Walker Bynum, *Holy Feast and Holy Fast: The religious significance of food to medieval women* (Berkeley and Los Angeles: University of California Press, 1987). Walker Bynum explores a range of literature relating to men and women, acknowledging the more general significance of food, but argues persuasively that symbolically, food 'was more important to women than to men'; *Holy Feast and Holy Fast*, 74.
42 Osbert of Clare, *Vita et translacione et miraculis beatae virginis Abburgae premissa* (Oxford, Bodleian Library MS Laud. Misc. 114, fols. 85–'120'), where Edburga's vocal abilities are noted on f. 91^v. See Braswell, "Saint Edburga of Winchester," 303.
43 See Katherine J. Lewis, *The Cult of St Katherine of Alexandria in Late Medieval England* (Woodbridge: Boydell, 2002). On the musical materials of St Katherine's

cult see James Blasina, "Music and Gender in the Medieval Cult of St. Katherine of Alexandria, 1050–1300." (PhD diss., Harvard University, 2015).
44 http://cantusdatabase.org/id/205272. My thanks to James Blasina for his assistance here.
45 Lefferts, *The Motet in England*, 177. Lefferts's view of this was more cautiously expressed in a previous publication, in which he qualified that the evidence is 'by no means clear cut'; "Text and Context in the Fourteenth-Century English Motet," 176.
46 Text edited and translated in Harrison and Lefferts, *Motets of English Provenance*, 225. Lefferts notes that Christopher Hohler had drawn attention to the fact that Edburga was not martyred, and thus that the text is more suitable for St Katherine. Christopher Hohler, "Reflections on Some Manuscripts Containing Thirteenth-Century Polyphony," *Journal of the Plainsong and Medieval Music Society* 1 (1978): 24–25; Lefferts, *The Motet in England*, 346.
47 *De sancta Edburga virgine* is found in three English manuscript sources. The text is edited in Braswell, "Saint Edburga of Winchester," 325–9.
48 This biography of Richard Scrope is reliant on Peter McNiven, "Scrope, Richard (c.1350–1405)." In *Oxford Dictionary of National Biography*, edited by H. C. G. Matthew and Brian Harrison (Oxford: Oxford University Press, 2004. Online edn. Edited by Lawrence Goldman, May 2008). Accessed 23 December 2015 www.oxforddnb.com/view/article/24964.
49 Patricia H. Cullum, "*Virginitas* and *Virilitas*: Richard Scope and his Fellow Bishops." In *Richard Scrope: Archbishop, rebel, martyr*, edited by P. J. P. Goldberg (Donington: Shaun Tyas, 2007), 96.
50 James Raine, ed. *The Historians of the Church of York and its Archbishops*, Rolls Series 71, 3 vols (London: Longman, 1879–94; repr. Cambridge: Cambridge University Press, 2012), II, 429. My thanks to Patricia Cullum for first drawing my attention to this reference.
51 The earliest source the Mass for the Holy Name dates to *c.* 1383. See Richard W. Pfaff, *New Liturgical Feasts in Later Medieval England* (Oxford: Clarendon Press, 1970), 65–6; David Mateer and Elizabeth New, "'In Nomine Jesu': Robert Fayrfax and the guild of the Holy Name in St Paul's Cathedral," *Music and Letters* 81 (2000). See also Aveling, "The Late Medieval Mass and Office of the Holy Name of Jesus in England".
52 Goldberg, "Introduction," *Richard Scrope: Archbishop, Rebel, Martyr*, 6.
53 David Hiley, ed., *Oxford Bodleian Library MS. Lat. liturg. b. 5* (*The York Gradual*) (Ottawa: Institute of Mediaeval Music, 1995). On the problems of defining the various uses of medieval England, see Matthew Cheung Salisbury, *The Use of York: Characteristics of the medieval liturgical office*, Borthwick Papers, 113 (York: Borthwick Institute, University of York, 2008). This theme is further developed in Matthew Cheung Salisbury, *The Secular Liturgical Office in Late Medieval England* (Turnhout, Belgium: Brepols, 2015).
54 Nicolas Sandon, ed., *The Use of Salisbury: The Proper of the Mass from Advent to Septuagesima* (Newton Abbot: Antico Edition, 2000), where items for the Mass on St Thomas's day are edited on pages 78–82. See also Kay Slocum, *Liturgies in Honour of Thomas Becket* (Toronto: University of Toronto Press, 2004), though Slocum's book does not discuss the sequence in question.
55 On British chant traditions and sources, see David Hiley, "The Norman Chant Traditions–Normandy, Britain, Sicily," *Proceedings of the Royal Musical Association* 107 (1980–81). See also David Hiley, "The Rhymed Sequence in England: A Preliminary Survey." In *Musicologie Medieval: Notations et sequences, Actes de la table ronde du C.N.R.S. à l'Institut de Recherche et d'Histoire des Textes, 6–7 septembre 1982*, edited by Michel Huglo (Paris, Librairie Honoré Champion, 1987).

84 *Authorship, musicianship and value*

My thanks to Helen Deeming for spotting the melodic concordance between 'In hoc mundo' and 'Spe mercedis'.
56 Translation provided by David Hiley, personal correspondence.
57 Hiley, Oxford Bodleian Library MS. Lat. liturg. b. 5, ix.
58 Walter Howard Frere, "The Newly Found York Gradual," *Journal of Theological Studies* 2 (1901), 583.
59 Hiley lists the melody as that commonly found with the texts 'Rex omnipotens' and 'Sancti spiritus assit'; Hiley, Oxford Bodleian Library MS. Lat. liturg. b. 5, ix.
60 A full edition can be found as free download on the Plainsong and Medieval Music Society website http://plainsong.org.uk/wp-content/uploads/2014/06/scrupulosa_colton.pdf edited by Lisa Colton, with translation by Leofranc Holford-Strevens. Paul Barnwell, Claire Cross and Ann Rycraft eds. *Mass and Parish in Late Medieval England: The Use of York* (Reading: Spire, 2005). Surviving sources of 'Scrupulosa' are: Oxford, University College, 78b, fol.138r (15th-century York Missal); Oxford, Latin Liturgical b. 5, ff. 115^{r-v} (15th-century York Gradual, with musical notation); Cambridge, Fitzwilliam, MS 34 (15th-century Missal); Cambridge, Sidney Sussex College, MS 33 (olim Δ 2. II), ff. 247 (York Missal, *c.* 1470s or early 1480s, not fourteenth century as stated in *Analecta Hymnica*; I am grateful to the archivist of Sidney Sussex College, Nicholas Rogers, for providing me with an image and accurate date for the manuscript); London, Sion College, MS A. 34. 3f (16th-century York Hymnal and Sequentiary); printed York Missals from [1509], 1516, 1517, 1530 and 1533.
61 Hiley suggests that eighteen sequence texts in the York Gradual 'may have been composed at York'; Hiley, *Oxford Bodleian Library MS. Lat. liturg. b. 5*, ix.
62 For a full discussion of the sources, see Ruth J. Dean, "Elizabeth, Abbess of Schönau, and Roger of Ford," *Modern Philology*, 41 (1944).
63 Anne L. Clark, ed., *Elizabeth of Schönau: The complete works* (New York: Paulist Press, 2000), 18. An edition of the *Regnante Domino* can be found in Pamela Sheingord and Marcelle Thiébaux eds. *The Passion of Saint Ursula [Regnante Domino]*, translated, with notes and introduction (Toronto: Peregrina Publishing, 1991).
64 Marsha Genensky and Johanna M. Rose, CD liner notes to Hildegard von Bingen, *11,000 Virgins: Chants for the Feast of St. Ursula*, Anonymous 4 (Harmonia Mundi, 907200, 1997). Jacobus de Voragine, *The Golden Legend, Readings on the Saints*, 2 vols, edited by William Granger Ryan (Princeton, NJ: Princeton University Press, 1993), II, 256–60. See also Manfred Görlach, *The Textual Tradition of the South English Legendary*. Leeds Texts and Monographs, New Series 6 (Leeds: University of Leeds, 1974), 198; Caxton's version is attributed to Elizabeth of Hungary, and is inserted into his edition of Raymund de Vineis's *Life of St. Catherine of Siena*; Dean, "Elizabeth, Abbess of Schönau," 212.
65 Dean, "Elizabeth, Abbess of Schönau," 217. James G. Clark, "Trevet, Nicholas (*b.* 1257x65, *d.* in or after 1334)." In *Oxford Dictionary of National Biography*, online edn. Edited by Lawrence Goldman. (Oxford: Oxford University Press, 2004). Accessed 16 September 2016 www.oxforddnb.com/view/article/27744.
66 Rodney N. Swanson, *A Calendar of the Register of Richard Scrope, Archbishop of York, 1398–1405*, 2 vols (Borthwick Institute of Historical Research, York, 1981 and 1985), II, 9.
67 Cullum, "*Virginitas* and *Virilitas*," 96.

4 Who was John Dunstaple?

Accounts of fifteenth-century music would seem incomplete without John Dunstaple's name.[1] His reputation was clear even during his own lifetime when the influence of his musical talents was reflected in the complimentary verses of Martin le Franc.[2] Histories of Western music have continued to feature Dunstaple as representative of a flowering of English music in the fifteenth century; Davey's *History of English Music*, for example, portrayed Dunstaple as a man whose musical contribution was revolutionary:

> As with the sound of trumpets, announcing the arrival of high personages or the preparation for solemn ceremonies, even so should this chapter begin; for now I have to relate how Englishmen led musicians out of the arid desert where for centuries they had wandered since escaping from the bondage of Greek theories [...]. England may well be proud that the one evergreen refreshing spot in the long wilderness is the Rota of Reading Abbey; and England may well be proud that the Pisgah-sight into the Promised Land, and the first footing on its pastures, were granted to a school of English musicians, of whom the chief was John Dunstable.[3]

As Zon has shown, Davey continued to credit Dunstaple with the invention of composition itself, and saw his music 'as a source of national identification'.[4] Although misconceptions about Dunstaple's responsibility for the development of counterpoint were effectively debunked by Bukofzer several decades ago, the image of the composer remains as one of the most outstanding artists of his age – a reputation supported in no small part by the beauty of his music.[5] Most of the works attributed convincingly to Dunstaple were probably already circulating by about 1430.[6] Dunstaple's sizeable output has continued to serve as a yardstick for excellence and innovation in musical form and style in modern accounts, just as it did in early ones. It is difficult to avoid the rhetoric of previous histories, in part because music attributed to him – whether securely or not – is frequently sophisticated, musically effective and innovative, even for his early pieces.[7]

One important area of Dunstaple's story has continued to frustrate those working on his music: the lack of firm biographical data through which one might appraise

86 *Who was John Dunstaple?*

his creative development. My archival research has led me to examine Dunstaple's biography in the light of previously unexplored documents. These can enrich the historical record, even though they also raise further questions. Who was John Dunstaple? It is by no means a simple question to answer, not least because various men of that name can be identified in archival sources (see Appendix A: Listing of members of Dunstaple and his family in historical records). This chapter will explore evidence that the composer (whose accepted death date is 1453) may be identified with a man about whom a great deal of information is retrievable, and who has been overlooked or misidentified in previous publications; this man was John Dunstaple, Esquire, of Steeple Morden in Cambridgeshire (d. 1459).[8]

* * *

Let us start by revisiting the generally accepted biography of the man believed to be the composer John Dunstaple. The date of Dunstaple's birth is estimated to have been *c.* 1390 or shortly after, and is usually projected backwards from his accepted death date. This is in relation to the documented performances of two of his motets, and from the dates of manuscript sources preserving his music.[8]

Dunstaple's motets *Veni sancte spiritus* and *Preco preheminencie* were among six sung on 21 August 1416 at Canterbury Cathedral, in celebration of English military success across the Channel and the signing of the Treaty of Canterbury.[9] The occasion is described in a chronicle attributed to Thomas Elmham. Margaret Bent notes that:

> the date is surprisingly early, and the first of the two motets is the only work of Dunstaple's present in the Old Hall manuscript, the first layer of which was probably compiled for Thomas, Duke of Clarence, killed in battle in 1421; it appears there as an addendum, perhaps implying that Dunstaple was newly known as a composer.[10]

Robert Nosow argues that *Preco preheminencie* was written in honour of John, Duke of Bedford between September 1416 and December 1418. This would be important because a late fifteenth-century inscription in Cambridge, St John's College, MS 162 indicates that musician John Dunstaple enjoyed the patronage of John of Bedford.[11] Nosow's analysis is based on the movements of court and on the date of the chronicles that records the motet's use.[12] He outlines ways in which the motet carries upper texts whose original and unique content both honours John the Baptist and contains topical allusions to John of Bedford himself.[13] These two isorhythmic motets provide the most precise chronological data about Dunstaple's musical career.

Early writings on the composer associated his birth with the town of Dunstable in Bedfordshire, and this inference has been repeated in recent scholarship.[14] There is, however, no proof that he was born there; in any case, the use of a town as surname is insufficient evidence by this time. Among sources that relate John

Dunstaple to noble patronage, the most helpful is a book inscription in which the composer is styled by the scribe as 'cum Iohanne duce Bedfordie musico' (Cambridge, St John's College, MS 162); Rodney Thomson has shown that this book once belonged to Dunstaple.[15] There is some evidence to associate Dunstaple with St Albans: one of his possible other patrons, Humphrey Duke of Gloucester, was buried at St Alban's in 1447, and an Abbot of St Alban's – John of Wheathamstead – wrote at least one of two epitaphs on the composer's death.[16] Andrew Wathey and Judith Stell have provided evidence that Dunstaple was also under the patronage of Queen Joan of Navarre (the wife of Henry IV) from the late 1420s.[17] After Dunstaple was buried at St Stephen's, Walbrook in London, an elaborate poetic epitaph outlining his musicianship against classical and philosophical references to astronomy decorated his tomb. The church and its monuments were destroyed in the Great Fire of London in 1666.

John Dunstaple's tomb at St Stephen's, Walbrook

Since the John Dunstaple that I am arguing might be identified as the composer died in 1459, it is vital first to consider the evidence for the composer's accepted death date of 1453, a date that is found in only one place: within a poetic epitaph that was recorded as having decorated his tomb. The inscription, first recorded in 1618, is thought once to have read:

> Clauditur hoc tumulo, qui caelum pectore clausit,
> Dunstable Ioannes, astrorum conscius. Illo
> Judice novit Urania abscondita pandere caeli.
> Hic vir erat tua laus, tua lux, tibi, musica, princeps,
> Quique tuas dulces per mundum sparserat artes.
> Anno Mil. C quater semel L tria jungito, Christi
> Pridie natalem, sidus transmigrat ad astra.
> Suscipiant proprium civem caeli sibi cives.

> Is enclosed in this tomb he who enclosed Heaven in his breast, John Dunstaple, the confederate of the stars. In his judgement Urania knew how to unfold the secrets of the heavens. This man was thy glory, thy light, thy chief, O Music; and one who had scattered thy sweet arts through the world. In the year one thousand four hundred and fifty three, on the day before Christ's Birthday, he passes as a constellation to the stars. May the citizens of Heaven receive him as a citizen, one of themselves.[18]

John Stow's *Survay of London* (1598) recorded that Dunstaple's epitaph was found on 'Two faire plated Stones in the Chancell, each by other'. It is not clear from any account whether the text was presented in a block or around the edge of the brass plates, or whether there was additional text or a likeness; however, all of these are features typical of the time and the adjective 'faire' may indicate decoration.

The parish church of St Stephen was completed in 1439, replacing a former church on land purchased from the Worshipful Company of Grocers, and enjoyed the patronage of an important local elite, including mayors William Stondon and Robert Chichley. It stood as one of five churches in the ward of Walbrook.[19] Robert Whittingham (d. 1452), an Alderman of Walbrook at various times, laid the church's foundation stone in 1429; he owned a considerable amount of property in the ward and remained patron of St Stephen's. Perhaps significantly, Whittingham acquired the advowson of the church and bought several properties in the area from John, Duke of Bedford (hereafter John of Bedford) in 1432. Whoever 'held the advowson' of a church or chapel had the right to appoint a candidate to a vacant ecclesiastical benefice or church position. These transactions imply a strong business association between the two men. Whittingham was responsible for the export of food and wine to John of Bedford's household in France, and was named co-executor in his will.[20] Dunstaple's tomb was therefore housed in a building that was still relatively new, and which had benefitted from the support of both merchants and the nobility, not least from Dunstaple's most securely associated patron, John of Bedford.

The St Stephen's epitaph may have been transcribed by John Stow himself but he did not record it in the 1598 edition of his *Survey*, which was subsequently reprinted in numerous revisions. The most significant changes to Stow's text were those made by Anthony Munday. His version of the epitaph may have been influenced by papers left by Stow, but certainly also included new materials from somewhere else. Munday's 1618 publication was the first to carry the epitaph in full: previous editions had only acknowledged the presence of his memorial in the church. Munday's transcription was definitely corrupt in details of its Latin. As Charles Maclean explained in examining the full range of versions of Dunstaple's epitaph in 1910:

> The authority for the details is dubious. If Munday obtained his version from Stow's papers, we do not know what state those were in, nor what use he made of them. If he obtained it from the slab, it is certain that the latter was more or less dilapidated [. . .]. It is useless to give an English translation of this original record of the epitaph, for it is only the first, fourth and eight lines which can be translated, and the rest are jargon [. . .]. It may be surmised that Munday knew but little Latin.[21]

By the time Thomas Fuller published his independent transcription of the brass in 1662, the lettering was already heavily worn and much of the text unrecoverable, including the lines relating to the year of Dunstaple's death. Rather than drawing on Munday's expanded text to fill in the blanks, though he certainly had this to hand, Fuller simply placed dotted lines in his transcription where portions were unreadable. As a result, the crucial date line is, tantalisingly, just ellipses.

Fuller's accompanying discussion is worth citing in full, since it is not reproduced elsewhere in the musicological literature and because it contains a different death date: 1455. This date has not been favoured by many subsequent writers, and there is no further evidence to support it; it may well have been a simple typographical error.[22] Fuller criticised the overblown claims of both known epitaphs in honour of John Dunstaple:

> What is true *of the bills* of some unconscionable Trades-men, *if ever paid, overpaid*; may be said of this [these] *hyperbolical Epitaphs, if ever believed, over believed*. Yea, one may safely cut off a *Third* in any part of it, and the remainder will amount to make him a most admirable person. Let none say that these might be two distinct persons, seeing (besides the concurrence of *time* and *place*,) it would *bank-rupt* the *Exchequer* of *Nature* to afford two such persons, *one Phoenix at once* being as much as any will believe. This *Dunstable* died an. 1455 [original emphasis].[23]

The St Stephen's epitaph is thus highly problematic as evidence, surviving only in very imperfect transcriptions from the seventeenth century. Maclean had to edit the epitaph to make sense of any of it, including the death date, although it is nearly impossible to adjust to read anything other than the date of 1453 while maintaining the sense and poetic features.[24]

The second epitaph does not explicitly contain a date, and is not thought to have been associated with any presentation on a monument or tomb. It is focused, as is the other, on diverse attributes, which John Weever recorded as relating to 'John Dunstable, an astrologian, a mathematician, a musician, and what not?':

> Musicus hic MICHALUS alter, novus & PTHOLOMEUS,
> Junior ac ATHLAS supportans robore celos,
> Pausat sub cinere; melior vir de muliere
> Nunquam natus erat; vicii quia labe carebat.
> Et virtutis opes possedit unicus omnes.
> Cur exoptetur, sic optandoque precetur
> Perpetuis annis celebretur fama JOHANNIS
> DUNSTAPIL; in pace requiescat & hic sine fine.[25]

> Here a musician who was another Mikkalos, and a new Ptolemy, and a younger Atlas holding up the heavens with his strength, rests beneath the ashes; a better man was never born of woman, since he was without the stain of vice and alone possessed all the wealth of virtue. Wherefore let him be wished for, and let the wish accompany the prayer that the fame of John Dunstaple may be celebrated for years everlasting; let him rest in peace here too without end.[26]

The author, in this case at least, was certainly John of Wheathamstead, whose flowery Latin has attracted more than its fair share of stylistic criticism. As David Carlson has written in relation to Wheathamstead's poems on the fifteenth-century English civil war: 'Wheathamstede's poetry is confused, characterized by an effort to adhere to competing, even antagonistic literary traditions: scholasticism, on the one hand, in Wheathamstede's espousal of the tradition of florid, ornate verse [. . .] and humanism, on the other'.[27]

Wheathamstead was Abbot of St Albans from 1420–40 and again 1452–65, and the stylistic similarity of the epitaphs has led to some conjecture that they were both penned by him.[28] Although it was once thought that Wheathamstead was a patron of the composer, Alessandria Petrina considers the evidence too slight.[29] There is, however, evidence to support some relationship between Dunstaple, Wheathamstead and St Albans. Wheathamstead was possibly responsible for adapting a text for Dunstaple's isorhythmic motet *Albanus roseo rutilat*; the dedication of the motet would have made it particularly appropriate for performance at the abbey, for example as part of the John of Bedford's visit to St Albans in 1426. Furthermore, Wheathamstead may have consulted Dunstaple for astrological advice in relation to ending his first abbacy; Hilary Carey has used the identification of Dunstaple's hand in astrological writings to explain the composer's possible role in the Abbot's decision.[30]

I have noticed an aspect of the Wheathamstead epitaph that, perhaps unexpectedly, reveals the Abbot's knowledge of one of Dunstaple's motets, *Preco preheminencie*. This new discovery merits some discussion here. Many epitaphs make reference to aspects of biography or personal piety, but at first glance, Dunstaple's are somewhat opaque in this respect – surprisingly so for a composer whose output is dominated by sacred music appropriate for use in the liturgy. Instead, Dunstaple is – in both cases – praised in reference to the most well-regarded scholars and even to gods: Urania was daughter of Zeus and muse of astronomy, reputed to encourage men to gaze towards heaven, and those who learned from her were raised there after their deaths. Dunstaple's keen interest and skill in astronomy make sense of this allusion. 'Michalus' is the musician Mikkalos mentioned in a piece of false reasoning analysed by Aristotle.[31] Ptolemy (d. *c*. 168) was both astronomer and musician, so that association is clear. Maclean notes that 'The Abbot praises Dunstable's personal virtues, it must be admitted, rather fulsomely', but it is the references to astronomy and astrology, rather than to music, that dominate.[32]

The most significant – and so far neglected – part of Wheathamstead's epitaph is the reference to Dunstaple's status as someone born without stain, there never having been a better man born of woman 'melior vir de muliere nunquam natus erat'. The line goes beyond direct praise, it recalls Biblical accounts such as Matthew 11: 11, in which John the Baptist is praised by Jesus:

> Amen dico vobis, non surrexit inter natos mulierum major Johanne Baptista: qui autem minor est in regno caelorum, major est illo.
>
> Truly, I say to you, among those born of women there has arisen no one greater than John the Baptist. Yet the one who is least in the kingdom of heaven is greater than he.

The Gospel of St Luke gives the fullest account of John the Baptist's infancy, and of Jesus's relationship with John. At Luke 7: 28, Jesus says:

> Dico enim vobis: major inter natos mulierum propheta Johanne Baptista nemo est: qui autem minor est in regno Dei, major est illo.

I tell you, among those born of women there is no one greater than John; yet the one who is least in the kingdom of God is greater than he.

It is without question that Wheathamstead's line 'melior vir de muliere nunquam natus erat' was deliberate in drawing on this very well-known Biblical text, which itself provided the basis for the liturgy on the Nativity of John the Baptist. The Baptist's feast was placed in the Christian calendar on 24 June, precisely six months before Christmas Eve, to highlight the relationship between him and Christ. The fact that, of the two Dunstaple epitaphs, each refers to either the 24 June (by implication, through the quotation of a well-known part of that day's liturgy) or to 24 December, therefore suggests significance in terms of their interrelationship. A reader of the two epitaphs might be encouraged to understand Dunstaple's reputation as a second John the Baptist.

Perhaps Wheathamstead's hand is among the many examples of marginal graffiti in Oxford, Bodleian Library, Rawlinson G.99, f. 82r and f. 76r, a collection of grammatical treatises that belonged to St Alban's Abbey in the fifteenth century, which includes the added acrostics 'Amen dico vobis pro omina [sic]' and 'Fuit homo missus a Deo cui nomen erat Iohannes' (A man was sent by God whose name was John; John 1: 6)?[33] The latter is part of the liturgy of St John the Baptist, and was often set polyphonically or provided the text for the second section of polyphonic settings of the antiphon 'Inter natos' for the feast of John the Baptist, while the former recalls the opening of both Matthew 11: 11 and Luke 7: 28.

There is a closer and more specific link to Dunstaple's music. The tenor of Dunstaple's isorhythmic motet *Preco preheminencie* (*Musica Britannica*, No. 29) is the Magnificat antiphon 'Inter natos mulierum non surrexit major Johanne ba[ptista]' ('Born of woman there has never arisen one greater than John the Baptist'), drawn from the Sarum rite for the Nativity of John the Baptist. Setting 'Inter natos mulierum' polyphonically was not in itself unusual, with examples even in the central sources of 13th-century polyphony.[34] 'Inter natos mulierum' was set by other fifteenth-century and early sixteenth-century composers, although not English ones. For example, 'Inter natos mulierum' was set twice, in three parts, by Gilles Binchois (Kaye, No. 41 and No. 42), a composer who may have visited England and whose music shows evidence of borrowing and appropriation from English music.[35]

Nevertheless, relatively few polyphonic works have survived from medieval England that honour John the Baptist. It is plausible that having been used to celebrate military success and flatter John of Bedford (for whom John the Baptist was patron saint), as Nosow has argued, Dunstaple's motet *Preco preheminencie* became synonymous with the composer more generally. Perhaps John of Wheathamstead embedded the relevant Biblical reference into the memorial in order to reference to one of the composer's most impressive pieces of polyphony? The intertextual reference to John the Baptist would have been obvious to readers with even a basic knowledge of liturgy, but its significance could only be properly understood by those who knew Dunstaple's motet. Indeed, the reference to the motet implies that the piece was sufficiently well-known not only to Wheathamstead but to a wider circle to merit its inclusion, offering a window into the reception of *Preco preheminencie* in the middle of the fifteenth century.

The reason why Dunstaple's body came to be buried in the chancel of St Stephen's is not found in any surviving record, though there were clear conventions for such matters in the later Middle Ages from which it is possible to surmise some context. It was common for a member of the gentry to maintain strong links with his or her main property and elsewhere, and it was within canon law for an individual to choose the site of his or her burial.[36] Since over 90 per cent of Londoners who left wills between 1380 and 1520 indicated their preferred place of burial, it is likely that Dunstaple, too, chose the site of his tomb, and exercised 'place-loyalty' of some sort.[37] Within the church, the chancel was the most high-ranking burial location because it was close to the main altar at which Mass was celebrated; this place was usually filled by local, high-status individuals and the clergy.[38] Deborah Youngs has discussed the competing reasons for the placement of such tombs, such as family and family allegiance, residence, age, political statement and economic status, as well as to ensure the future presence of the deceased individual within cultural memory.[39] Floor or wall brasses were more common than standing monuments for members of the gentry, and many contained stylised imagery of the person there interred. The text or iconography on memorials might also refer to family members buried adjacently, or to the ancestral links that supported their burial in a high-ranking architectural position. If such references were made elsewhere on the St Stephen's brass plate, Stow, Munday and Fuller did not report them.

The primary stumbling block for identifying the composer buried in St Stephen's Walbrook and the owner of property discussed below – and it is a significant one – is that the date on the brass plates has been reported as Christmas Eve, 1453. While the majority of scholars have accepted the date as accurate, Roger Bowers expressed some caution in the mid-1970s, calling it only 'the generally accepted date of 24 December 1453'.[40] In her monograph, Bent included the warning that 'the garbled transmission casts doubt on the security of Dunstaple's hitherto unquestioned death date'.[41] Arguably, the range of evidence discussed above raises important questions about the accuracy and authenticity of the tomb's epitaph, allowing the opportunity to question it in relation to the poetic allusions to John the Baptist in the second epitaph.

If the composer is also to be identified with John Dunstaple Esquire of Steeple Morden in Cambridgeshire, whose biography will be explored below, there are two problems with the date: the year and the month. The matter cannot be a simple error in the transmission of the anonymous epitaph, since 24 December 1459 is too late in that year; we know from the records that the Cambridgeshire man was dead by the autumn. On the other hand, it is difficult to reimagine the anonymous text in such a way that would rectify the problem. Instead, to reconcile the identification of John Dunstaple the composer with the man from Cambridgeshire, it is necessary to take the entire dating in the epitaph as a piece of poetic licence, perhaps created around 1460 or even later. Perhaps by this time it was not possible or necessary to be so precise about the date as it would have been to create a fanci-ful picture of the astronomer musician dying on a day associated with the Nativity of Jesus, in which the star of Bethlehem played its part in guiding people to him between his birth and Epiphany.[42] To give full weight to this suggestion, it is necessary to look more closely at the Cambridgeshire Dunstaple's will and at his property holdings and social circles, since they bring relevant evidence into the picture. Finally, this context will be extended by consideration of the relationship between Dunstaple's musical, devotional, astronomical and astrological interests.

John Dunstaple's will

Although it has not been widely noticed, the catalogue of Hertfordshire Record Office includes reference to a copy of a will of a certain John Dunstaple Esquire (see Appendix B: Hertfordshire Record Office MS 44505, hereafter GB-HFr 44505).[43] The document in question is heavily abbreviated and includes sections of three other legal texts that concern the manor of Broadfield in Hertfordshire; the original sources were probably copied in abridged form for legal purposes in the early part of the sixteenth century. Since only portions of the original documents were recorded, several pieces of stock information found in wills and other legal records, such as the names of witnesses, are frustratingly absent. Such details would certainly have proved useful for cross-reference. For example, the opening of the will lacks what would be details of how and where John Dunstaple wished to be buried; since we know the location of the composer's burial, this would have provided an instant opportunity for verification. It would likewise have been useful to find references to financial donations to specific parish churches, repair costs for local religious monuments or buildings, or even for the payment of singing men for memorials as was customary, but no such details were included. The final information excluded from the sixteenth-century copy was the bequest of movable goods to his heirs, institutional patrons or associates such as items of furniture, plates or books. But the absence of such facts is also compounded by the specific inclusion of another: the will was made out on 7 July 1459.

It has long been commented upon that composer John Dunstaple was probably also a landowner, in line with several contemporaries working for high-status chapels, churches or cathedrals. In 1910, Maclean suggested six historical John Dunstaples who had at some point been individually connected with the composer, namely:

1 Alderman of London in 1303
2 Monk of St Albans by 1326
3 Gentleman [sic] of Cambridgeshire in 1436
4 Owner of Hertfordshire manor of Broadfield in 1449
5 Person commemorated in the chancel at St Stephen's, Walbrook
6 Goldsmith living in London in 1461

Options (1) and (2) are too early to be the composer, though the fact that a high-ranking John de Dunstaple (option 1) lived in the ward of Walbrook is potentially interesting, given the lack of evidence for the composer's family origins. Maclean's list can be expanded in this case to reveal that this man, the skinner John Dunstaple, was elected (or re-elected) as an alderman of Walbrook as early as 1293, and that his will of October 1307 indicates that he died in that year, after which his duties were replaced by John of Wengrave.[44] The list can also be extended with another name: Richard L. Greene identified a man or men by the name of John Dunstavylle (listed also as John Dunstaple) who was a canon of Hereford between 1419 and 1440 and whose title of 'clerk' would not have necessitated his residency for all of that time.[45] This man was named in the records on account of holding the prebendary of Putson Minor in Hereford.[46] Some accounts have consolidated various combinations of (3), (4) and (5) into a single man, thought to have been the composer. Options (3) and (5) were linked in particular by Andrew Wathey, who, with Judith Stell, published taxation records showing that John Dunstaple had a high taxable income from lands in Cambridge, Essex and London, and that he received a substantial annuity from Queen Joan (d. 1437) of £80, both in 1436. Wathey remained cautious, referring to 'a John Dunstable who it seems may be the composer' at the outset.[47] In exploring the implications of such a grant from Queen Joan, Wathey encouraged speculation as follows:

> Nothing in the documentation of Joan's household and estates suggests that our John Dunstable was active as an administrative official, and the failure of central government sources to betray even minor activity in local political affairs must suggest that some other form of service – of exceptionally high value – was involved.[48]

Naturally, Wathey's hint was that 'some other form of service' might have had a musical flavour, though he did not say so explicitly. His archival research had additionally noted Dunstaple as a beneficiary in the Queen's New Year's gifts of 1428, including what must have been a striking scarlet gown with fur – matching the livery of the highest-ranking men of her household – and a silver cup worth 78s.[49] A result of this article in particular, whose identification of the musician with the landowner has since been generally accepted, was that the composer was linked with income from an additional royal patron. It also supported the idea that the composer held lands in Cambridgeshire, Essex and London. Additionally, Wathey's research identified Dunstaple with lands held in Normandy. This all built a picture of a man of substantial financial means, effectively earning a living as a professional musician, presumably writing for royal or noble patrons.[50]

But was Wathey's identification of the John Dunstaple in the tax records with the composer convincing? Roger Bowers did not think so, as he expressed in his review of the published version of Wathey's doctoral thesis:

> It is much to be hoped that the author will persevere with this research, and will presently be able to complete his work by supplying the last, but crucially

important, piece in this most impressive jigsaw puzzle of evidence – namely, some good grounds for believing that this John Dunstable may legitimately be identified with John Dunstable the composer. The name is not so singular or unusual that any such identification can simply be assumed as axiomatic; and it would seem at present that no truly convincing case can be built on the rather circumstantial and fugitive evidence so far available.[51]

It is my contention that the Dunstaple identified by Wathey – consistently styled 'esquire' or 'armiger' (the equivalent Latin term) in formal documents – were all John Dunstaple of Steeple Morden, and that this man is also most likely the composer.

In order to explore the possible identification of the Cambridge and Hertfordshire landowner with John Dunstaple the composer, it is necessary to examine the legal documents that lay out the landholdings, including the re-examination of documents outlined by Stell and Wathey, and to set aside the musical elements for the time being. One would style this man officially as John Dunstaple, Esquire, of Steeple Morden, Cambridgeshire, because this is how he and his heirs are identified in legal and papal records. A particularly useful feature that can help to combine identifications is his styling as 'armiger' or 'esquire', a title that was bestowed on those with a landed income significantly above that of a gentleman, usually alongside some form of administrative function for the government. From the early fifteenth century, it was the law that anyone who held a title should be so named in legal papers, whatever the nature of the case. Wathey notes that:

> Dunstable is consistently styled esquire or armiger and other composers traceable as landowners frequently receive this designation. Lionel Power was styled thus at Canterbury in 1438, and John Plummer appears first as a gentleman and later as armiger at Windsor between 1442 and 1480.[52]

The earliest reference to Dunstaple with this title is with the gifts from Queen Joan in 1427/8, implying a change of status by this point in his life. As such, the listing in Appendix A pays close attention to the title of the individuals named in each case, reproducing it as closely as possible from the original.

Dunstaple's principal manor was the manor of Brewis in Steeple Morden where he was tenant-in-chief, a title that indicates that he held the land directly from the Crown, rather than from the church or another nobleman. Brewis was part of linked landholdings in the Armingford Hundred, in which out of ten main vills (parishes, manors or tithings), Dunstaple held property in five: Steeple Morden, Gilden Morden, Bassingbourn, Abington and Litlington. Dunstaple's role of tenant-in-chief also resulted in his death being reported in a writ of *diem clausit extremum* on 14 September 1459, indicating that he died between 7 July (when the will was written) and that date.[53] A writ of *diem clausit extremum* ('he has closed his last day') was issued by king's chancery when a tenant-in-chief died in order to trigger the *inquisition post mortem* that would establish legal heirs and land holdings.[54]

96 Who was John Dunstaple?

The most crucial identification to make is arguably with properties in the city of London itself. We know from the will of John Dunstaple Esquire, and from the tax records of 1436, that he owned property in Essex and London by this date, but the precise locations are unknown. Dunstaple's will made potential provision for his goods to be divided between the priory of Stratford-at-Bow and the monastery of Stratford Langthorne in the event that his daughter produced no legitimate heirs; his grandson Thomas eventually disposed of lands at Stratford Langthorne in 1484, but it is unknown how or when Dunstaple had acquired them.

By 1445/6, John Dunstaple Esquire had become co-owner of a string of properties that are identified in London, Metropolitan Archives, Husting Roll 175 (membranes relating to 1445–6) (hereafter GB-Llma 175), which largely match a set of properties that had previously belonged to William Gawetron. These assets were likely acquired *en masse* by Dunstaple in years following Gawetron's death in 1434/5 (see Figure 4.1).[55]

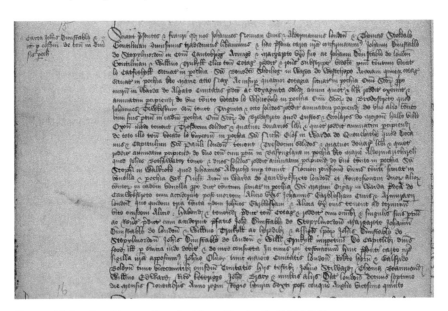

Figure 4.1 London, Metropolitan Archives, Husting Roll 175 (16)
Reproduced with the permission of London Metropolitan Archives, City of London.

The properties can be summarised as follows, according to the Husting Roll entry for November 1446, which are listed here to confirm the earlier ownership:

1 tenement called Le Catsethall in the parish of St Benet Sherehog, Westcheap ward.
5 cottages situated in the parish of St Mary Axe.
4 cottages situated in the parish of All Hallows London Wall in the parish of Aldgate.

1 tenement called The White Bull in the parish of All Hallows, Bread Street, which John Tewkesbury senior held.[56]

1 other tenement in the parish of All Saints Bread Street that the Wardens and Scholars of Merton Hall in the town of Oxford lately held.

1 tenement called The Unicorn in the parish of St Nicholas Olave in the ward of Queenhithe that the Dean and Chapter of St Paul's held.

1 tenement and its parts in Basing Lane in the parish of St Mary Aldermanbury that John Bethewater held.

1 tenement in the parish of St Stephen in Walbrook that John Aldriche lately held.[57]

1 tenement situated in the lane and parish of St Nicholas Acons in the ward of Candlewick Street, London.

2 tenements in the parish of St Martin Orgar in Candlewick Street ward (after the death of Alice, wife of John Garblesham, citizen and armourer, London).

The property most of interest here is the tenement in the parish where the composer John Dunstaple was buried that had formerly belong to John Aldriche (whose identity remains unclear). There is no reason to assume that Dunstaple was personally resident in any of the properties listed. This tenement was later in the possession of John Dunstaple Esquire's daughter, Margaret. Wathey had identified Margaret as John's wife, but using his will and other evidence this can now be corrected: John had both a wife and a daughter named Margaret (see Figure 4.3).[58] According to the churchwardens' accounts of St Stephen's, Walbrook, a payment of 2 shillings was made to Margaret (the daughter) in November 1485 by the churchwardens. This Margaret was being paid rent for this property by tenant Thomas Ingram, rather than the other way round:

> Item. Paid the 9th day of November in the first year of the reign of Henry VII [1485] Margaret Dunstable [Margarete donstabyl] for quarter rent at Michaelmas to Thomas Ingram [Yngram] 2s.[59]

Thomas Ingram's will (12 January 1500/1) confirms that he left 10 shillings each to the churches of St John the Baptist, Cottered ['Codred'] in Broadfield and Rushden ['Russheden'], indicating that he too had personal ties both in St Stephen, Walbrook and with the Dunstaple landowners of those places in Hertfordshire.[60]

Arguably the most jointly frustrating and illuminating element of the GB-Lma 175 is one that has not been reported by Wathey, who first drew attention to the document in his article 'Dunstable in France'; this is the list of co-owners found on the roll. The opening of the document lists the owners as: 1. John Dunstable of Steeple Morden in the county of Cambridgeshire, Armiger, and Margaret his wife, 2. John Dunstable of London, Gentleman, and 3. William Trukyll, clerk (see Figure 4.1).

Who were these other two men? I will deal first with William Trukyll (also found as Trokyll, Trokill), who is certainly the rector of St Stephen's,

98 Who was John Dunstaple?

Walbrook, serving there between 1440 and 1474. Here, then, is a second clear connection between John Dunstaple Esquire, landowner of Broadfield and Steeple Morden, and the parish church of St Stephen's. As James White's *History of the Ward of Walbrook* records, following the death in the Tower of London of Robert Southwell, accused of treason, Trukyll was appointed to the post of rector; he was presented for the post by Robert Whittingham. The vestry minutes record that:

> Owre p'son [parson] Sir W^m Tr'klye hath ij dedes of the gr'nte [grant] of ye Chirche, one is a dede of Rob' Chichele and a nother dede of ye Kynge's graunte of hys grete Seale.[61]

William Trukyll is also known from other records. A memorandum of 1 August 1441/2 confirms the passing of all goods and properties formerly belonging to John Harrys the elder, citizen and skinner of London – recently deceased – to the joint ownership of Trukyll, listed as clerk, and Robert Whittingham, Esquire, citizen of London (d. 1452). That the properties were referred to as 'in London and elsewhere' suggests considerable holdings, and that Whittingham and Trukyll were increasing landholdings as well as further establishing themselves in Walbrook.[62] Trukyll continued to acquire property through inheritance. A notice of 18 January 1450/1 records the gift of goods from Agnes Hoccle to both William Trukyll, again styled as clerk, and bell founder Thomas Pykworth:

> Agnes Hoccle, widow, of [Saffron] Walden co. Essex to William Trokyll clerk and Thomas Pykworth citizen and foundour of London, their executors and assigns. Gift of all her goods and chattels in Walden, London and elsewhere within the realm, and all debts to her due.[63]

A certain John Hurst (Herst), whose identity is otherwise unclear, left a further tenement to Trukyll and to the churchwardens of St Stephen's, Walbrook and their successors, in 1461/2:

> To be buried according to directions contained in another testament touching his movables. To Agnes his wife a certain tenement in the parish of S. Stephen de Walbrook for life; remainder to William Trokyll, the rector, and churchwardens of the church of S. Stephen de Walbrook and their successors, charged with keeping the same in repair, with the maintenance, out of the issues and profits, of a chantry, and with the observance of his obit, &c., in manner as directed. The devisees are enjoined not to remove the glass windows and lattices from out of the tenement, nor the lavatory, nor the beam for the candle of *coton*, nor the large cupboards, but the same are to be left for the benefit of the tenement. In case of default the tenement is to go over to the Mayor and Commonalty of the City of London to the use and maintenance of London Bridge, charged with keeping his obit as above.[64]

This evidence illustrates that both John Dunstaple Esquire, landowner of Steeple Morden, and William Trukyll were active in the parish of St Stephen, Walbrook and held a number of properties in common.

The appearance of the second 'John Dunstaple' in GB-Llma 175, here styled 'gentleman', is more of a puzzle. No other extant records contain such a reference. It seems fair to speculate that this John Dunstaple was family, given the co-ownership and common name. His status is indicated by his name falling between the esquire and the clerk, so it would be appropriate for him to be brought into a property agreement as a means of building his status as a young man. I would further propose that John Dunstaple, Gentleman, was the esquire's eldest son (or perhaps nephew), who then disappeared from legal documents because of premature death; there is no mention of a child of that name in the Hertfordshire will. A single document, now lost, but whose content is indicated by a catalogue entry in the National Archives, holds some support for this conjecture. Dating from 1436/7, the document styles John Dunstaple of Steeple Morden 'the elder'. Such an appellation really must presuppose that there is a John Dunstaple 'the younger' – a close, but more junior family member.

One calculation that does not sit well, chronologically, is if the landowner's son was the composer; records show the composition of the two motets performed in Canterbury must have existed by 1416, and any child of the landowner would not have reached adulthood by that date. While, then, GB-Llma 175 might at first seem to undermine the plausible linkage of the composer's biography with John Dunstaple, Esquire of Steeple Morden, its existence, in fact, only more securely links all *three* John Dunstaples with the rector of St Stephen's, Walbrook. Moreover, it is worth imagining how William Trukyll would have been involved with the arrangements made for the composer's burial and memorial in the church, a service that he undertook both as part of his duties as rector and through his personal and business associations.

In light of the assertions above, a closer examination of further property dealings will help to enrich the picture of John Dunstaple Esquire as a man whose business, career and devotional interests sit equally well with him being the composer.

The acquisition of John Dunstaple's properties

John Dunstaple's properties came to him by two main routes: some from individuals and some from the Crown. Dunstaple's co-owned properties in London were acquired from previous landowners in the city. His lands in Cambridgeshire were grants by the Crown, which was responsible for making him and his heirs tenants-in-chief of Steeple Morden. This is supported by an *inspeximus* (essentially a charter that confirms the validity of an earlier charter) made on 30 November 1435 at Westminster, naming 'John Dunstaple, Esquire' as 'the present tenant of the lands referred to in the charter'. Although the lands are not listed explicitly, separate records indicate that the manors of Brewis and Avenels, and lands in Steeple and Guilden Morden, passed from Hugh Haselden (d. 1433) to John

Dunstaple in or by 1435.[65] The related landholdings at Abington, Litlington (115 acres descended with Brewis manor), Bassingbourn and so forth descended with the property, but are not always specifically listed in the records.

It may be significant that at his death, out of his considerable holdings, John of Bedford's landed interests included property and income from a court in Abington and Bassingbourn. The Duke's Cambridge entry in his *inquisition post mortem* (a list drawn up to document the properties held at death) included: 'Bassingbourn, the manor, annual value £46 16s. 51/2d.' and 'Little Abington, a court of view of frankpledge, held once a year', plus knight's fees in a range of vills including Little Abington.[66] These were essentially economic benefits from the area in which John Dunstaple Esquire held property. While there is no evidence that English properties passed directly between John of Bedford and John Dunstaple, the possession of landed income in the same part of the county is worth consideration, especially since Wathey has shown that property in Normandy passed to Dunstaple in the wake of Bedford's death.

The general receiver for John of Bedford's properties in England and abroad was Robert Whittingham, and Whittingham provides us with a further potentially fruitful link between the activities at court and with the career of John Dunstaple Esquire. Whittingham's background was mercantile but became increasingly central to high profile civic affairs though the 1420s, including acting as an Alderman of Walbrook ward from 1422. There is insufficient space to outline Whittingham's career in full. One highlight was his role as receiver-general of the duchy of Cornwall (21 March 1433–4 November 1439) and of the English estates of John of Bedford by 10 September 1435. After Bedford's death on 14 September 1435, Whittingham continued to manage his estates and other Crown property as well as to travel abroad on diplomatic and financial matters. Whittingham's own properties were numerous, but the majority were concentrated in the parish of St Stephen, Walbrook. Whittingham's association with the parish was thus very strong: as patron of the church, he even laid its third foundation stone in May 1429. Roskell, Clark and Rawcliffe noted:

> [Whittingham] acquired the advowson of the church and several houses in that area from the duke of Bedford in 1432, thus adding to other premises which had been in his hands from 1418 if not before, and, incidentally, cementing an already close relationship with the most powerful nobleman in England.[67]

A musician working in some prominent capacity within the household of John of Bedford would have had cause to know, and benefit from, the actions of Robert Whittingham. We have already seen that Whittingham appointed Trukyll as rector, a man who held property jointly with John Dunstaple of Steeple Morden, with Dunstaple's wife Margaret, and with John Dunstaple, Gentleman of London (as confirmed by GB-Llma 175). Whittingham's role in Bedford's household and with his estate after 1435 therefore offers a further link between the composer John Dunstaple and the parish church of St Stephen where the musician was later buried.

Who was John Dunstaple? 101

On 16 March 1449, the manor of Broadfield in Hertfordshire was granted by John Suthrey and Richard Whaplode, who was vicar of the parish church of Steeple Morden, to four named individuals: John and Margaret Dunstaple, Ralph Grey, and Henry Wells.[68] An engraving made *c.* 1700 shows the manor house as it was rebuilt in the mid-1650s, but gives some indication of the scale and value of the land (see Figure 4.2)

Whaplode, like all the priests of the church of Steeple Morden, had been appointed on the recommendation of New College, Oxford, which had held the advowson there since 1378.[69] Whaplode had been admitted as a scholar to New College in October 1415, becoming a fellow of that college two years later. Presented to Steeple Morden some time after 1421, and certainly having vacated his position at Oxford by 1431, he had died by February 1454. The conveyance of the Hertfordshire property from Whaplode to Dunstaple probably stems from

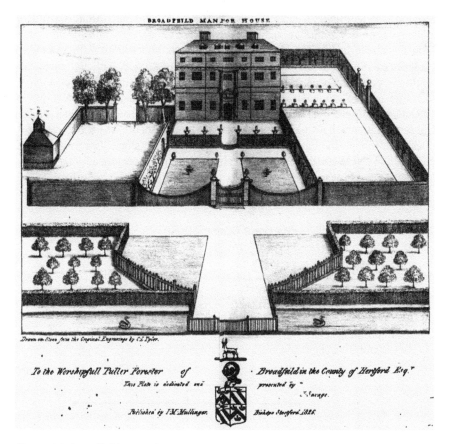

Figure 4.2 Broadfield manor house. Drawn on stone from the original engraving by C. L. Tyler

Image made by John Savage (*c.* 1700)[70]

their relationship in Steeple Morden, where Dunstaple had owned a range of property for 14 years by the time the Broadfield grant was made.

The heirs of John Dunstaple Esquire

To what extent might the family of John Dunstaple of Steeple Morden help us to consider the possibility that he was the composer? Dunstaple's heirs continued to have a strong relationship with the areas of Hertfordshire, Cambridgeshire, London and Essex. Dunstaple's daughter Margaret and son-in-law Richard Hatfield (also spelled Hatfeld in historical records), and his grandson Thomas Hatfield, styled themselves 'of Steeple Morden', but maintained involvement in both Cambridgeshire and London throughout their lives (see Appendix A for the legal titles of Dunstaple's heirs).

Unlike his father-in-law, Richard Hatfield Esquire was regularly involved in taxations and reparation work in his local area as tenant-in-chief of Steeple Morden after Dunstaple's death; for example, Richard was listed alongside others to assess a tax in Cambridge in 1463. These were the sorts of duties from which John Dunstaple had been exempted by the Crown, and which Wathey took as evidence of Dunstaple providing some other form of service. Although musician might be one such role, other options present themselves from Dunstaple's scientific and philosophical interests, and these will be considered below.

Richard Hatfield held an official position at court, Sergeant Avener of the Household, in which he assisted the Master of the Horse, one of the highest court roles even though the duties may to modern eyes seem slight. For example, on 20 June 1461 at Westminster, Richard Hatfield's duties were listed: 'To provide hay, oats, beans, peas, straw, litter and other necessaries for his office'.[71] The

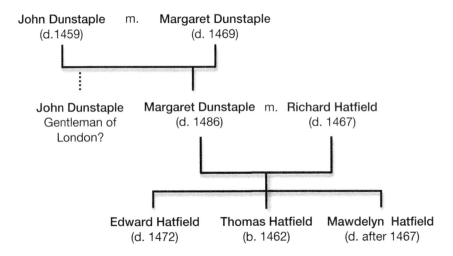

Figure 4.3 Family of John Dunstaple, Esquire, of Steeple Morden in Cambridgeshire

Sergeant Avener was also in charge of the expense accounts of the stable and was responsible for the payroll. The role came with material benefits, evidenced by Richard Hatfield's will, as dictated on 28 February 1467. In the will, Richard lists various items of bequest, including the following – evidently of considerable value:

> Item. I will that my hors trappes [ornamental covering for a horse] of goldsmythes werk and bawderyk of silver in abagge [in a bag] eqally be devyded disposed and departed in ij partes that is to say unto Edward my son one part and to Thomas my son the other part. Item. I biquith unto the same Edward myne harnys complete. And unto thesaid Thomas an other harneys complete.[72]

Although Richard Hatfield made various provisions for the church of St Peter in Steeple Morden (20s. for the church work; 6s. 8d. for the high altar; provision for an honest man to sing for his soul for one year), his main financial donations were to St Mary Woolchurch in Walbrook. To this church he gave 6s. 8d. to the high altar, but also funds for the provision of a stone tomb with epitaph and £3 6s. 8d. for a stained glass window to be made in the design chosen by his executors. It was St Mary Woolchurch that maintained his memory through his substantial patronage after death.[73]

The will of John Dunstaple, even in its abbreviated form, gives clear indication as to how his properties should descend, and it seems from the evidence that they did so according to his wishes. Dunstaple's wife Margaret died in 1469 leaving his daughter Margaret as his main heir, perhaps having become so as result of the early death of a son named John. Following the death of Richard Hatfield, daughter Margaret married William Hyde. Under the terms of the will, Dunstaple's daughter passed the manors of Broadfield and Mounseys in Cumberlow to her son Thomas Hatfield at her death in 1486.[74] In the years following John Dunstaple's death, a considerable volume of property changed hands, and usefully this was sometimes done under the name of Dunstaple, by which name Margaret Hatfield was still occasionally known for legal purposes.

The majority of properties of Thomas Hatfield were set up for dispersal in 1484, and at this point included Steeple Morden, Litlington and Abington in Cambridgeshire; Broadfield and Cumberlow Green in Hertfordshire; lands, tenements, rents, reversions and services in Stratford Langthorne and elsewhere in Essex and in the city of London. In 1485, Thomas also granted Guilden Morden, naming John Dunstaple as its former owner, to the same recipients – all of whom were either clerks or gentlemen. On 7 June 1492, a memorandum of acknowledgement confirmed his wishes.

On 26 October 1486, Thomas described himself as 'Thomas Hatfeld de Steple Morden in Com' Cantebr' Armiger filius et heres Margarete Hatfeld' in a quitclaim (a charter used to transfer property) relating the two tenements that had previously belonged to John Dunstaple in the parish of All Saints, Bread Street.[75] The Bread Street properties were named as the Woolsack ['Wolsak'; tenant Philip Ball, Haberdasher, 38 shillings rent] and The Three Kings of Cologne ['Lez Three

Kynges Coleyn'], *alias* The White Bull, £3 rent. This quitclaim awarded the property to John Breton (citizen and salter of London), John Gibbs and Thomas Goldhurst.[76] Thomas Goldhurst can be found regularly in the churchwarden's accounts of St Stephen's, Walbrook, where he was an active parishioner, rented property from the church in the early 1480s, buried his deceased children in the church and provided torches for graves by way of his profession as skinner. Reference to the former ownership of the Bread Street ward properties – to Thomas Hatfield and his mother Margaret – was made as late as 1510 in a further grant.[77] It seems plausible that at least the majority of the properties that were owned by Thomas Hatfield had descended directly from John Dunstaple Esquire, his grandfather.

The Three Kings of Cologne, Bread Street

The twice-named tenement in Bread Street offers interesting evidence that further establishes the link between Dunstaple the landowner and the composer in terms of their apparently duplicated aspects of personal piety, astronomy and astrology. During the ownership of the property by the Dunstaple/Hatfield family, one of the Bread Street properties can be found in the records variously as The Three Kings of Cologne, as well as by its alternative name, The White Bull, establishing that these were one and the same and inviting us to speculate on why the two different names may have been used.

Although neither property name was unique, the appellation of The White Bull was by far the more commonplace across England for properties than The Three Kings of Cologne. The closest property geographically, to be named after the king's cult was the Three Crowns, Coleman Street, in London, identified in records only from the late sixteenth century and thought by Jacob Larwood and John Camden Hotten to have taken its name from the trade between London and the Mercers of Cologne, following their source, antiquarian Mr Bagford:

> The origin of the sign of the Three Crowns is thus accounted for by Bagford: – 'The mercers trading with Collen [Cologne] set vp ther singes [signs] ouer ther dores of ther Houses the three kinges of Collen, with the Armes of that Citye, which was the Three Crouens of the former kinges, in memory of them, and by those singes the people knew in what wares they deld in.' Afterwards, like all other signs, it was used promiscuously, and thus it gave a name to a good old-fashioned inn in Lichfield, the property of Dr Johnson, and the very next house to that in which the doctor was born.[78]

Although signboards continue to be used to the present day for pubs, in the fifteenth century they were used for any form of property that needed to be distinguished from its neighbours; this was an era before houses were numbered or numeracy and literacy could be relied upon, but when property boundaries were just as important. The records indicate that tenants of The White Bull/Three Kings of Cologne were consistently either Haberdashers or Mercers, that is they were –

as was typical of that area of London – traders in silk, linen, worsted and small items such as buttons, now understood as haberdashery. Of the twelve great livery companies of London, the Mercers and the Haberdashers were related by some of their activities but it was the Mercers who were by far the most prominent and wealthy, developing trade links with the Low Countries and coming to administer the charitable estates of their wealthiest members – such as Richard 'Dick' Whittington (d. 1423).[79] The sign of The Three Kings of Cologne invoked a number of topics: travel; the continental trade links of linen merchants; pilgrimage; and religious devotion to the wise men of the East, whose relics were translated to Cologne in 1164 spreading the popularity of the cult across northern Europe.[80]

Richard Pfaff's exploration of England's medieval liturgy discusses two books relevant to this matter. A printed missal, made in London in December 1498, includes a mass for travellers labelled as a Mass of the Three Kings, and Pfaff notes that 'each of the proper prayers contains the names of Jaspar, Melchior, and Baltasar', making it unique among printed Sarum missals.[81] He argues that although it is possible that the printer had to hand a mass text from Cologne, and included it as a novelty, the same liturgical material appears in a second source, London, British Library Additional 25588 (hereafter GB-Lbl 25588), an early fifteenth-century manuscript Sarum missal. GB-Lbl 25588, from the diocese of Norwich, includes 'Missa pro itenerantibus de Sanctis tribus Regibus Colonie' (f. 252) as one of the additions in a later hand than the main content. The later devotions, all only textual rather than noted, at the end of GB-Lbl 25588 comprise a very interesting set of materials, not least the liturgical items for the Three Kings that imply the user's interest in travel and pilgrimage. These devotions include liturgical items for the cult of the Holy Name of Jesus (popular among elite and noble women in particular) and, fascinatingly, a sequence 'Jubilemus pia mente', found in a concordant manuscript (London, Lampbeth Palace 213, an early fifteenth-century missal used at one point in Meath, Ireland) as 'Missa pro rege pro mortalitate evitenda': a Mass for the King, to avoid or escape his mortality.[82] The sequence 'Jubilemus pia mente' had been created during the Black Death – under the orders of Pope Clement VI – and was thus, in the later Middle Ages, circulating as a potentially occult liturgical rite, warding off death for members of the nobility.[83]

Who owned GB-Lbl 25588? Pfaff speculated that the final three leaves of GB-Lbl 25588 were in the hand of Henry Wells (Wellys, Welles), the owner and later donor of the book. The provenance of the book rests in part on two later inscriptions: 'Obiit dominus Henricus Wellis qui hunc librum dedit huic ecclesie' (19 June, f. 4v) (Obit of Henry of Wells who gave this book to this church) and 'Orate pro anima Henrici Wellys Capellani domine Alicie Wiche et Johannis Dunstaple et cetera' (f. 250): 'Pray for the souls of Henry of Wells, chaplain to [both] Lady Alice Wiche and John Dunstaple, et cetera'.[84] The church itself is unnamed, but its dedication was on 5 June, as evidenced by the book's calendar. The 'etc.' at the end of the inscription has not been previously noted; it may indicate only the absence of some standard closing formula – liturgical or titular – rather than additional names of those whose souls might receive prayers.

Given that the liturgical additions on the final folios of GB-Lbl 25588 were part of a book owned by Henry Wells, he may have inscribed them, or had them inserted, in order to support his spiritual guidance of Alice Wiche (will made 27 September, 1474) and John Dunstaple. Alice Wiche was the wife, later widow, of Sir Hugh Wiche (Wyche) (d. May 1468), Master of the Mercers Company of London in 1450, and Lord Mayor of London in 1461.[85] The book inscription links men by the names of Henry Wells and John Dunstaple, but can we be sure the latter is relevant to the current discussion? The Broadfield documents show us that he is; GB-HFr 44505 mentions both men in relation to the property that passed to Dunstaple on 16 March 1448/9, indicating that they held Broadfield and its related properties jointly at that date.

What was the relationship between Wells and Dunstaple? GB-Lbl 25588 indicates Wells was an ordained chaplain of Lady Alice, which encourages us to identify this man as the Henry Wells who had been employed by New College, Oxford, on 4 March 1422.[86] Wells is recorded as having acted as one of the executors of the will of Alice Wiche, whose testament – confirmed in the Mercers' Company record in 1475 – indicates not only the movement of valuable items of property such as plate, but also the foundation of annual memorial masses for Alice and her husband, which were to be performed with music.[87]

Alice's will indicates that the chaplains of the Mercers' Company should pray for her and her two late husbands' souls (both Hugh Wiche and William Holt were special benefactors of the Company) for a period of sixty years in the parish church of St Denis (known as St Dionis Backchurch) in the ward of Lime Street, London, 'solemply by note by Prestes & Clerkes of the same Churche there to pray for the Soules of her & her husbonds'.[88] Alice's husband Hugh's will indicates that Henry Wells, styled there as priest, witnessed the making of the document; Hugh's extensive will also lays out a considerable requirement for masses to be said and sung in the memory of him, his relatives and friends.[89] The lack of Sir Hugh Wiche's name in the obit is because he predeceased Alice, who then remarried: this helps to date the inscription in GB-Lbl 25588 as made after September 1474, by which time John Dunstaple, Hugh Wiche and Alice Wiche were all dead.

A further clue as to the specific working relationship between Dunstaple and Wells is the rare papal indulgence awarded to a number of noble recipients, including John Dunstaple, allowing them to choose their own confessor. David Smith points out an increase during the later Middle Ages of the employment of private confessors, especially within the upper hierarchy of the church and amon the nobility.[90] Such confessors were often close friends, and intellectual as well as spiritual advisors, able to give deeply personal dimensions to religious contemplation.[91] Family confessors were often remembered in wills, and were party to private issues; it was John Sibsun, the private confessor of Richard Scrope, for example, who confirmed the virginity of the Archbishop upon his martyrdom.

The papal Register, dated 13 December 1434 (Florence), grants to 'John Donstaple, esquire, nobleman, of the diocese of Lincoln', indulgence to 'choose their confessor, who may as often as they please, after hearing their confession, grant them absolution, enjoining a salutary penance'.[92] As a landowner in

Hertfordshire, Dunstaple's property lay within the diocese of Lincoln, so this is doubtless the same man.[93] It seems, then, that Wells was chosen as Dunstaple's personal confessor, and as such would have been more likely to copy in items to his missal that reflected the private devotions of individuals – such as a Mass for the Three Kings or a Mass to help a king evade death – for a man for whom the feasts were of special significance. Hugh Wiche did not receive his equivalent papal indulgence until 1451, so may not have appointed Wells until considerably later than John Dunstaple.[94] Wells's broader interests are elucidated by a book (now Munich, Staatsbibliothek, Clm 26887), which once belonged to him and may contain his handwriting.[95] This book collects together various texts by Aristotle, including Aristotle, *On the Soul*, *On Generation and Corruption*, and *On the Heavens*; the last of these gives an outline of the philosopher's astronomical theory.

There is thus additional evidence to support the identification of the John Dunstaple Esquire with the composer, specifically in the composer's expertise in astronomy and his evident interest in The Three Kings of Cologne. Thomson's extensive work has identified the composer's connection to books on a range of subjects, including music and astronomy, sources that may also include examples of his hand.[96] Dunstaple's authorship of a treatise on astronomy is as yet unproven. However, the manuscript now known as Cambridge, Emmanuel College 70 preserves a scribal annotation 'Dunstaplus conscripsit hunc librum' (Dunstaple wrote this book), supported by a marginal gloss naming The Three Kings of Cologne in Hebrew, Greek, and Latin: 'Nota quod nomina trium regum sunt hec ut scribit magister in historia scolastica. Hebraice Appelius Amerus Damascus. Grece Galgalat Malgaleb Serachin. Latine Jaspar Balthesar Melchior'.[97] Consistent with later medieval devotion to the Holy Name of Jesus, it would seem that the names of the Kings themselves also held some spiritual power for Dunstaple at the time he wrote this marginal note. A man so personally invested in the cult of the Three Kings might plausibly have renamed one of his properties after it as an act of piety.

Conclusions

This chapter offers a clear and internally consistent biography for John Dunstaple Esquire, of Steeple Morden in Cambridgeshire. His financial and legal dealings allow us to connect him further – by evidence such as his styling as esquire and the complex but secure association of various properties within England and northern France – to the known taxation records that show his direct patronage from such high social class figures as Queen Joan of Navarre, John of Bedford and Richard Whittingham. The same man moved in high circles, sharing close company and his choice of private confessor with the one-time Lord Mayor of London and his wife (Hugh and Alice Wiche), as recorded by confessor Henry Wells's mass book. This rather beautiful missal shows signs of adaptation to suit the devotional interests of its owner or owner's patrons, specifically in the addition of a Mass for celebration on the feast day of The Three Kings of Cologne – men whose cult revolved around astronomy and who were most often celebrated as part of Epiphany.

108 *Who was John Dunstaple?*

Dunstaple and his heirs' connections with diverse properties, individuals, churches, parishes and drapery companies shows a strong relationship with the city, even though his official residence was elsewhere. In particular, his heirs bestowed their patronage on Steeple Morden in Cambridgeshire and on a second parish church in Walbrook: St Mary Woolchurch, where Richard Hatfield was buried.[98] Two men in particular – William Trukyll and Thomas Ingram – help us to connect the Cambridgeshire Dunstaple with St Stephen's Walbrook where the composer was buried. A further man, Henry Wells, shows the importance of astronomy and astrology within a devotional context, and was a close business acquaintance of John Dunstaple Esquire and possibly his private confessor. None of the contextual detail here would be inconsistent with the otherwise poorly documented composer, John Dunstaple, if he is indeed a separate figure. Nosow notes that Dunstaple the musician wrote a Gloria and Credo pair *Jesu Christe fili Dei*, based on a responsory for the Feast of the Epiphany.[99] Indeed, it is perhaps astronomy more than music that offers most of the contextual evidence in the discussion of connections between composer John Dunstaple and the various individuals, books and other evidence discussed in this chapter.

There is no single, incontrovertible piece of evidence that John Dunstaple Esquire of Steeple Morden was the musician buried at St Stephen's, Walbrook, given the conflict of reported death dates (which, within the literature of the past 400 years, have included 1453 (Munday), 1455 (Fuller), 1458 (Chappell), and now 1459). However, with an abundance of evidence relating to a high-status individual of that name who had clear business and personal links with the specific London church and its environs, and a range of supportive contextual evidence, it is high time for the date allegedly found on the tomb to be seriously challenged. Certainly, those who do not find this identification compelling will be required to remove almost all of the generally accepted biography of the composer, leaving us with the puzzling situation of a man whose reputation stretched across the English Channel but who otherwise left almost no archival record beyond manuscripts of his music, a record of early motet performances, and a tomb engraving with a 1453 death date as part of its epitaph.

Instead, I have presented biographical evidence that arguably presents one man: a polymath whose special skills in astronomy, astrology and music enabled him to become established within the mercantile and noble circles of fifteenth-century England. My proposal allows us to view the man consistently titled John Dunstaple Esquire in legal documents as the recipient of noble patronage from the leading figures of his day. He was a man whose learning in astronomy and astrology made him an authoritative figure, someone up-to-date with modern devotional practices. John Dunstaple was not a professional composer, or at least composition cannot have been his sole focus; the books that he owned demonstrate his expertise in matters that might well have been too sensitive to document officially, such as astrology used in judicial or state matters.[100] His income was likely related initially to his skills and talents but increasingly to landholding and business. By the time of his death in 1459, John Dunstaple was almost legendary; it is little wonder that he continues to be presented as a Moses-like figure, leading English composers out of the wilderness of anonymity, a champion of the most heavenly music.

Notes

1 Although some modern accounts use the spelling 'Dunstable', the composer's name was found more frequently as 'Dunstaple' during his lifetime.
2 Martin le Franc's comments about English musicians are discussed in Chapter 6.
3 Henry Davey, *History of English Music* (London: Curwen and Sons, 1895, 2nd edn, 1921), 45.
4 Bennett Zon, *Music and Metaphor in Nineteenth-Century British Musicology* (Aldershot: Ashgate, 2000), 185–7.
5 Manfred Bukofzer, "John Dunstable: A Quincentenary Report," *The Musical Quarterly* 40 (1954).
6 Margaret Bent, "A New Canonic Gloria and the Changing Profile of Dunstable," *Plainsong and Medieval Music* 5 (1996): 45–67, 46. Bent explores Dunstaple's claim as composer of the four-part setting of *Descendi in ortum meum*, and other pieces such as the Marian antiphon *Gaude flore virginali* (London, British Library, Additional 54324, hereafter GB-Lbl 54324), which might be identified with the (missing) piece of that name listed in the Eton Choirbook. For GB-Lbl 54324 (*c*. 1475), rediscovered by Thurston Dart, see Margaret Bent and Ian Bent, "Dufay, Dunstable, Plummer – A New Source," *Journal of the American Musicological Society* 22 (1969).
7 Bowers, accepting Dunstaple as the composer of *Descendi in ortum meum*, notes that it demonstrates that 'in circles which may well be expected to have been at the forefront of enterprise and experiment, the very beginnings of the use of the boy's voice in composed polyphony were already in evidence by the early 1450s'; "To Chorus from Quartet: The Performing Resource for English Church Polyphony, *c*. 1390–1559." In *English Choral Practice, 1400–1650*, edited by John Morehen (Cambridge: Cambridge University Press, 1995), 27.
8 Bent, *Dunstaple*, 5.
9 *Veni sancte spiritus* was likely the isorhythmic motet *Veni sancte spiritus/Veni sancte/Veni creator*. See Manfred Bukofzer, ed. *John Dunstaple: Complete works*. Musica Britannica 8. Revised by Margaret Bent, Ian Bent, and Brian Trowell (London: Stainer & Bell, 1970), No. 32, for Pentecost. Dunstaple wrote another setting of the same text (Bukofzer, *John Dunstaple: Complete works*, No. 33); Bent urges caution of assuming one over the other, since the text is not unique, but Nosow has demonstrated the strong relationship between this four-part motet and *Preco preheminencie*, structurally speaking and in their placement in manuscript sources; *Ritual Meanings in the Fifteenth-Century Motet* (Cambridge: Cambridge University Press, 2012), 23–43. Bent notes that Bedford's victory at Harfleur and the Battle of the Seine was celebrated the very same day, and as such it would be unlikely that an elaborate motet such as *Preco preheminencie* would have been prepared on that date; *Dunstaple*, 8. A further analysis of *Preco preheminencie*, in the context of English and continental isorhythmic motets, is given in Julie E. Cumming, *The Motet in the Age of Du Fay* (Cambridge: Cambridge University Press, 1999), 208–15. A fragmentary Canterbury source for *Preco preheminencie* (Bukofzer, *John Dunstaple: Complete Works*, No. 29), potentially one used in fifteenth-century performances at the cathedral, is discussed in Nicholas Sandon, "Fragments of Medieval Polyphony at Canterbury Cathedral," *Musica Disciplina* 30 (1976).
10 Margaret Bent, "Dunstaple, John (d. 1453)," *Oxford Dictionary of National Biography* (Oxford University Press, 2004; online edn, May 2006). Accessed 15 November 2015, www.oxforddnb.com/view/article/8286.

110   *Who was John Dunstaple?*

11 On the appearance of John Dunstaple's name in several fifteenth-century manuscripts not containing music, see Rodney M. Thomson, "John Dunstaple and his Books," *The Musical Times* 150 (2009), where this well-known inscription is discussed on page 12.
12 Nosow, *Ritual Meanings in the Fifteenth-Century Motet*, 37.
13 Nosow, *Ritual Meanings in the Fifteenth-Century Motet*, 34–6.
14 Thomson, "John Dunstaple and his Books," 3.
15 Thomson, "John Dunstaple and his Books," 12–13.
16 On the epitaph by John of Wheathamstead in relation to the motet *Preco preheminencie*, see below.
17 Judith Stell and Andrew Wathey, "New light on the biography of John Dunstable?" *Music and Letters* 62 (1981).
18 Charles Maclean, "The Dunstable Inscription in London," *Sammelbände der Internationalen Musikgesellschaft*, 11. Jahrg., H. 2. (1910), 247–8. The Latin text provided here is Maclean's corrected version, in the light of errors probably made by the seventeenth-century writers who transcribed it, and with some minor amendment using the more recent presentation of the Latin by Bent, *Dunstaple*, 2.
19 See James G. White, *The Churches and Chapels of Old London, with a Short Account of those who have Ministered in them* (London: C. E. Gray, 1901), and James G. White, *History of the Ward of Walbrook in the City of London: Together with an account of the Aldermen* (London: 1904. Reprint London: Forgotten Books, 2013).
20 For a detailed biography of Whittingham, see www.historyofparliamentonline.org/volume/1386-1421/member/whittingham-robert-1452.
21 Maclean, "The Dunstable Inscription in London," 237.
22 One publication for which Fuller's work presumably provided a source was William Chappell, ed., *A Collection of National English Airs, Consisting of Ancient Song, Ballad* (London: Chappell: 1838), Chappell's introduction was speculative at best: 'John Dunstable, famous for his superior skill in music and astronomy, flourished in the former part of the fifteenth century, and died in London, A.D. 1458, or according to some, A.D. 1455'; Chappell, *A Collection of National Airs*, 17.
23 Thomas Fuller, *The Worthies of England* (London: J. G., W. L. and W. G., 1662), 116–17, at 117. Fuller died in 1661, and the volume was published by his son. See P. Austen Nuttall, *A History of The Worthies of England by Thomas Fuller*, 3 vols (London: Thomas Tegg, 1840), where the passage from Fuller, relating to John Dunstable, is re-edited at volume I, 169–70. The date of Dunstaple's death remains presented as 1455, and the Latin epitaphs are the same except for Latin abbreviations – which have been expanded – and capitalisation, which has updated in style.
24 Equater mistaken for *C quarter* (i.e. CCCC for 400); 'trius' (for 1453) also a corruption that was not corrected until 1720 by John Strype as 'tria'; John Strype (1720) cited in Maclean, "The Dunstable Inscription in London," 241. Although there is no direct evidence that the word recorded was once the Latin for five (quinque), eight (octo), or nine (nove), the syllable count would work; I am grateful to Margaret Bent for this point. The task of recovering the original Latin text remains open, in my view.
25 John Weever, *Antient Funeral Monuments of Great-Britain, Ireland, and the Islands Adjacent* (London: W. Tooke, 1631), 341.
26 The translation is drawn from Bent, *Dunstaple*, 3, with amendments by Leofranc Holford-Strevens. Holford-Strevens notes that 'Although *precetur* ought to mean "let him pray", here it seems to be an impersonal passive, "let it be prayed"; emendation to *precemur*, but "let us pray", is discouraged by the internal rhymes' (personal correspondence).
27 David R. Carlson, "The Civic Poetry of Abbot John Whethamstede of St. Albans," *Mediaeval Studies* 61 (1999), 206.
28 David Howlett, "Studies in the Works of John Whethamstede." (PhD diss., University of Oxford, 1975); the suggestion is reported in Bent, *Dunstaple*, 4. Thomson considers

Wheathamstead the probable author of both epitaphs; "John Dunstaple and his Books," 5.
29   Alessandria Petrina, *Cultural Politics in Fifteenth-Century England: The case of Humphrey Duke of Gloucester* (Leiden, Netherlands: Brill, 2004), 51.
30   In Cambridge, Emmanuel College I. 3.18, MS 70, f. 151, a manuscript identified by Thomson as an autograph of John Dunstaple, 'there is a scheme for a judicial question: "on the resignation of a benefice, whether it is good or not". This is dated 1449, and the topic of the question, if not the date, would correspond to Wethamstede's [sic] dramatic decision to step down as Abbot—only to take on the mantle again later in his career. Wethamstede gives us a very full account of this in his Register'; Hilary M. Carey, "Judicial Astrology in Theory and Practice in Later Medieval Europe," *Studies in History and Philosophy of Biological and Biomedical Sciences* 41 (2010), 97. Dunstaple himself obtained a number of benefices in Northern France, and the date by which these had been lost or surrendered remains unclear in the records. Since the date of 1449 also corresponds with that of the collapse of Lancastrian Normandy, it is plausible that Dunstaple's judicial question related to his own landholdings.
31   As Bent has pointed out, the reference to Mikkalos was probably based upon Wheathamstead's misunderstanding of his source, assuming it to have indicated a musician; *Dunstaple*, 2. I am also grateful to Leofranc Holford-Strevens for the reference to the poetic specific lines; Aristotle, *Prior Analytics* Book 1, Chapter 33 (47b29–37).
32   Maclean, "The Dunstable Inscription in London," 235.
33   James G. Clark notes the marginal notes of medieval readers in various St Alban's manuscripts, including this one, in *A Monastic Renaissance at St Albans: Thomas Walsingham and his Circle, c. 1350–1440* (Oxford and New York: Clarendon Press, 2004), 139. The manuscript was brought to St Albans by Hugh Legat in 1400; Clarke, *A Monastic Renaissance*, 144. GB-Ob G.99 has miscellaneous contents mainly dating to the thirteenth centuries, including a treatise on Latin verbs, Ovid's *Heroides*, and part of a late twelfth-century missal that may have originated in Reims. The volume includes indications of use or ownership by Abbot John Stoke (who served in between John Wheathamstead's two periods of office, 1440–51) as well as other names that relate to the abbey's history such as Hugh of Eversden (Abbot of St Albans 1308–27).
34   Thirteenth-century Parisian sources F, W1 and W2 all contain concordant settings of 'Inter natos'; Heinrich Husmann and Gilbert Reaney, "The Origin and Destination of the 'Magnus liber organi'," *The Musical Quarterly* 49 (1963), 314–15.
35   See especially Peter Wright, "Binchois in England: Some Questions of Style, Influence, and Attribution in his Sacred Works." In *Binchois Studies*, edited by Andrew Kirkman and Dennis Slavin (Oxford: Oxford University Press, 2000), 95–9. A six-part setting of the text 'Inter natos mulierum', with the second part 'Fuit homo missus', has received attention for its problematic attributions to Josquin, though it is not based on the antiphon's melody; see Rob C. Wegman, "The Other Josquin," *Tijdschrift van de Koninklijke Vereniging voor Nederlandse Muziekgeschiedenis* 58 (2008).
36   See Deborah Youngs, *Humphrey Newton (1466–1536): An early Tudor gentleman* (Woodbridge: Boydell, 2008), especially 136–7.
37   For the term 'place-loyalty' see Philip Morgan, "Of Worms and War: 1380–1558." In *Death in England: An Illustrated History*, edited by Peter C. Jupp and Clare Gittings (Manchester: Manchester University Press, 1999), 140.
38   Youngs, *Humphrey Newton*, 137.
39   Youngs, *Humphrey Newton*, 136, 141.
40   Roger Bowers, "Some Observations on the Life and Career of Lionel Power," *Proceedings of the Royal Musical Association* 102 (1975–6), 103.
41   Bent, *Dunstaple*, 2.

112 *Who was John Dunstaple?*

42 For a detailed examination of Dunstaple's astrological interests as evidenced by the books owned and written by him, see Carey, "Judicial Astrology in Theory and Practice". Margaret Bent also discusses astrology in "a new Canonic *Gloria* and the Changing Profile of Dunstable," *Plainsong and Medieval Music* 5 (1996).
43 Robert Nosow subsequently, and independently, noticed the will in the records. I am grateful to Robert for both his willingness to discuss his own research, and for his voluntary withdrawal from his own detailed investigation upon realising that I was already pursuing it. Any information offered to me by Robert that I had not already discovered is acknowledged.
44 Alfred P. Beaven, "Aldermen of the City of London: Walbrook Ward," in *The Aldermen of the City of London Temp. Henry III–1912* (London: E. Fisher, 1908), 216–24 www.british-history.ac.uk/no-series/london-aldermen/hen3-1912/pp216-224 [accessed 4 August 2015]. A Robert de Dunstaple was the queen's clerk in 1329, as confirmed in papal records in which he was provided with a canonry and prebend of St John's, Beverley, and that he was rector of Tunstall; "Regesta 91: 1329." In *Calendar of Papal Registers Relating to Great Britain and Ireland*, edited by W. H. Bliss, II, 1305–42 (London: Her Majesty's Stationery Office, 1895), 290–6, www.british-history.ac.uk/cal-papal-registers/brit-ie/vol2/pp290-296 [Accessed 7 August 2015].
45 Richard L. Greene, "John Dunstable: A Quincentenary Supplement," *The Musical Quarterly* 40 (1954).
46 Joyce M. Horne, ed. "Prebendaries: Putson Minor." In *Fasti Ecclesiae Anglicanae 1300–1541: II, Hereford Diocese*, 47–8 (London: Athlone Press, 1962).
47 Judith Stell and Andrew Wathey, "New Light on the Biography of John Dunstable?" *Music and Letters* 62 (1981), 60.
48 Stell and Wathey, "New Light," 62.
49 Wathey, "Dunstable in France," 6.
50 See Wathey, "Dunstable in France" and Andrew Wathey, *Music in the Royal and Noble Households in Late Medieval England: Studies of Sources and Patronage* (London and New York: Garland, 1989).
51 Roger Bowers, "Review of Music in the Royal and Noble Households in Late Medieval England, by Andrew Wathey." *Music and Letters* 73 (1992), 640.
52 Wathey, "Dunstable in France," 27.
53 Writ issued at Winchester; *Calendar of the Fine Rolls, Volume 29, Henry VI, 1452–1461*, edited by C. T. Flower (London: Her Majesty's Stationery Office, 1939), 245.
54 The AHRC project to publish all such records by Boydell and Brewer has been discontinued, and I am very grateful to Christine Carpenter, former editor of the series, for her advice and for confirming that, to her knowledge, the relevant *Inquisition post mortem* for John Dunstaple no longer exists.
55 The rents for the tenement in St Stephen's Walbrook are recorded on GB-Llma 175 (15) and (16) (*olim* City of London Record Office Husting Roll 175 (15) and (16)). They record property held at the time of the records: November 1445 and November 1446. William Gawetron's inquisition post mortem (Middlesex) can be viewed at London, National Archives, C 139/68/10 (August 1435). He was a draper of the city of London and the son of Walter Gawetron, also a draper, who previously owned the same tenement in St Stephen's, Walbrook, in addition to a further tenement in the parish not later owned by Dunstaple. Wathey said this was not owned by John Dunstaple until after 1437/8, according to the Merton College manuscript, which would mean that Aldrich held the property for two years.
56 Tempting as it would be to identify property passing between a man of this name and John Dunstaple in relation to music theorist and astronomer John of Tewkesbury (*fl.* 1351–92), author of the *Quatuor principalia*, there is no evidence to do so, and the chronological gap would argue against it.

57 Presumably John Aldriche, a skinner, held the property between William Gawetron and John Dunstaple and his co-owners.
58 Wathey, "Dunstable in France," 27.
59 London, London Metropolitan Archives, MS 593/1, f.22v. These churchwardens' accounts (formerly London Guildhall Library, MS 593/1) cover the period 1474–1538. The Thomas Ingram in GB-HFr 44505 was probably dead by this time.
60 The will of Thomas Ingram is GB-Lna, PROB 11/12/309. Ingram's Hertfordshire connections were evidently still strong, since he was buried in St Michael's church at Bishop's Stortford and left donations to various churches and fraternities in that area.
61 White, *History of the ward of Walbrook*, 320.
62 "Close Rolls, Henry VI: 1441–1442." In *Calendar of Close Rolls, Henry VI: Volume 4, 1441–1447*, edited by A. E. Stamp (London: His Majesty's Stationery Office, 1937), 45–7.
63 "Close Rolls, Henry VI: 1450–1451." In *Calendar of Close Rolls, Henry VI: Volume 5, 1447–1454*, edited by C. T. Flower (London: His Majesty's Stationery Office, 1947), 248–58.
64 "Wills: 1 Edward IV (1461–2)." In *Calendar of Wills Proved and Enrolled in the Court of Husting, London: Part 2, 1358–1688*, edited by R. R. Sharpe (London: Her Majesty's Stationery Office, 1890), 545–8.
65 A. P. Baggs, S. M. Keeling and C. A. F. Meekings, "Parishes: Steeple Morden." In *A History of the County of Cambridge and the Isle of Ely* 8, edited by A. P. M. Wright (London: Victoria County History, 1982).
66 *Calendar of Inquisitions Post Mortem, Henry VI*, edited by M. L. Holford, S. A. Mileson, C. V. Noble, and Kate Parkin (Woodbridge: Boydell and Brewer, 2010), 380–81. Between Haselden's death and Dunstaple's award of the property, the lands would have been held by the King.
67 J. S. Roskell, L. Clark and C. Rawcliffe, eds, *The History of Parliament: The House of Commons 1386–1421* (Woodbridge: Boydell and Brewer, 1993).
68 Previous owners included John Tyrrel of Essex (until 31 January 1425/6), Humphrey, Earl of Stafford and others; John Hughesson of Asshewell, and John and Thomas Clerke (citizens and grocers of London). The advowson of Broadfield church descended with the manor. See Henry Chauncy, *The Historical Antiquities of Hertfordshire* (London: Ben Griffin, 1700), 2nd edn (Bishops Stortford, J. M. Mullinger, 1826), 144.
69 'Bishop William of Wykeham, under a bull of 1378 and a royal licence of 1379, gave the church [of Steeple Morden] to his new college at Oxford, to which it was appropriated in 1381. A vicarage was ordained, of which New College held the advowson until the 1970s'; Baggs, Keeling, and Meekings, "Parishes: Steeple Morden," 111–24.
70 Savage's image appeared as a plate in Chauncy, *The Historical Antiquities of Hertfordshire*, and is reproduced here from the 2nd edn (Bishops Stortford, J. M. Mullinger, 1826), plate 3, p. 145a. The book is freely available in digital form online.
71 *Calendar of the Patent Rolls, Edward IV, Volume II, 1468–1476*. Edited by W. H. B. Bird, and K. H. Ledward (London: Her Majesty's Stationery Office, 1953), 12.
72 Richard Hatfield's will is at London, National Archives, PROB 11/5.
73 Richard Hatfield's tomb confirmed 1467 as the year of his death. The writ of *diem clausit extremum* for Richard Hatfield was not issued until 19 March 1468 and probate made at Lambeth on 3 July 1468; it might therefore be estimated that he died towards the end of 1467.
74 A dispute over bequests seems to have arisen in 1486, on Margaret's death, with the manor of Broadfield briefly being held by a Robert Hyde, presumably a further

(unlawful) heir from her second marriage to William Hyde. At this point the manor was worth £10.
75   This confirms that although Thomas Hatfield had set up the transfer of his property in 1484, the dispersal of Steeple Morden had not yet occurred.
76   Thomas Goldhurst and other co-owners, including John Gybbes, were granted the Angel in Friday Street in the parish of St Matthew, Bread Street. On 12 October 1501 he surrendered property including that at Friday Street. In 1510 he made a grant to Robert Bailly (citizen and Sherman) and his wife Ann of a yearly rent from a tenement held by Richard Lakyn: The Three Kings of Cologne *alias* The White Bull and a tenement called the Wool Sak, lately held by Philip Ball (Haberdasher).
77   The property passed twenty years later to the Wardens of the Fraternity and Guild of Corpus Christi in All Saints, Bread Street, and to the male and female members of that fraternity.
78   Mr Bagford, GB-Lbl Harley 5910, vol. I, f. 193; cited in Jacob Larwood and John Camden Hotten, *The History of Signboards from the Earliest Times to the Present Day* (London: Chatto and Windus, 1866; 12th edn, 1908), 102.
79   See Ann F. Sutton, *The Mercery of London: Trade, Goods and People, 1130–1578* (Aldershot: Ashgate, 2005). After Thomas Hatfield quit the property, it remained under the ownership of the Salters, another of the Great 12 Livery Companies of London.
80   Hugh Mountney, *The Three Holy Kings* (Leominster: Gracewing, 2003).
81   Richard W. Pfaff, *The Liturgy in Medieval England: A history* (Cambridge: Cambridge University Press, 2009), 421.
82   I am grateful to Gregorio Bevilacqua for confirming my translation of this line.
83   Although *Analecta Hymnica* lists only other copies of the sequence, the editors do not list the copy in GB-Lbl 25588.
84   The British Library's transcription of the phrase reads 'Johanni' rather than 'Johannis'; *Catalogue of Additions to the Manuscripts in the British Museum in the Years 1854–1875* (London: British Museum, 1877), 204. Having viewed the manuscript, and following discussions with Leofranc Holford-Strevens, I am confident that the correct reading is 'Johannis', indicating that Wells served as chaplain to both John and Alice.
85   My thanks to Robert Nosow for confirmation that Alice Wiche was Hugh's wife. Hugh Wiche's will is held as National Archives, PROB 11/5/56.
86   Alfred B. Emden, *A Biographical Dictionary of the University of Oxford to AD 1500*, 3 vols (Oxford: Clarendon Press, 1957–59). He may also be the Henry Wells who worked as the rector of Little Hinton in Dorset (1434–39) and then at All Hallows, London Wall (6 August 1439–July 1440), but the name is too common to be sure.
87   Laetitia Lyell and Frank D. Watney, eds. *Acts of Court of the Mercers' Company 1453–1527* (Cambridge: Cambridge University Press, 1936; reprinted 2012), 82–4.
88   Lyell and Watney, *Acts of the Court of the Mercers' Company*, 82. This church later lay in the ward of Langbourn but was situated on the south-west corner of Lime Street.
89   Hugh Wiche's will requested for memorial masses and Lady masses to be sung 'by note' in the church of St Margaret Lothbury, at the church of St Dionis Backchurch, and by the nuns of Stratford-at-Bow.
90   David Michael Smith, *Studies in Clergy and Ministry in Medieval England* (York: University of York, Borthwick Institute of Historical Research), especially 108–9.
91   Virginia Davies, *Clergy in London in the Late Middle Ages: A Register of Clergy Ordained in the Diocese of London Based on Episcopal Ordination Lists, 1361–1539* (London: University of London Centre for Metropolitan History, 2000). My thanks to Virginia Davies for allowing me access to her database during my research.
92   I am grateful to Robert Nosow for bringing this document to my attention. The document, *Archivio Apostolica Vaticana, Regestra Lateriana, vol. 326, f. 300 d.*, in the section 'De plenaria remissione' (Indults of Plenary Indulgence). The reference

is published in *Calendar of Papal Registers Relating to Great Britain and Ireland*, Volume 8, 1427–47, edited by J. A. Twemlow (London: His Majesty's Stationery Office, 1909), 510–16. Nosow considers the mention of Lincoln evidence that he was working for Joan of Navarre in 1434, whereas I would see it as relating to Dunstaple's other landholdings.

93 Nosow notes that there is a possible avenue for enquiry here between King's Langley, the palace and manor that formed part of the dowry of Queen Joan of Navarre, which was also within the diocese of Lincoln. It seems clear that Queen Joan spent considerable time there.

94 Hugh received papal indulgence to choose his confessor when he was still married to Joan; 'To Hugh Wyche, nobleman, dwelling at London [. . .] and Joan his wife, noblewoman. Indult to choose . . .'; 'Lateran Regesta 467: 1451', f. 272. In *Calendar of Papal Registers*, edited by J. A. Twemlow, 517–26.

95 The manuscript is described in Karl Halm, Georg von Laubmann, and Wilhelm Meyer, *Catalogus codicum latinorum Bibliothecae Regiae Monacensis* (1881), 225; this catalogue entry was viewed through the library's webpages.

96 Thomson, "John Dunstaple and his Books."

97 I was informed of the inscription of these names in the Cambridge manuscript by Nosow (personal correspondence, 8–9 November 2012), though its significance in relation to other evidence only later occured to me.

98 For lost sources of music from the Walbrook ward, see Magnus Williamson, "Liturgical Polyphony in the Pre-Reformation English Parish Church: A Provisional List and Commentary," *Royal Musical Association Research Chronicle* 38 (2005), 32 (St Mary, Woolchurch; St Mary, Woolnorth) and 34 (St Stephen, Walbrook). Evidence of polyphony and the cultivation of polyphonic music exists from the ward, though not with any reference to music directly relevant to Dunstaple.

99 Personal correspondence (8 November 2012).

100 One of his patrons, Queen Joan of Navarre, was convicted and imprisoned from 1419–*c*. 1423, for trying to poison Henry V through witchcraft. It would be easy to see the specific relevance of the fourteenth-century sequence 'Jubilemus pia mente', part of a Mass to allow his heir, Henry VI, to escape death. There is, unfortunately, insufficient evidence through which this idea might be pursued here.

5 The idea of English music
Identity, ethnicity and musical style

English music reflects influence from further afield as well as contributing to ideas outside its borders, and the ways in which this has occurred has been imagined and documented in many accounts from the Middle Ages to the present day. Music moved with musicians, and there were numerous reasons for musically trained people – especially but not exclusively those employed by the church – to take their practices around the country and beyond. Whether for study, diplomatic service or pilgrimage, many musicians would have travelled, taking with them current knowledge of repertoire and notation. Nevertheless, we have a limited picture of such movement. Crucial data have been lost, such as the records of many noble household chapels. Some travels have left little impression on the records: consider, for example, the musical sounds associated with pilgrimage to major sites such as Canterbury or Santiago de Compostela. What songs and vocal styles did someone like lay pilgrim Margery Kempe (*c*. 1373–after 1439) hear on her journey to the Holy Land? What music did she hear at Mass or in the streets of Venice, Rome, Lincoln, Aachen, Calais, London or Jaffa? What differences between English and foreign musics and performance styles would Margery have perceived as an active and sensitive listener at Mass, 'herying hir messe' as she put it?[1]

The surviving manuscripts of medieval English music are relatively poor witnesses to the sorts of musical exchanges to which I have alluded. Sources of polyphony can give us clues as to their ownership and to the provenance of their contents; concordances demonstrate something of patterns of transmission, for example.[2] Texted music can, in particular, guide us to the origin of pieces for which we have no information about their composers; the use of a particular tenor and the choice of language for texted parts can help connect anonymous music with local practices. Beyond that, evidence of creative origin becomes more speculative, based on the analysis of aspects such as structure, codicology, contrapuntal properties, melodic shape or notational style. Anglo-continental relations between composers, performers and their music continue to fascinate scholars for a range of reasons, some of them stemming from a long-held desire to demonstrate the particular, perhaps superior, qualities of English music before the renaissance.

To what extent have writers about English music been influenced by national or nationalist agendas? How have they sought to identify markers of Englishness

118 *The idea of English music*

in fourteenth- and fifteenth-century repertoire? Did English musicians of the Middle Ages express, or aim to express, notions of national identity through copying or composition? In this chapter, I will explore a variety of musicological texts that exemplify some of the common tropes in accounts of Englishness in relation to music. In particular, I will demonstrate how, historically, musicologists have used language that has treated musical properties as if they related to ethnic fingerprints, revealing anxieties that have been mapped from cultural debate about nationalism and migration onto creative practice. This chapter is largely historiographical, tracing the complexities of retelling the history of English music. I will concentrate primarily on the relationship between English and French music, partly because there is clear evidence of cultural exchange between the two countries at various points, and to varying degrees, between 1300 and 1450, and partly because many of the published examinations of repertoire have centred on trying to separate French and English repertory.[3]

The musicological studies that I have chosen to discuss have been selected because they are well-known, influential and have been widely disseminated through publication. This chapter will firstly examine the way in which English musical language has been conceptualised and historicised. Then, having understood the prevailing features of the discourse, I will focus more fully on the relationship between compositional practice and musical style, investigating what it might mean when writers use terminology relating to national and ethnic markers for music. The point here is not to blame writers for (inevitably) approaching music in ways that reflect the attitudes and research priorities of their time. Rather, I wish to examine the interrelationship between writers' own historical placement and the history that they chose to write about medieval English music, tracing the concept of nationality and ethnicity across diverse texts in ways that demonstrate the magnetic attraction of much older stories.

Manuscripts as sources of identity

The sources that preserve medieval music behave in similar ways to music repositories of the digital age, in which songs enjoy popularity with individuals for different reasons. They therefore often rub shoulders in their owners' personal collections – which may not be physical – with diverse genres, styles and sounds. Manuscript collections of monophonic and polyphonic music were highly individualised, perhaps even more than record collections in the twentieth century, about which Martin Stokes has made the following comment:

> A private collection of records, tapes or CDs [...] articulates a number of highly idiosyncratic sets of places and boundaries. A moment's reflection on our own musical practices brings home to us the sheer profusion of identities and selves that we possess.[4]

Stokes's words are equally applicable to English music manuscripts, each of whose unique content can reveal something about their owners' interests, institutional priorities or contact with networks of copying activity. Consider manuscript collections in fourteenth-century England, in which every one of approximately one hundred sources appears to contain a one-off selection of pieces, even though there is a striking number of concordances across surviving fragments.[5] Summers estimates that 40 per cent of the fourteenth-century fragments of polyphony include music found in at least one other source, and notes the 'shocking fact' that 'no two sources seem to have been produced by the same hand'.[6] Each manuscript thus has the potential to be read as an expression of musical, spiritual and other forms of identity at a particular place and time, acknowledging that in some cases, music was copied from items that were conveniently available rather than being indicative of a coherent individual collection strategy.[7] A well-known source such as GB-Lbl 978 – probably compiled by a number of religious men in thirteenth-century Reading – bears witness to the scribes' diverse interests both locally and more widely: Deeming argues that its copyists 'were able to tap into international networks of song, as well as gaining access to items less well distributed', from 'Sumer is icumen in' and other unica to items known in France, Ireland and Spain.[8] A brief consideration of a handful of sources can suggest myriad ways in which we might reshape our understanding of music along lines that are not dominated first and foremost by nationalist agenda.

A prestigious source copied in just one or two stages has exceptional potential to show the driving agenda of a patron or institution at a particular moment in time. The largest and most complete and coherent source for English music is the Old Hall Manuscript. Old Hall contains nearly 150 compositions, and others have no doubt been lost by damage since there is evidence that the codex contained at least a further twenty-five folios. Non-English work is represented, such as music by Antonio Zacara da Teramo, though the collection is certainly dominated by pieces whose composers known to have lived and worked across England.[9] Old Hall is a key witness to Anglo-Continental exchange in the first decades of the fifteenth century and to the richness of musical practice in England at that time. This one source contains strikingly different stylistic approaches, from relatively straightforward settings of Mass Ordinary texts to those involving complex canonic or isorhythmic devices. It would be possible to build a case that Old Hall was copied primarily as a celebration of the achievements of English composers of the present and recent past, but there are more stories to tell.

The majority of work on Old Hall has been undertaken by Bent, who has shown the earliest layer of the collection to have been copied between 1415 and the death of Thomas, Duke of Clarence in 1421, and the second layer over one or more subsequent years after the manuscript had passed to Henry V's chapel.[10] The manuscript's contents offer rich opportunities for the exploration of questions of identity, not least in relation to the devotional practices of the household chapels, but also in relation to the input of King Henry (probably Henry V) as composer. The copying practices of its scribes have been examined in detail, but it is likely that more information might emerge in the current era of digitisation.[11] Some of the later pieces may have been copied in by their composers – perhaps by Burell, Cooke, Damett and Sturgeon – and personal intervention in copying practice is also worthy of greater scrutiny in relation to other sources. Questions of identity can also be explored through the votive purpose of some of the items such as Masses on tenors taken from particular liturgies (notably that of Thomas of Canterbury) and Byttering's motet *En Katerine solennia/Virginalis contio/Sponsus amat sponsum*, a likely candidate for origin at the time of the wedding of Henry V to Catherine of Valois in 1420.

Examinations of miscellanies, or commonplace books, have no less to offer; such apparently messy or haphazardly compiled sources allow us to view the changing interests of one or more owners over time. The work of Andrew Taylor and Deeming has already been outlined in relation to the composite collection, GB-Lbl Harley 978. Lesser-known sources containing rather less music can repay close study. York Minster Library, xvi.N.3 (hereafter GB-Yc xvi.N.3), for example, includes parts of just three pieces of music: the English motet *Zelo tui langueo/Reor nescia/T. Omnes de Saba*, also found in GB-Lbl Sloane 1210; *Inter amenitatis tripudia/O livor anxie/T. Reverenti*, a motet known from the *Roman de Fauvel* and elsewhere on the continent in two- and three-part versions; and a monophonic presentation of *Ad rose titulum*, preserved polyphonically in Cambridge, Gonville and Caius College, 512/543 (probably copied in or around Norwich). A critical assessment of codicological and paleographical evidence, patterns of transmission, art history and the relationship between piety and gender has established that GB-Yc xvi.N.3 was owned by the house of Gilbertine nuns and monks at Shouldham in Norfolk.[12] GB-Yc xvi.N.3 thus bears witness to a network of musical transmission that resonated both locally and internationally. As a monastic institution attracting men and women from the gentry and nobility, Shouldham also sat at the apex of lay and monastic cultures; its residents would have used not only Latin but at least two vernaculars (French and English). The collection contains textual items in three vernaculars, including the popular devotional text in Anglo-Norman, *La Lumiere as Lais* by Pierre d'Abernon (d. 1293).[13] GB-Yc xvi.N.3 was not a liturgical book. It was at various times a personal or library copy, bringing together a unique combination of devotional and practical items relevant to women and men. Music was one of its several types of content: some parts (such as the liturgical calendar and the instructions for calculating Easter) were eminently practical, some were for religious contemplation, some for entertainment.

Finally, even fragmentary sources can convey a surprising level of information if thoroughly investigated. A prime example is the work of Bent on isolated leaves that once formed part of a choir book of similar proportions to Old Hall, probably compiled a little later than its equivalent, for an unidentified royal patron.[14] The majority of surviving English music is preserved in a fragmentary state or exists as musical items added alongside non-musical texts. Most sources were connected not to royal households but to monastic libraries and wealthy individuals.[15] Benedictine monasteries at Durham and Bury St Edmunds, for example, once owned substantial collections of polyphony in which English and French motets were copied adjacently. There was no conflict, it would seem, for Durham monks to sing a troped Kyrie in honour of their patron St Cuthbert (as found in Durham, Cathedral Library A.III.11, f. 4v) or a well-travelled motet such as *Apta caro/*

Flos/Alma redemptoris mater, sometimes attributed to Philippe de Vitry (Durham, Cathedral Library, C.I.20, ff. 338v–339r and five continental sources).[16] Appraised primarily within a national framework, it is easy to lose the nuanced picture that any one source might offer. Manuscripts frequently show a multi-local identity, not usually through changing hands but through the nestling together of repertory from diverse places.[17]

Native, endemic and indigenous English music

The classification of a native English musical language springing 'naturally' from the people of England, without outside influence, was a particular feature of early-to-mid twentieth-century examinations of the repertory. This approach extended from nationalistic sentiments developed during the nineteenth century in particular. Some writers were motivated by a desire to identify music that might be described as endemic to England. Endemic music would not only be native but also restricted to practices within the island rather than travelling further afield. We might think, here, of studies of the English carol or of the practice of composing Masses upon 'squares'.[18] Other writers' nets were cast more widely, examining localised English practices that were native but that were indigenous rather than endemic: found beyond the English coastline in ways suggestive of English influence abroad. Most accounts have focused on music emanating from England and France; Italy enters discussions more prominently after *c.* 1430 because of the preservation of English pieces in continental sources such as the Trent codices. France is geographically and politically close to England, not least during periods of intertwined genealogies and periods in which parts of modern France were officially parts of England. Lengthy periods of military and diplomatic activity brought ample opportunities for cultural exchange between the two countries. As Lefferts observed in relation to the fourteenth century:

> The English and the French knew each other's music. Politics and intellectual life made this inevitable, and it is testified to by the theoretical tradition as well as the musical sources [. . .]. The timing and degree of influence exerted by each culture on the other are, however, issues on which scholars have come to very different conclusions.[19]

Lefferts's book centred on the motets cultivated in England, examining provenance, notation, sources, texts and structural and stylistic features. He emphasised the importance of striking a balance between the position of two groups of scholars: the first who saw indigenous English music as cut off from continental practice between *c.* 1300 and *c.* 1415, after which its influence spread across the Channel and maintained clearly identifiable English stylistic features; and a second group who saw little that was peculiar to the English motet tradition after the middle of the fourteenth century. Lefferts's study found that English music from the early part of the fourteenth century was 'insular in its antecedents, richer in its variety of formal approaches than continental practice, more reflective on the whole of

122 *The idea of English music*

the versification of the texts set to music and innovative in notation and in numerical control of phrase lengths'.[20] In comparison, later fourteenth-century music (found across relatively few surviving sources) included 'many more continental motets, some given new texts to suit English preferences [. . . and] insular pieces with varied approaches to the reconciliation of continental notation and style with local practice'.[21] Overall then, Lefferts aimed to examine the compositional traditions that were current in England however, in doing so, he sought to distinguish between these practices in terms of origin and influence. Defining the motet as known in England required separating it from contemporary non-English models. Lefferts's study is a remarkably objective one, informed by knowledge of the genre from diverse perspectives, and stands out in part because of his careful avoidance of loaded terminology. This sort of objectivity can only really be gained from examining musical history through intimate knowledge of individual manuscript sources, as the precursor to embedding that knowledge into broader historical narratives, rather than the other way around.

Earlier twentieth-century accounts tended to embrace more subjective language, not least within general surveys of the later Middle Ages. One particular concept that recurs is the quest to find musical practice that was indigenous to England, a term properly used to describe something that occurs naturally in a specific location. Once a writer has identified the indigenous nature of a particular stylistic trait, their assertion can then be employed to build a case of the role of that trait in influencing traditions elsewhere. The final chapter of Gustav Reese's *Music in the Middle Ages* (1940) outlined what he saw as naturalness in English musical expression. Reese used the question of English cultural influence in the fifteenth century as a platform on which to place English compositional practices at the vanguard of the development of tonality itself, which he argued stemmed from a sophisticated musical nature. His argument was formed in relation to what he considered distinctively English approaches to voice-leading:

> The *enormous influence* exerted by English methods on Continental voice-leading is evident in the widespread adoption of the fauxbourdon style about the middle of the 15th century. The dissatisfaction with the old interval theory [. . .] was now replaced by an *apparently unconscious desire* to bring some order into the progressions of chords, to relate them somehow to each other, as chords. It is possible to see, in English, as well as Continental compositions of the first half of the 15th century, the first attempts at what we should call functional harmony [emphasis added].[22]

Reese distinguished here between the continental musicians' path towards tonality and that followed by the English. It was only the English who were credited with a natural, 'unconscious desire' to relate chords to one another, though similar effects were identifiable in 'Continental compositions', a phrase belying deliberate and intellectual motivation. Reese avoided marking this important shift in musical technique as one by design. Rather, his chapter on English music – which appears to crown his book with these concluding remarks – argues that:

Yet in no case, at this period, is there any question of a *systematic approach* towards harmony in the modern sense, or even of the *awareness* of the possibility of building such a system. Such relationships as may be found are of the *simplest* sort and seem *entirely instinctive* [emphasis added].[23]

It is difficult to miss the way in which the development of polyphonic music in fifteenth-century England was being positioned here as a primitive form of tonality: one that would naturally evolve over time until more enlightened individuals would formalise the seminal harmonic gestures found in the earlier period into the rules governing harmony and counterpoint.

For Reese, the innate English desire for harmonic relationship was combined with his observation that English music was naturally more melodious. English and French polyphonic repertoire *c.* 1350–*c.* 1425 were compared, measured in ways that would have found sympathy from Burney and other Enlightenment scholars:

[English music] seems to consist largely in the invention of melodies more pleasing than the French to ears trained chiefly on 18th- and 19th-century music.[24]

In this way, English music was highlighted as combining a natural skill for the regulated behaviour of tonal music with an inherent national inclination to tunefulness. Reese argued here that cultured, civilised Western listeners, who grew up on a diet of Mozart and Beethoven, would have recognised and enjoyed melodic contours within English music more than the, by implication, learned melodic accomplishments of French composers.

With its vibrant style and broad, detailed knowledge of repertoire, Reese's work became a standard reference work for those researching medieval music, and as such his book influenced later writers. Henry Raynor's *Music in England* (1980), for example, shared some common themes. Raynor drew on the established division between natural English musicality and technical French music, emphasising the 'more poignant, sensuous direction' taken by English music *c.* 1200.[25]

Raynor's language placed the music itself as agent of choice and change rather than the musicians who were composing and performing it. This approach may have been encouraged by the anonymity of the repertoire, but the effect was to side-step problems with holding individuals responsible for stylistic shifts. He went further in his discussion of medieval music more generally, linking English music not only to the melodic sensitivities of the nineteenth century but also to the expressive and romantic core of that later period:

It would really not be too much to suggest that in its early days, as in its later, English music aimed at frank emotionalism.[26]

The idea that English music was linked to the emotional (as opposed, perhaps, to the rational) had been foregrounded in various earlier histories – not least Davey's

History of English Music, which had noted the coincidence that: 'the earliest composition ["Sumer is icumen in"], being English, should be inspired by the thoroughly English sentiment, joy in country life'.[27] In this way, Davey, Reese and Raynor sought to identify a natural English musical spirit common to all time, a kind of indigenous binding agent based on rural idyll, melody, sweet harmony and expression, dominating matters of formal structure and design. The priorities of Beethovenian Romanticism, placing expression above structural limitations, may have been in their minds as a later equivalent. If French musical history was dominated by modal rhythm, isorhythmic devices and authorial poet-composers such as Machaut, the parallel English musical culture was one based on primitive, emotional expression that naturally achieved a more progressive outcome in its foreshadowing of markers of genius in tonal music.

Ethnicity and anonymity in English music

A fundamental pillar of musico-historical writing involves outlining who composed what, where and when; consequently, national boundaries have traditionally been an important part of musicological discourse. Only with authorship and provenance clearly established can lines of development and influence be traced and innovators celebrated. As I explored in Chapter 3, the unclaimed status of almost all English repertoire before the fifteenth century makes answering questions relating to place of origin difficult. Music with English text makes the association between genesis and the nationality of its author (at least for the text) more convincing, as English was not a vernacular regularly cultivated further afield. Unfortunately, English lyrics are relatively rare outside the paraliturgical repertory of thirteenth-century devotional items and fifteenth-century carols. English composers, and especially those associated with royal or noble patrons, continued to set French texts right into the sixteenth century because of the higher courtly status of French.

Musical style alone is a problematic aspect on which to rely for a secure attribution to an English composer. Though aspects of musical language have sometimes been associated with English compositional practice, those features are often found in pieces that have uncontested origins from beyond the coastline. The need to satisfy the question of a piece of music's 'ethnicity' (that is, in addition or in place of similar information about the composer him/herself) pervades much of the writing about medieval English music.[28] Discussions identifying Englishness in musical style were particular energetic in articles by Jacques Handschin and Ernest Sanders in the 1940s, 50s and 60s. In Nicky Losseff's discussion of some of these authors' approaches, especially research that saw the use of thirds as a consonance or the use of voice exchange as proof of Englishness, she queried the validity of mapping musical style firmly onto the identification of national origin:

> It does now seem that a more cautious attitude towards real or imagined ethnic differences should be taken, and that a more imaginative approach to questions of reception and influence is needed.[29]

The idea of English music 125

As Stokes has commented, 'musical styles can be made emblematic of national identities in complex and often contradictory ways'.[30] Thus, in musicology – a discipline whose origins lie in the classification of musical repertories, genres and styles – there has been a historical trope in writing that aims to separate characteristics, to identify differences, along a number of lines that include ethnic boundaries. It should be clear from my discussion so far that setting up a binarism of English/non-English ethnicity for music of this period may have been standard in earlier historical writing, but it is not in itself necessary or desirable. Although many of the earlier writers discussed in this chapter lived during a time in which national identity was more of a pressing concern – not least during the First or Second World Wars – it is arguably less appropriate to continue to place emphasis on musical ethnicity in a world in which migration continues to be at the forefront of political debate. Furthermore, such questions go beyond whether nuances of notational or musical style were common to particular locations; rather the identification of Englishness in music has been made used to establish notions of ethnicity that have been successfully challenged by postcolonial approaches in other disciplines.

Given the anonymity of works found in musical codices, it is highly possible that scribes were unaware of the precise origin of some individual works, unless this was marked by some very specific details of the musical notation in exemplars. Exceptions – notably in relation to fifteenth-century continental sources that identify what they believe to be English pieces with the designation 'de anglia' or similar – are in themselves informative on this point. The need to separate English from non-English pieces was something that caused anxiety in more recent accounts. Richard Hoppin's 'English Epilogue' from his book *Medieval Music* is a representative example from a key text, and is worth reproducing in extended form:

> A distinction must be made between English music and music in England. To do so, however, is not always a simple matter. The liturgical repertory of the School of Notre Dame was known and used in England throughout the thirteenth century [. . .]. We only presume that additions to this repertory in English sources are the work of English rather than French composers. The conductus and motet were also known in England, and again we cannot always be sure whether a particular piece is of continental or insular origin. Similarly, in the fourteenth century the innovations and at least some of the music of the French Ars Nova penetrated England with evident effects on the work of presumably native composers. The unfortunate anonymity of almost all of this music does nothing to remove our uncertainties.[31]

Hoppin's account is loaded with anxiety about how a history of English music might be written if it is based on pieces whose ethnic heritage cannot be confidently demonstrated. Not only might some of the music in England be hiding its origin elsewhere – France in particular – but also even nationally pure music by English composers was likely diluted by the influence of the ars nova, which 'penetrated' the country. It is one thing to note early fourteenth-century French music, such as motets found in the *Roman de Fauvel*, appeared in English manuscripts alongside local pieces, and may have influenced local tastes. The reception of French music and ideas in England is worthy of further research. In discussions like Hoppin's, the importance of input from both sides is side-lined in favour of the dominant narrative of French technical innovation invading or disrupting natural, naive English culture. A quasi-gendered discourse, and certainly one that reflects notions of pure musical ethnicities, can be detected in such descriptions, sometimes in language that is suggestive of broader cultural concerns of the twentieth century.[32]

To examine similar concerns in fifteenth-century repertory, we can look at Harrison's *Music in Medieval Britain*: a survey of the country's music that has yet to be surpassed in many ways. Harrison puzzled over how to distinguish between pieces that should form part of his history, and whether their authorship by someone born in Britain was sufficient grounds for inclusion:

> Some of these composers [Dunstaple, Pyamour, Benet, Bedyngham, Forest, Plummer, Sandley, Frye] may have spent their lives abroad, like Robert Morton, whose extant work consists entirely of French chansons, and it may always remain uncertain how much of this great store of expatriate music belongs to the history of music *in* Britain [Harrison's emphasis, reflecting his book's title].[33]

Harrison's account questions whether the music of a composer is truly part of the history of music in Britain – for example, if he lived abroad or if his music was composed outside of his homeland. Indeed, if the genre and textual language are French, to what extent can the music be British?

The ethnic origin of musical style, and of the composers that produced this music, is a line of investigation that can easily lead to simplistic distinctions between authentically 'English' (or 'French', 'German', etc.) practices or cultural expressions. I do not suggest that stylistic traits within surviving repertory are unimportant. Nor am I denying that certain repertories appear not to have found favour on the opposite side of the Channel.[34] What I highlight is the way in which such investigations are reported in language that speaks of an anxiety about the ethnicity of the repertory itself: that perhaps French pieces might be lurking in English collections but hidden by a new text or by aping insular style.

Compositional style as proof of ethnicity: *Sub Arturo plebs*

One English composer with whom a specific, extant composition may be identified is Johannes Alanus, who may have worked on the continent *c*. 1400. Alanus is credited as composer of the 'musicians' motet' *Sub Arturo* [or *Arcturo*] *plebs*. *Sub Arturo plebs* is an unusual example of a piece whose text reveals the identity of its author and lists many musicians in both duplum and triplum; many of them are likely to have been genuine English musicians of the composer's time or of recent history.[35] The origins of the piece have been widely debated. Brian Trowell and Roger Bowers located the genesis of *Sub Arturo plebs* in the third quarter of the fourteenth century, drawing on evidence from the text that named the composer and his musical companions, and linking the biographies of Alanus (a common name, and one that still requires convincing disambiguation) and other musicians to potential identities in those decades. Trowell had linked the motet to a Garter occasion at Windsor in 1358 on account of its nationalistic sentiment. Bowers argued for a date in the 1370s, using a range of archival evidence. In 1973, Bent expressed her doubts, on stylistic grounds, that the piece could be so early, since comparable works dated to the early fifteenth century. In Bent's more recent scholarship on the motet, she has placed it in the 1410s, recognising that this leaves many of the biographical elements unexplained.[36] A later dating locates the motet within the clutch of repertoire that found its way from England to the European mainland in the early 1420s, alongside the English pieces in Bologna, Museo Internazionale e Biblioteca della Musica di Bologna, Q15 (hereafter Bologna Q15) by Dunstaple, Gervays and Benet.[37] *Sub Arturo plebs* therefore sits more comfortably within a compositional and copying context: its three sources are certainly later than the 1370s (though this in itself would not preclude an earlier compositional date).[38] It is the various discussions of the piece and the conclusions drawn in terms of its relationship with musical style and English national sentiment that make it a relevant case study here.

The initial dislocation of style, provenance and date for *Sub Arturo plebs* offered writers a thorny problem. What could account for the discrepancy? In 1973, Bent had made the following observation:

> Should further evidence in support of an early dating of the triplum text be forthcoming, the stylistic discrepancy between it and the music seems so irreconcilable that it might be preferable to assume the use of the early text for a later musical setting, than to envisage the adoption by an Englishman, in 1358, of an exaggerated (and very advanced) French musical idiom in order to sing the virtues of his compatriots.[39]

The remarks here relate origin, political intention and style to one another. If an English composer wished to write a work in praise of English musicians, why would he choose such a radical French style in which to do it? In effect, Bent's purpose was not to argue that this was the case but to add weight to her argument that the piece may have been conceived much later than previously accepted. Her words were later echoed and taken further by Strohm, who also found Trowell's 1358 provenance untenable, asking:

> In that case, *would he not have adopted a more indigenous style*? It is perhaps more likely that this 'musicians' motet', which amounts to political propaganda, was written during an English campaign in southern France, and in a style familiar to musicians at the Avignonese orbit [emphasis added].[40]

The expectation here is that the compositional intentions, and cultural or political motivations, of the composer may be retrievable from musical language. Not only that, but a disjunction between origin and style can be seen as just as meaningful as the more sympathetic pairing of the two. The interpretative remarks of Trowell and Strohm can be seen as part of a fashion for collapsing together notions of musical style common within England or France and the use of such stylistic features seen as being used for political purposes. The direct relationship between the sentiment ('nationalist' or otherwise) of a piece of English-texted music and its chosen musical language remains unproven.

Conclusions

The definition of unequivocal 'Englishness' in musical style has proven elusive, in part because there is a distinction to be made between stylistic gestures more popular in England than elsewhere (the preponderance of thirds and sixths being the most commonly cited) and the exclusivity of melodic or harmonic features to music from any one region, which is essentially a myth. The picture of Anglo-Continental cultural exchange is limited by the number sources and their fragmentary state, but what has survived reveals a striking diversity in how pieces were transmitted. Collections large and small carry the potential to be read in relation to systems of patronage, notational practice, musical style and devotional cultures in ways that benefit from de-prioritising national categorisation.

Through examining the ways in which writers have identified Englishness (or not) in music and in sources, it is possible to unpick the repertoire from some of the prevailing attitudes of twentieth-century scholarship – often apparently anxious about the ethnic origin of musicians *and* the music they produced. In so doing, new ways might be forged in analysing the relationship between music and cultural identity during the later Middle Ages. This work might benefit from revisiting questions of musical style, notation, function, devotional context and social practice, without the need to weave answers into predominantly national frameworks. It may take a fresh look at manuscript sources not simply as containers of repertory, but as meaningful expressions of diverse cultural identities.

Such work would be a positive step to move beyond the competitive rhetoric of earlier accounts in which English, French and German nations were pitted against one another for their particular contributions to the history of music as were outlined by Warren Dwight Allen in 1939:

> English and French scholars, thanks, possibly, to more favorable political circumstances than those in Germany and Italy since the World War, need not argue about music history; they need only tell about it. Both point calmly and dispassionately to records of early achievement; England to the account given by Giraldus Cambrensis, in the twelfth century, of part singing in the British Isles; and France to the music of the troubadours and trouvères with which the history of secular art usually begins. John Dunstable is also the stand-by for English claims for priority (in spite of the fact that he spent most

of his life on the continent) and the Reading rota, 'Sumer is icumen in,' is an indispensable beginning for every history of counterpoint. But thanks to German research [Friedrich Ludwig], the center of thirteenth-century activity in polyphonic music proves to have been in the great scholastic center in Paris and Notre Dame.[41]

On the subject of architecture, and to some extent the visual arts as a whole, Binski argued that 'there was no simple corollary between ideas of nationhood and style', a conclusion that serves equally well for music.[42] The connection between nationalist sentiment and perceptions of national style that was evident in music at the beginning of the twentieth century is not directly comparable to the English repertory of the Middle Ages. English adoption of aspects of certain compositional and notational techniques first developed or favoured in France seems to have been relatively swift. Any attempt to separate French pieces from English ones does not reflect the reality of the fourteenth century in which cultural products could be both nationalist and sensitive to continental influence, both capable of retaining independent characteristics and emulating the latest trends. The preservation of music that originated in France next to music that originated in England within surviving manuscript fragments shows openness to diverse stylistic approaches.

There were clearly particular approaches that were favoured in some regions of Europe over others, at different times and in contrasting cultural circumstances. English-texted motets, for example, never seem to have gained favour beyond the occasional use of a vernacular tenor. The sonorous thirds and sixths commonly found in medieval music seem favoured especially, if not exclusively, in England. Cumming points out that, musically, the 'real fusion of English and continental music would come in the 1440s and 1450s', a time in which some historical accounts have sought to see Dunstaple's influence on continental models.[43] It is therefore to the *contenance angloise* – a term associated with the influence of English music in Europe – that the final chapter of this book will turn.

Notes

1   In the devotional texts of later medieval England, the phrase 'hearing' Mass appears frequently. It is a commonplace, but one that might remind us that in addition to simply hearing, we also listen, compare, analyse and understand. Margery Kempe's accounts are full of sensory references, including hearing, smelling and tasting. Barry Windeatt, ed., *The Book of Margery Kempe* (London: Longman: 2000). See also Anthony Goodman, *Margery Kempe and Her World* (London: Longman, 2002). A map of the sites visited by Kempe is given in Anthony Bale, transl. *A Book of Margery Kempe* (Oxford: Oxford University Press, 2015), xliv.
2   The transmission of music between England and the continent has been treated extensively, but a clear summary of the difficulties and implications of patterns of transmission can be found in Margaret Bent, "The Transmission of English Music 1300–1500: Some Aspects of Repertory and Presentation." In *Studien zur Tradition in Der Musik: Kurt von Fischer zum 60. Geburtstag*, edited by Hans Heinrich Eggebrecht, and Max Lütolf (Munich: Musikverlag Emil Katzbichler, 1973). See also

130 The idea of English music

      Theodor Dumitrescu, *The Early Tudor Court and International Musical Relations* (Aldershot: Ashgate, 2007).
3   Important studies that go beyond Anglo-French relations include Reinhard Strohm, *The Rise of European Music 1380–1500* (Cambridge: Cambridge University Press, 1993) and Reinhard Strohm, *Music in Medieval Bruges* (New York: Clarendon Press and Oxford Universtiy Press, 1985).
4   Martin Stokes, "Introduction." In *Ethnicity, Identity and Music: The Musical Construction of Place*, edited by Martin Stokes (Oxford: Berg, 1994), 3–4.
5   Peter M. Lefferts, "The Motet in England in the 14th Century," *Current Musicology* 28 (1979), 57.
6   William John Summers, "To Trope or Not to Trope? Or, How was the English Gloria Performed?" In *Music in Medieval Europe: Studies in Honour of Bryan Gillingham*, edited by Terence Bailey and Alma Santosuosso (Aldershot: Ashgate, 2007), 96.
7   On reading the relationship between surviving sources of polyphony and an individual monastic community, see Lisa Colton, "Music and Identity in Medieval Bury St Edmunds." In *St Edmund, King and Martyr: Changing images of a medieval saint*, edited by Anthony Bale (Woodbridge: Boydell, 2009).
8   Helen Deeming, "An English Monastic Miscellany: The Reading Manuscript of *Sumer is icumen in*." In *Manuscripts and Medieval Song: Inscription, performance, context*, edited by Helen Deeming and Elizabeth Eva Leach (Cambridge: Cambridge University Press, 2015), 139.
9   On concordances see Margaret Bent, "Sources of the Old Hall Manuscript," *Proceedings of the Royal Musical Association* 94th Session (1967–8).
10 Margaret Bent, "Old Hall Manuscript," *Grove Music Online. Oxford Music Online.* Oxford University Press, accessed 13 August 2015, www.oxfordmusiconline.com/subscriber/article/grove/music/20296.
11 The most thorough paleographical study of the manuscript, undertaken when it belonged to the College of St Edmund (Old Hall, Hertfordshire), is Margaret Bent, "The Old Hall Manuscript: A Palaeographical Study." (PhD diss., University of Cambridge, 1969).
12 See Lisa Colton, "Languishing for Provenance: *Zelo tui langueo* and the Search for Women's Polyphony in England," *Early Music* 39 (2011).
13 The York copy of this text is described in M. Dominica Legge, "'La Lumiere as Lais': A postscript," *The Modern Language Review* 46 (1951).
14 Margaret Bent, "A Lost English Choirbook of the Fifteenth Century," *International Musicological Society: Report of the 11th Congress, Copenhangen, 1972*, 2 vols, edited by H. Glahn, Søren Sørensen, and Peter Ryom (Copenhagen: Wilhelm Hansen, 1974); Margaret Bent, "The Progeny of Old Hall: More Leaves from a Royal English Choirbook." In *Gordon Athol Anderson (1929–1981) in Memoriam* 2 vols, Musicological Studies 49 (Henryville, Ottawa and Binningen: Institute of Mediaeval Music, 1984).
15 On records that relate to lost sources, showing a surprising range of possible owners of polyphonic music, see especially Andrew Wathey, "Lost Books of Polyphony in England: A List to 1500," *RMA Research Chronicle* 21 (1988).
16 On fourteenth-century sources from Durham and Bury St Edmunds within the context of Anglo-Continental musical exchange, see in particular Frank Ll. Harrison, "Ars Nova In England: A New Source," *Musica Disciplina* 21 (1967).
17 The phrase 'multi-local' has been encouraged by writer and musician Taiye Selasi in relation to the challenge of the question 'where are you from?' to those whose parentage, upbringing, career and relationships have been experienced across more than one geographical location, and for whom associating their identity primarily with the concept of an individual country is problematic. I use it here in a context not envisaged by Selasi.

18   Hugh Baillie, "Squares," *Acta Musicologica* 32 (1960).
19   Peter M. Lefferts, *The Motet in England in the Fourteenth Century* (Michigan: Ann Arbor, 1986), 2.
20   Lefferts, *The Motet in England*, 2.
21   Lefferts, *The Motet in England*, 2.
22   Gustav Reese, "Polyphony in the British Isles from the 12th century to the Death of Dunstable." In *Music in the Middle Ages* (London: J. M. Dent, 1940), 387–424, at 424.
23   Reese, "Polyphony in the British Isles," 424.
24   Reese, "Polyphony in the British Isles," 414.
25   Henry Raynor, *Music in England* (London: Robert Hale, 1980), 26.
26   Raynor, *Music in England*, 18.
27   Henry Davey, *History of English Music* (London: Curwen and Sons, 1895; 2nd edn, 1921), 23.
28   The term 'ethnicity' was first used by Fredrik Barth, *Ethnic Groups and Boundaries: The social organisation of culture difference* (London, George Allen and Unwin, 1960), cited in Stokes, *Ethnicity, Identity and Music*, 6.
29   Nicky Losseff, *The Best Concords: Music in thirteenth-century England* (New York: Garland, 1994), 15.
30   Stokes, *Ethnicity, Identity and Music*, 13.
31   Richard Hoppin, *Medieval Music* (New York: Norton, 1978), 502–03.
32   Hoppin's *Medieval Music* continues to form a key part of university curricula and has been made available in languages including French (1991), Spanish (2000) and Slovak (2007).
33   Frank Harrison, *Music in Medieval Britain* (London: Routledge and Kegan Paul, 1958), 250.
34   Bent, "The Transmission of English music," 65.
35   Margaret Bent, ed., *Two 14th-Century Motets in Praise of Music* (Newton Abbot: Antico Edition, 1977). The piece is also discussed in Roger Bowers, "Fixed Points in the Chronology of English Fourteenth-Century Polyphony," *Music and Letters* 71 (1990), 313–15.
36   Margaret Bent, "The Earliest Fifteenth-Century Transmission of English music to the Continent." In *Essays on the History of English Music: Sources, Style, Performance, Historiography. In Honour of John Caldwell*, edited by Emma Hornby and David Maw (Woodbridge, Boydell and Brewer, 2010), 88.
37   The copying process of Bologna Q15 – which appears to have been the responsibility of a single scribe – is explained in detail by Margaret Bent; Bent argues that the scribe uses the term 'de Anglia' as a form of 'designer label': 'Johannes dunstaple anglicus; Jo bent Anglicus and Jo Bent de Anglia'. Margaret Bent, "The Earliest Fifteenth-Century Transmission of English Music to the Continent." In *Essays on the History of English Music: Sources, style, performance, historiography. In Honour of John Caldwell*, edited by Emma Hornby and David Maw (Woodbridge: Boydell and Brewer, 2010), 94.
38   Ipswich, Suffolk Record Office, HA 30: 50/22/13.15 is likely the earliest source, probably dating to no earlier than the end of the fourteenth century; the Chantilly Manuscript dates from *c*. 1400; Bologna Q15 can be dated to the early 1420s. See Bent, "The Earliest Fifteenth-Century Transmission," 87.
39   Bent, "The Transmission of English music," 72.
40   Strohm, *The Rise of European Music*, 82. Strohm was responding to Brian Trowell, "A Fourteenth-Century Ceremonial Motet and its Composer," *Acta Musicologica* 29 (1957). Strohm notes that Trowell's dating of 1358 was contested in Bent, "The Transmission of English music," 70.

41 This quotation from the reprint of the book: Warren Dwight Allen, *Philosophies of Music History: A study of general histories of music 1600–1960*, 2nd edn (New York: Dover Publications, 1962), 161.
42 Paul Binski, *Westminster Abbey and the Plantagenets: Kingship and the representation of power 1200–1400* (New Haven and London: Yale University Press, 1995), 44.
43 Julie E. Cumming, *The Motet in the Age of Du Fay* (Cambridge: Cambridge University Press, 1999), 154.

6 *Contenance angloise*
A reappraisal

The phrase *contenance angloise* appears just once in the literature of the Middle Ages, yet it holds a prominent place in musicological discourse. The source of the phrase is Martin Le Franc's *Le Champion des Dames*, a poem from 1440–2 in which, in a relatively fleeting moment within the 24,000 verses about the end of the world, he appears to describe the influence of the English on the innovative works of continental composers Dufay and Binchois.[1] Le Franc's comments chime with the words of Tinctoris, who named John Dunstaple as leading English composers responsible for a new art in his *Proportionale Musices* (1472–5). In a further treatise by Tinctoris, the *Liber de arte contrapuncti* (1477), Dunstaple, Binchois and Dufay (all by this point deceased) were hailed as teachers (*praeceptores*) of the next generation. Tinctoris claimed the influence of their works (*opera*) on the generation of composers that included Ockeghem, Regis, Busnois, Caron and Faugues.[2] Originating from the pens of two authors writing from distinctly different perspectives, these texts have been used to identify the 1430s as a period of significant change, one that announced the flowering of the renaissance.

Numerous studies have sought to map le Franc's *contenance angloise* onto the repertoire that survives from the composers named by le Franc and Tinctoris, composers capable of writing music that could be seen as part of Tinctoris's putative 'new art'.[3] The results have been largely unconvincing, serving only to support Theodor Dumitrescu's arguments that Englishness is 'an extremely slippery concept', and that even English discant can be shown to be a construct largely developed by Bukofzer.[4] Philip Kaye and Gareth Curtis, for example, have outlined the difficulties of relating the notion of an 'English style' onto the way that English composers treated consonance and dissonance, with Curtis concluding that:

> to refer to a specific English style whose characteristics are broadly common to the whole repertory is positively misleading. There is, in fact, no single style at all, but a number of individual styles and sub-styles, each of which has its own conventions and rules.[5]

In a similar vein, Wegman has argued that:

134 *Contenance angloise*

Attempts to establish the precise nature of the *contenance angloise* in compositions from the early fifteenth century have proved inconclusive at best. [...] Whatever the poet may have meant, there is no indication in the 1430s that the premises of musical practice and theory were being fundamentally reconsidered, no evidence of a conceptual change in the realms of music philosophy and aesthetics – nothing, in short, that could be helpfully explained by positing the beginning of a new era in music history, let alone the advent of the Renaissance.[6]

The purpose of this chapter is thus to propose a very different reading of le Franc's text, an extra-musical definition of *contenance angloise* that resonates strongly with devotional and political literature in the fifteenth century.

Rereading le Franc

In order to re-examine le Franc's words, it is first important to recall their detail in poetic context. For musicologists, the section of the poem that includes composers' names is the most significant part of *Le Champion des Dames*: it is both temptingly specific and frustratingly oblique, using a variety of musical (or pseudo-musical) words in a manner that feels historical and authoritative. It was, of course, a poetic conceit to include technical terms in poetry to add intellectual weight, but the incorporation also of composers' names tempts the reader to consult le Franc's description as if it were an elegant, versified musical history.[7] Below is an extract from this section of the poem, with significant words emphasised. The translation that follows is an adaptation of previously published versions, and an attempt to avoid loading it at this stage of my discussion with precise musical terminology:

> Car ilz ont *nouvelle pratique*
> De faire *frisque concordance*
> En *haulte* et en *basse musique*,
> En *fainte*, en *pause* et en *muance*,
> Et ont prins de la *contenance*
> *Angloise* et ensuÿ *Dunstaple*;
> Pour quoy merveilleuse plaisance
> Rend leur *chant* joieux et *notable*.

> For theirs is a new practice of making joyful consonance in high and low music, in its articulation in performance, and they take of the contenance angloise and follow Dunstaple; whereby wondrous pleasure makes their music joyful and notable.[8]

Many attempts have been made to pin down the meaning of the music-related words. The poet appears to use them to indicate Dunstaple's leadership of some form of new practice, performance tradition or compositional technique associated with a national (English) trend. Such a story has been of particular appeal to those with a nationalist agenda for English culture. Dunstaple, an Englishman, would effectively head the musical canon of renaissance Europe.[9]

The phrase *contenance angloise* has been variously translated as English countenance (Strohm), contenance (Kaye), manner (Wright and Gallagher), guise (Perkins) and style (various), and has been explored in terms of its origin as a contrapuntal feature, as a style in its own right, a practice, as related to performance or as reflective of rhetorical principles. The consideration of *contenance angloise* as a discernable set of stylistic fingerprints can be traced within the literature in several ways. These might usefully be grouped into those who imply that *contenance angloise* displays evidence of the roots of tonality in its emphasis on vertical consonance; writers for whom English music's textural simplicity and euphony are its distinctive features;[10] those who emphasise English music's melodic grace;[11] and finally analysts who have identified certain rhythmic and mensural elements that unify fifteenth-century English repertory and distinguish it from continental pieces within common codices.[12]

The term *contenance angloise* has been a major part of discussions of compositional technique.[13] An early (erroneous) identification of Dunstaple as the inventor of counterpoint was partly responsible for the collapsing together of *contenance angloise* and contrapuntal innovation. Davey had maintained Dunstaple's responsibility for the invention of counterpoint even in the face of significant criticism to the first edition of his *History of English Music*.[14] Even after Bukofzer's debunking of Dunstaple mythology, the possibility that the English were admired for innovative vertical sonorities resulting from the grammar of two-part counterpoint and from English discant still appealed.[15]

Still smarting, perhaps, from the ubiquitous accusation that England was *Das Land ohne Musik*, writers of the twentieth century were encouraged by the thought that an Englishman might have led the field.[16] Fifteenth-century English music could be associated with a homogenous 'national school' of composition, a unified approach to that most central aspect of musical writing (for the modern period): the vertical alignment of parts, a proto-harmonic, chordal polyphonic style. Hoppin, for example, regarded the consonant English style as a watershed between 'linear aspects' of medieval composition, and the shift of 'emphasis to the vertical aspect of polyphony'.[17] These statements have been challenged in more recent literature in which analysis has shown the common approaches to composition on each side of the English Channel. Philip Kaye, for example, has warned that 'Even the high use of the 6/3 – the combination often seen as synonymous with and quintessentially the sound of English music – does not differ markedly from continental music in many ways'.[18]

I am not the first to seek an alternative to the interpretation of le Franc's lines as stylistic. Strohm, for example, speculated that the term might reflect the poet's lack of precise technical knowledge for things that he recognised aurally as well as raising the possibility that the term *contenance angloise* indicated performance practice rather than style *per se*.[19] He also advised that le Franc did not write that the musical techniques he listed were English.[20] David Fallows warned against assuming too direct a link between music by Dunstaple and Dufay.[21] Fallows was one of the first to challenge the idea of a shift in style in the 1430s.[22] Based on a thorough consideration of both le Franc's poetic text and of the repertoire of the time, Fallows suggested that Dufay was a possible reference point in the communication of historical trends in music between le Franc and Tinctoris.[23] Affirming a position in line with Fallows, and having considered the broader poetic context of the 'musical' stanzas, against Tinctoris's *Proportionale musices* (1472–3) and *Liber de arte contrapuncti* (1471), Wegman put the case more strongly still:

> The truth of the matter [. . .] is that the case for a musical Renaissance in the 1430s cannot be sustained without doing considerable violence to Le Franc's text. His six stanzas on music have been made to bear far more explanatory weight than they could realistically carry, and the poem in which they appear has been allowed to explain far less than the stanzas might be expected to require.[24]

Sceptical of the way in which the terms within le Franc's text have been aligned largely with written, compositional practices, Bent's consideration of the musical stanzas in *Le Champion des Dames* made a strong case for le Franc's prioritisation of the experiential in music, the practical performance itself and the implied listener in such performances. Situating le Franc's words within the rhetoric of his age, Bent's focus on the 'richly attested perspective of sounding performance and its effect on the listener' convincingly demonstrated the danger of assuming that witnesses such as le Franc were describing a tradition in which the written text enjoyed primacy.[25] Bent also viewed the question of Dufay and Binchois's 'imitation' or 'following' of Dunstaple as being part of the rhetorical practice of *imitatio*, in which great composers would only be able to become so, in part, by emulating their forebears.[26]

Angels and angles in medieval texts

One difficulty of interpreting the phrase *contenance angloise* is that the presentation of the words in the text is ambiguous: unlike other terminology in le Franc's musical stanzas, the phrase appears split between poetic lines. Its treatment as a conjoined phrase ignores the internal dislocation, one that hints at its representation as something rather different to the ostensibly musical (or performative) terms that precede it. I want to respond to the visual and poetic division of *contenance* from *angloise*. In so doing, I hope to illustrate that le Franc was drawing attention to a particular play on words that was well-known to him and that had a rich heritage in the way in which English national identity had been understood for many centuries. Ignoring for the time being the musical context of the words in question, *angloise* (here 'Angloise', capitalised only because it lies at a line break) could also be seen as typical of the wordplay common between the words angel/Angle and their Latin equivalents – effectively 'angelic' or 'English-ish' (or 'Anglish'). Puns are ubiquitous in medieval literature across England and France, and the discussion below will explore this particular device in relation to devotional and liturgical texts from these two countries. In particular, I will draw examples from texts associated with saints prominent in England whose cults encouraged authors to explore, through literary devices, these saints' identities as a combination of Englishness and holiness. It is the heritage of historical and devotional texts that I argue lie at the heart of le Franc's poem.

The text of the seventh lesson at Matins in the Office for the translation feast of St Thomas of Canterbury, written in the early part of the thirteenth century, claimed that natives of England shared a special place in God's creation, a status that was central to Thomas's own holiness:

> Exultet in Domino gens Anglorum universa, quam Rex celestis specialius ceteris insignivit, dum ex ea virum sine macula preelegit, ut sic unus ex Anglicis inter angelos constitutus, intercessor sit pro salute populorum.
>
> Let all the English people exult in the Lord, since the heavenly King particularly distinguished this people above all others when he forechose from it a man without spot, in order to make one of the English, set among the angels, an intercessor for the people's salvation.[27]

The English may not have been alone in considering themselves as God's chosen people during the Middle Ages, but the effects of this view were felt in every artistic field from liturgical prose to the visual arts.

The concept of sanctity was defined by the holiness of an individual's life, but the precise grounds for canonisation were ambiguous in this period.[28] A person could be elevated towards the status of the divine through a life of pious works. Posthumous miracles performed at the individual's tomb were considered additional proof of sanctity, but they were not an essential element of it. By the later Middle Ages, many of the ancestors of the English ruling and religious classes had been canonised; for this sector of society, beatification was not considered out of reach.[29] English kings and high-ranking officials noted for their sanctity included St Edmund King and Martyr, St Edward the Confessor, St Edward King and Martyr, and St Thomas of Canterbury. Further, various noblemen acquired a cult status, even if they were not fully canonised. These included Simon de Montfort, Thomas of Lancaster and Edward II. Some English saints such as St Edburga of Winchester/Pershore, St Wulstan and St Oswald were known for lives of piety rather than a worldly role in government even though their blood lines were noble. Overall, English history was replete with people whose lives and reputations were a blend of devotion to Christ and political influence; many of these figures enjoyed a cult that extended well beyond the English coast, most notably St Thomas of Canterbury.

The wordplay that reads 'angel' for 'Angle' (or vice versa) has already featured in the title of Chapter 2, and it is now time to consider it more directly. The pun has its origin in the work of Bede, whose *Historiam Ecclesiasticam Gentis Anglorum* (Ecclesiastical History of the English People, completed in 731) related the story of how and why Gregory the Great was inspired to bring the English

138 *Contenance angloise*

people into the Christian church. It is clear that Bede credited Gregory more fully than Augustine with the conversion of the English, though he treats all the various stages of conversion including Augustine's mission. The passage is worth presenting in full. In Book 2, Bede writes:

> Nec silentio praetereunda opinio, quae de beato Gregorio traditione maiorum ad nos usque perlata est; qua uidelicet ex causa admonitus tam sedulam erga salutem nostrae gentis curam gesserit. Dicunt, quia die quadam cum, aduenientibus nuper mercatoribus, multa uenalia in forum fuissent conlata, multi ad emendum confluxissent, et ipsum Gregorium inter alios aduenisse, ac uidisse inter alia pueros uenales positos candidi corporis, ac uenusti uultus, capillorum quoque forma egregia. Quos cum aspiceret, interrogauit, ut aiunt, de qua regione uel terra essent adlati. Dictumque est, quia de Brittania insula, cuius incolae talis essent aspectus. Rursus interrogauit, utrum idem insulani Christiani, an paganis adhuc erroribus essent inplicati. Dictum est, quod essent pagani. At ille, intimo ex corde longa trahens suspiria: 'Heu, pro dolor!' inquit, 'quod tam lucidi uultus homines tenebrarum auctor possidet, tantaque gratia frontispicii mentem ab interna gratia uacuam gestat!' Rursus ergo interrogauit, quod esset uocabulum gentis illius. Responsum est, quod Angli uocarentur. At ille: 'Bene,' inquit; 'nam et angelicam habent faciem, et tales angelorum in caelis decet esse coheredes. Quod habet nomen ipsa prouincia, de qua isti sunt adlati?' Responsum est, quod Deiri uocarentur idem prouinciales. At ille: 'Bene,' inquit, 'Deiri; de ira eruti, et ad misericordiam Christi uocati. Rex prouinciae illius quomodo appellatur?' Responsum est, quod Aelli diceretur. At ille adludens ad nomen ait: 'Alleluia, laudem Dei Creatoris illis in partibus oportet cantari'.[30]

Nor is the account of St Gregory, which has been handed down to us by the tradition of our ancestors, to be passed by in silence, in relation to his motives for taking such interest in the salvation of our nation. It is reported that some merchants, having just arrived at Rome on a certain day, exposed many things for sale in the marketplace, and abundance of people resorted thither to buy: Gregory himself went with the rest, and, among other things, some boys were set to sale, their bodies white, their countenances beautiful, and their hair very fine. Having viewed them, he asked, as is said, from what country or nation they were brought? and was told, from the island of Britain, whose inhabitants were of such personal appearance. He again inquired whether those islanders were Christians, or still involved in the errors of paganism? and was informed that they were pagans. Then fetching a deep sigh from the bottom of his heart, 'Alas! what pity,' said he, 'that the author of darkness is possessed of men of such fair countenances; and that being remarkable for such graceful aspects, their minds should be void of inward grace.' He therefore again asked, what was the name of that nation? and was answered, that they were called Angles. 'Right,' said he, 'for they have an Angelic face, and it becomes such to be co-heirs with the Angels in heaven. What is the name,' proceeded he, 'of the province from which they are brought?' It was replied, that the natives of that province were called Deiri. 'Truly are they *De ira*,' said he, 'withdrawn from wrath, and called to the mercy of Christ. How is the king of that province called?' They told him his name was Ælla: and he, alluding to the name said, 'Hallelujah, the praise of God the Creator must be sung in those parts.'[31]

Bede's account was used as the source for many later retellings of this legend, which tended to condense the story, leaving out the puns on 'De ira' and 'Hallelujah'. In the thirteenth century, Jacobus de Voragine's widely disseminated and translated thirteenth-century hagiographical text *Legenda Aurea* (Golden Legend) gave the same story, reporting Gregory's pun in response to seeing the blond hair of English slaves:

Tunc Gregorius acriter ingemiscens: heu proh dolor, inquit, quod splendidas facies princeps tenebrarum nunc possidet. Interrogat igitur, quod esset vocabulum gentis illius. Cui ille: Anglici vocantur. Bene, inquit, anglici quasi angelici, quia et angelicos vultus habent.[32]

Gregory groaned sadly and said: 'What a pity, that the prince of darkness should possess these radiant faces!' He then asked the name of that people and was told that they were called Angles. 'And well named!' he said, 'The name sounds like Angels and their faces are angelic.'[33]

The *South English Legendary*, which drew on many materials and whose compiler may have known Voragine's text, likewise enjoyed the fable and relished the wordplay in his relation of the same story, emphasising the importance of the appearance of the Angles in justifying bringing them closer to Rome and to Christ. The *South English Legendary*'s entry for Gregory concludes with lines that might even suggest that the saint's final rest was to be in heaven with the Angles/angels, a fitting reward for his mission:

Þus þe holie man seint Gregori: pope was in rome,
And sende us in-to engelonde: þe lawes of cristindome.
holi churche and cristindom: þoruȝ him was so i-loked here,
Þat he is nouþe in heouene: with Aungles i-fere.
Bidde we þanne þene holie man: apostle of Engelonde,
Þat he bi-fore ihesu crist: ore neode ounder-stonde.[34]

Over seventy copies of the *South English Legendary* are still extant, having circulated alongside the *Legenda Aurea* in England throughout the later Middle Ages in manuscript and later in print adaptations. The despair at the contradiction between heavenly angels and pagan Angles continued to be one of the *vita* (biographical account) of St Gregory's most stable elements. By the time William Caxton (c. 1422–91) printed his English translation of Voragine's text in 1483, the story was rendered as follows:

140 *Contenance angloise*

>The syght saint gregorye & sayd: alas what fayr peple hath the devyle in hys doctrine & in hys dominacyon? After, he demaunded how thies peple were called. He answered that they were called englisshe men. Thene he sayd: they maye well be so called for they have the visage of angelles.[35]

The passage was also found within the *vita* of St Augustine in many texts, including the *Legenda Aurea*, Caxton's translation and the so-called Gilte Legend, which continue to repeat the story of St Gregory's pun.

English plainchant and polyphony sometimes explored the same tropes of the English as a chosen, angelic people. Motets in honour of St Augustine or St Gregory were, as one might expect, especially likely to do so. St Augustine of Canterbury (d. 604, feast day 27 May) introduced monasticism to the country. Two motets in honour of St Augustine of Canterbury survive, both from sources dating to c. 1300–30: *Augustine par angelis* (fragmentary) and *Solaris ardor Romuli*.[36] The second of these motets offers ideas relevant to the present discussion.

Solaris ardor Romuli/Gregorius sol seculi/Petre nua navicula/T. *Mariounette douche* is jointly dedicated to St Augustine of Canterbury and St Gregory. It is constructed over a French secular song used also as a tenor in a motet (*Caligo terre*) found in the same polyphonic source. *Solaris ardor Romuli* revels in additional wordplay in relation to the words 'Cantuarie', 'Cancie' and 'cancro', mixing the importance of Canterbury and Kent with the description of Rome as the 'Cancer of Romulus' in the quadruplum and triplum. The importance of St Augustine to the English nation is emphasised through the appearance of various words to describe the British population. The words 'Anglos' for the English people (quadruplum) and 'Anglie' (triplum) are used to indicate the people of England in combination with the island of Britain ('insula Britannie') mentioned in the duplum.

The quadruplum opens by describing the way in which Augustine converted the pagans of Britain ('Britannie') but closes by stating that there is faith 'quocumque fluctus hodie claudet anglos equorei', 'wherever today the waves of the sea enclose the English'. There is suggestion in these combined texts that the main people of Britain are the English, but that the people of Kent and Canterbury were especially linked to Rome. It is possible that this sentiment, though doubtless more attractive to those in the South East than elsewhere in the country, was part of a wider understanding that saw the South East as connected, spiritually, to the continent through the cults of St Augustine and St Thomas. By extension, it would have been logical for composers connected with the royal family – concentrated in their insular movements to the south east of England and sometimes travelling to parts of France from Dover – to be associated with the heightened sense of Englishness and divine providence that had been established by legends of Augustine and Gregory: these angels/Angles were not just English but associated with the South East. Given what we know of the biographies of composers such as Power and Dunstaple, the divine providence of English musicians from this part of the country may even have been part of their reputation in England and further afield. GB-Lbl Onc 362, the only surviving source of *Solaris ardor Romuli*, contains pieces that hint at a provenance in Westminster, or more likely Canterbury, based on motet texts that reference Saints Augustine, Gregory, Peter and Edward the Confessor, for example.[37]

The saint with whose cult notions of the sanctity of the English were most associated was St Edmund, King and Martyr, whose cult was focused on his shrine at Bury St Edmunds.[38] By far the most prominent antiphon in Edmund's liturgy was the antiphon 'Ave rex gentis anglorum'. The antiphon's text explicitly draws on the Angle/angel pun in question: 'Ave rex gentis Anglorum, miles regis angelorum, O Edmunde, flos martirum, velut rosa vel lilium' (Hail, king of the English nation, soldier of the king of angels, O Edmund, the flower of the martyrs, just as the rose and the lily).[39]

'Ave rex gentis anglorum' was one of four plainchant items attributed by Thomson to Abbot Garnier (or Warner) of Rebais who composed them some time before 1087; the remaining three are 'O purpurea martyrum', 'Gaudes honore gemino' and 'Princeps et pater patriae'.[40] Thomson has argued that they are 'neither Bury nor English compositions' because their author was visiting Bury from Normandy rather than being a permanent resident there.[41] The composer's appropriation of the Angel/angle wordplay serves as an homage to his hosts. The significance of his four St Edmund antiphons is evidenced by a number of references to their texts in visual art and literature; in particular, 'Ave rex gentis anglorum' had a central role in connecting Bury to the English Crown more generally.[42] Of the motets and carols that survive from the later medieval period, three make explicit reference to this liturgical item. *Ave miles celestis curie/Ave rex gentis* opens with the same word as the chant, emphasising the relationship between the motet and its borrowed material.[43] Both *Ave miles celestis curie* and the motet *De flore martirum/Deus tuorum militum/Ave rex gentis* use the plainchant as a cantus firmus in their tenor lines. The chorus of the single surviving fifteenth-century English carol to St Edmund (which survives without music) also makes reference to the plainchant in its burden: 'Synge we now all and sum, *Ave rex gentis anglorum*'.[44]

The abbey at Bury was a royal foundation, and it was important for the monks to remind the English monarchy of their patron saint as part of broader political allegiance and patronage. Evidence of the power of the antiphon 'Ave rex gentis Anglorum' in establishing the relationship between the abbey and the king is found in the thirteenth century, when Henry III's clerks sang the plainchant during the queen's labour, ensuring the safe delivery of Henry's fourth child. The occasion was officially recorded in a letter from Henry III to the Abbot of Bury:

> Know that on Monday after the feast of St Hilary, when our beloved consort Eleanor, our Queen, was labouring in the pains of childbirth, we had the antiphon of St Edmund chanted for her, and when the aforesaid prayer was not yet finished, the bearer of this present letter, our valet [Stephen de Salines, told us that she had] borne us a son. So that you may have the greater joy from this news we have arranged for it to be told to you by Stephen himself. And know that, as you requested us if you remember, we are having our son named Edmund.[45]

142 *Contenance angloise*

Over a century later, when Henry VI arrived for his lengthy stay at Bury – from Christmas 1433 to St George's Day, 23 April 1434 – the monks processed him from the south side of the abbey to the high altar using the antiphon in procession.[46] The appearance of the plainchant 'Ave rex gentis anglorum' in narrative and musical contexts suggests that it represented both the local and national contexts of St Edmund's cult, emphasising the relationship between nation and heaven.

Outside of hagiographical items, one particular piece dating from the late fourteenth century offers an example of the potential confusion in the transmission of the appropriate or intended word: the five-part, isorhythmic motet *Are post libamina/Nunc surgunt* is by Matheus de Sancto Johanne (d. after 10 June 1391). It is found in two sources: the Old Hall Manuscript, and a later, now fragmentary, source that was perhaps associated with a royal patron during the 1430s.[47] Of the two copies, the triplum as copied in Old Hall suggests that the Latin-texted motet enjoyed a previous life with French lyrics, after which the music was made 'sweeter to the *English*' by the use of a new Latin text; the later copy states that the music was made sweeter to the *angels* by the same process.[48] The triplum closes:

> We should give forth sweet harmonies, highly lyrical, with joyful tone. Our sound should never be hastened or anticipated, but always restrained by listening with attention. The active, distinguished Frenchman composed this song on French melodies; but after he revised it with the Latin language, it more often became sweet to the English [angels], replacing Deo Gracias [later textual version in square brackets].

Wathey drew attention to the angel/Angle substitution as being predictable, perhaps on account of how easily the error could be made, whereas Bent expressed surprise that two manuscripts with such a close provenance should contain this 'classic confusion'.[49] One might even imagine a mischievous scribe adjusting the text from his exemplar deliberately; in the early part of the fifteenth century, it was clearly possible, for a variety of reasons, for the words to be exchanged.

In terms of opportunities for sharing cultural and political ideas, the visit of King Sigismund (later to become Holy Roman Emperor) to Westminster from May 1416 has long been held as crucial. The visit was expected to help foster negotiations of a peace between England and France, as well as being part of the important attempts to resolve the papal schism; however, it coincided with the battle at Harfleur in which the English destroyed much of the French navy. One account of Sigismund's visit, by chronicler and hagiographer John Capgrave (1393–1464), documented the parting of Sigismund, during which servants apparently released pieces of politically charged writing into the streets. Capgrave reports one such sample sentiment, underlining the expectation that texts expressing nationalist sentiment might feature the angel/Angle pun in relation to song:

> Farewel, with glorious victory,
> Blessid Inglond, ful of melody.
> Thou may be cleped [called] of Angel nature;

Though servist God so with bysy cure.
We leave with the this praising,
Whech we schul evir sey and sing.[50]

The meaning of contenance

Having explored the word 'angloise' in relation to notions of Englishness, Angles and angels, let us turn to the word with which it is paired in le Franc's lyric. The flexible word, 'countenance', was often used during the later Middle Ages in ways that meant aspects of appearance. Its first use to mean 'face' appears to have been English, but facial expression, comportment and demeanour were all common meanings in English and French in the appropriate period. Wegman has explored le Franc's poetry within the language of its time, examining the word 'contenance' in terms of its contemporary definition, and remarking that it did not mean 'face' until the sixteenth century. He has argued that the expected phrasing - 'maniere d'Angleterre' (that music might exhibit a demeanor relating to England) - was substituted with the word 'contenenance' primarily for a more flexible and satisfactory rhyme.[51]

The Middle English word 'contenaunce' was used from at least the early part of the fourteenth century to imply physical appearance and manner. Derived from the Old French 'cuntenaunce', it could be found regularly in vernacular texts between 1300 and 1500, especially in those whose authors, such as Chaucer, inflected their style with French. If used with a positive adjective such as 'fair', it also indicated chivalry and the bearing of a person of fine breeding and experience. The literature of the period records various uses of the word countenance; some uses imply appearance over authenticity of sentiment, that having a certain 'countenance' was a good veil for one's genuine views or intentions. The earliest English use of the word countenance to mean face is surprisingly early. John Gower's first extensive vernacular work, the *Confessio amantis* – a lengthy text on the seven deadly sins – was composed between about 1386 and 1390, with the third recension produced in 1393. The section of the poem discussing avarice includes the couplets:

To chirche I come, and there I stonde,
And though I take a boke on honde
My contenaunce is on the boke,
But toward her is all my loke.[52]

Such is his infatuation with the lady who he sees frequenting Mass and Matins in church or chapel that even though he has a devotional book in hand, and his face appears to look at it, his glances are constantly to the object of his affection. Gower's writings include works in English (approximately a third of his output), French and Latin; as such, he was well placed to use a word in full knowledge of its poetic resonance in both vernaculars, and to exploit the word's potential. Indeed, the *Confessio amantis* includes several terms borrowed from French or Latin which were later adopted into English more widely, as well as phrasing that would have been enjoyed by those with good linguistic skills in all three literary vernaculars. Gower's style is full of wordplay and innuendo, drawing on his understanding of law, French and Latin romance.[53]

Conclusions

The angel/Angle play on words found across diverse texts suited the English imagination very well. The point of the passage in the *vitae* of St Gregory and St Augustine was that the angelic looks that exemplified the country's men and women were matched, by the later Middle Ages, by their strong Christian faith. For the English, heaven was a reflection of their terrestrial existence since it contained choirs of angels cast in their own image. Just as Ardis Butterfield has shown in relation to literary history that Chaucer 'has been constantly mistaken as the inventor of a new English', underpinned by particular 'notions of English and Englishness' that are inappropriate and unsupportable, so too must Dunstaple's position in the history of music be challenged.[54]

The cross-channel heritage of the word 'angloise' would have been obvious to readers of le Franc's text, and perhaps more so to listeners for whom the speaker may have drawn attention to poetic subtleties. My interpretation of the poet's intention is supported by the placement of the second word at the line break, interrupting the flow and drawing the reader's/listener's attention to the alternative reading of a heavenly or angelic musical agreement of notes within English writing. Following the edition given in Bent's article of the stanza above, I would suggest that the following slight adjustment reflects the allegorical and playful nature of le Franc's intentions:

> For they have a new way of making lively concord, in loud and soft music, in *fainte*, in *pause*, and in *muance*, and they have taken something of the countenance of angels/Angles, and followed Dunstaple; this is why wonderful pleasure makes their song joyful and notable.

Comparison with heavenly music-making was a common literary conceit of the period. Stanza 2036 of *Le Champion des Dames*, for example, describes harp players 'who enliven their concords and their harmonies so perfectly that it seems that they strive to rival the melodies of angels'.[55] My interpretation does not undermine the central point of the literature regarding English music, which was admired and – to some extent – emulated by continental composers: it was 'notable' in its remarkable beauty, which derived from its notes, to draw on Le Franc's double meanings once more. However, it softens the literal level of translation found in previous discussions of the poem by writers who have sought to map the words directly onto English musical style. Instead it is possible to position Dunstaple as a dominant personality among lesser-known 'Angles' whose sweet sounding polyphony, achieved by means of a wide range of compositional techniques, was known to continental writers of the later fifteenth century. In a letter to the secretaries of the chancellery of Savoy in the mid-1430s, le Franc outlined the particular 'importance of the *imitatio* (the emulation of models) for the art of speaking well' in which, 'he drew one of his examples from music, noting that a musician was deemed excellent if in his compositions he imitated ('similfacit') the 'celestial chords' of Du Fay and the 'most agreeable songs' of Binchois'.[56] In all, le Franc's *contenance angloise* may have been paying a similar compliment by claiming that Dufay and Binchois took something of English composers' angelic reputations, honouring their predecessors by the employment of a well-known literary homage.

Notes

1 See Margaret Bent, "The Musical Stanzas in Martin Le Franc's *Le Champion des Dames*." In *Music and Medieval Manuscripts: Paleography and performance. Essays dedicated to Andrew Hughes*, edited by John Haines and Randall Rosenfeld (Aldershot: Ashgate, 2004). The poem may be consulted in Martin Le Franc, *Le Champion des Dames*, 5 vols, edited by Robert Deschaux (Paris: Honoré Champion, 1999).

2 Rob C. Wegman, "Johannes Tinctoris and the 'New Art'," *Music and Letters* 84 (2003), 173. The word 'teacher' here implies not a direct pedagogical experience, but some form of study by the younger men of the works of their predecessors. On this relationship, see Paula Higgins, "Musical 'Parents' and their 'Progeny': The Discourse of Creative Patriarchy in Early Modern Europe." In *Music in Renaissance Cities and Courts: Studies in Honor of Lewis Lockwood*, edited by Jessie Ann Owensand Anthony M. Cummings (Warren, Michigan, 1997), 172–3.

3 See especially Wegman, "Johannes Tinctoris and the 'New Art'".

4 Theodor Dumitrescu, *The Early Tudor Court and International Musical Relations* (Aldershot: Ashgate, 2007), 226.

5 Philip R. Kaye, *The 'Contenance Angloise' in Perspective: A study of consonance and dissonance in continental music c. 1380–1440* (New York and London, Garland: 1989), 1; Gareth Curtis, "Stylistic layers in the English Mass Repertory c. 1400–1450," *Proceedings of the Royal Musical Association* 109 (1982–3), 24.

6 Rob C. Wegman, "New Music for a World Grown Old: Martin Le Franc and the *contenance angloise*," *Acta Musicologica* 75 (2003), 208.

7 My thanks to James Cook sharing with me the Scots poetry by Gavin Douglas (*c.* 1474–1522) that is similarly peppered with references to musical sounds, techniques and practices.

8 The French text is that cited in Bent, "The Musical Stanzas in Martin Le Franc's *Le Champion des Dames*," 97, which draws on the edition by Deschaux. The translation draws on Bent's discussion of terminology in "The Musical Stanzas in Martin Le Franc's *Le Champion des Dames*".

9 Howard Mayer Brown's *Music in the Renaissance* (Englewood Cliffs, NJ: Prentice Hall, 1976) starts with a chapter dealing with John Dunstaple and his English contemporaries.

10 Reinhard Strohm, *The Rise of European Music 1380–1500* (Cambridge: Cambridge University Press, 1993), 79.

11 Thomas Brothers, "Contenance Angloise and Accidentals in some Motets by Du Fay," *Plainsong and Medieval Music* 6 (1997).

12 For a guide to English repertory in continental sources, see Gareth Curtis and Andrew Wathey, "Fifteenth-Century English Liturgical Music: A list of the surviving repertory," *RMA Research Chronicle* 27 (1994).

146 *Contenance angloise*

13 Andrew Kirkman, "Some Early Fifteenth-Century Fauxbourdons by Dufay and his Contemporaries: A study in liturgically-motivated musical styles," *Tijdschrift van de Vereniging voor Nederlandse Muziekgeschiedenis* 40 (1990).
14 Henry Davey, *History of English Music*, 2nd edn (London, Curwen and Sons, 1921), xii–xiii.
15 Manfred Bukofzer, "John Dunstable: A quincentenary report," *The Musical Quarterly* 40 (1954), 29–49.
16 The complaint that England had few native composers of significance was widely acknowledged in nineteenth-century literature, but it was Oskar Schmitz's phrase – the land without music – that has since been most commonly cited; Oskar Adolf Hermann Schmitz, *Das Land ohne Musik* (Munich: G. Müller, 1914).
17 Richard Hoppin, *Medieval Music* (New York: Norton, 1978), 523.
18 Kaye, *The 'Contenance Angloise' in Perspective*, 267.
19 Strohm, *The Rise of European Music*, 128.
20 Strohm, *The Rise of European Music*, 128–9.
21 David Fallows, *Dufay* (London: J. M. Dent, 1982), 246.
22 David Fallows, "The *Contenance Angloise*: English influence on continental composers of the fifteenth century," *Renaissance Studies* 1 (1987), 194.
23 Fallows, "The *Contenance Angloise*," 205. Although Strohm notes that a professional musician may not have been required as intermediary, if the story was by then a commonplace, he considers two further candidates in the transmission of these ideas: 'Éloi d'Amerval, a Savoy chaplain in 1455-7, who later met Tinctoris at Orléans, and Jacques Villette, a bachelor of Law at Cambrai, singer of the Savoy court and Geneva Cathedral, who in the 1470s was employed at the court of Naples'; Reinhard Strohm, "Music, Humanism, and the Idea of a 'Rebirth' of the Arts." In *Music as Concept and Practice in the Late Middle Ages*, edited by Reinhard Strohm and Bonnie Blackburn, New Oxford History of Music, iii/1 (Oxford: Oxford University Press, 2001), 384.
24 Wegman, "New Music for a World Grown Old," 212.
25 Bent, "The Musical Stanzas in Martin Le Franc's *Le Champion des Dames*," 122.
26 Bent, "The musical stanzas in Martin Le Franc's *Le Champion des Dames*", 121–2.
27 The Latin is from Sherry L. Reames, "Reconstructing and Interpreting a Thirteenth-Century Office for the Translation of Thomas Becket," *Speculum* 80 (2005), 168. The translation is taken from Sherry L. Reames, "Liturgical Offices for the Cult of St. Thomas Becket." In *Medieval Hagiography: An Anthology*, edited by Thomas Head (New York: Garland, 2000), 585–6.
28 Jennifer R. Bray, "Concepts of Sainthood in Fourteenth-Century England," *Bulletin of the John Rylands Library, Manchester* 66 (1984); Aviad M. Kleinberg, "Proving Sanctity: Selection and Authentication of Saints in the Later Middle Ages," *Viator* 20 (1989).
29 Gábor Klaniczay, *Holy Rulers and Blessed Princesses: Dynastic cults in medieval central Europe*. Translated by Eva Pálmai (Cambridge: Cambridge University Press, 2002), 78.
30 Bede, *Historiam Ecclesiasticam Gentis Anglorum. Liber Secundus* www.thelatinlibrary.com/bede/bede2.shtml (Accessed 21 December 2015).
31 Medieval sourcebook. Bede (673735), *Ecclesiastical History of the English Nation*, Book II www.fordham.edu/halsall/basis/bede-book2.asp (Accessed 21 December 2015).
32 Thomas Graesse, ed., *Legenda Aurea* (Leipzig: lmpensis Librariae Arnoldianae, 1850), ch. 46 'De sancto Gregorio', 188–202, at page 190.
33 Jacobus de Voragine, *The Golden Legend, Readings on the Saints*, translated by William Granger Ryan, 2 vols (Princeton: Princeton University Press, 1993), 172.

34 Oxford, Bodleian Library, Ms. Laud, 108. Edition by Carl Horstmann, *The Early South English Legendary*. Early English Text Society, Original Series 87 (London: Trübner, 1887), 359.
35 William Caxton, *The Golden Legend or Lives of the Saints Compiled by Jacobus de Voragine, Archbishop of Genoa, 1275*. Englished by William Caxton (Westminster, first Latin edition 1470, English translation 1483); *Early English Books Online* (image ID 3756).
36 [Summe presul Augustine?]/*Augustine par angelis*/T. *Summe presul Augustine* is found as an addition to a fourteenth-century cartulary from the chapel of St Mary at St Augustine's in Daventry, a Cluniac house. The duplum also survives without music in a hymnal from St Augustine's, Canterbury (Cambridge, St John's College, 262, ff. 74v–75), where it has an additional stanza. Lefferts comments that the surviving music is indicative that 'the harmony must have been very "English" '; see Peter M. Lefferts, *The Motet in England in the Fourteenth Century* (Michigan: Ann Arbor, 1986), 272. *Solaris ardor Romuli* is copied as part of Oxford, New College, MS 362, f. 89.
37 See the discussion of music for St Edward the Confessor in Chapter 2.
38 For a wider discussion of music associated with St Edmund, see Lisa Colton, "Music and Identity in Medieval Bury St Edmunds." In *St Edmund, King and Martyr: Changing images of a medieval saint*, edited by Anthony Bale (Woodbridge: Boydell, 2009).
39 The antiphon is reproduced in facsimile in Walter H. Frere, ed., *Antiphonale Sarisburiense: A reproduction in facsimile from early manuscripts with a dissertation and analytical index* (London, 1901–24, repr. Farnborough, 1966), VI, 597.
40 Thomson, "The music," 192. Hughes rejects Abbot Garnier's authorship of the first antiphon, since it appears in the Copenhagen source on its own, and considers that the Abbot wrote four antiphons in addition to those already in circulation; Andrew Hughes, "British Rhymed Offices: A catalogue and commentary." In *Music in the Medieval English Liturgy*, edited by Susan Rankin and David Hiley (Oxford: Clarendon Press, 1993), 260.
41 Thomson, "The Music," 192.
42 This melody was also employed later for the liturgy of saints including St Edmund of Abingdon, St Oswine and St Ethelbert; for a fuller account, see Thomson, "The Music," 193.
43 For a detailed analysis of the intertexuality in *Ave miles celestis curie*, see Lisa Colton, "Music, Text and Structure in Fourteenth-Century English Motets: The case of *Ave miles celestis curie*," *Early Music* 45 (forthcoming for 2017).
44 *The Early English Carols*, 2nd edn, edited by Richard L. Greene (Oxford: Clarendon Press, 1977), 190.
45 Margaret J. Howell, "The Children of Henry III and Eleanor of Provence." In *Thirteenth Century England* 4, edited by P. R. Coss and L. G. Lloyd (Woodbridge: Boydell and Brewer, 1992), 63.
46 Craven Ord, "An Account of the Entertainment of Henry the Sixth at the Abbey of Bury St. Edmunds," *Archaeologia* 15 (1806). 70; Ord prints the Latin account of Henry's visit, 'De adventu regis Henrici VI ad monasterium de Sancto Edmundo 1433', preserved in the Register of Abbot Curteys, now London, British Library, MS Additional 14848, ff. 128r–v.
47 See Andrew Wathey, "Matheus de Sancto Johanne." *Grove Music Online. Oxford Music Online.* Oxford University Press. Accessed 21 December 2015, www.oxfordmusiconline.com/subscriber/article/grove/music/18061. On the leaves that formed part of the later, unnamed manuscript source (formerly known as H6), see Margaret Bent, "The Progeny of Old Hall: More Leaves from a Royal English Choirbook." In *Gordon Athol Anderson, 1929–81, in Memoriam*, edited by Luther Dittmer (Henryville, Ottawa, and Binningen: Institute of Mediaeval Music, 1984), 7–10.

48 Andrew Wathey, "The Peace of 1360–1369 and Anglo-French Musical Relations," *Early Music History* 9 (1990), 149.
49 Wathey, "The Peace of 1360–1369," 149; Bent, "The Progeny of Old Hall," 7.
50 John Capgrave, *The Chronicle of England*, edited by F. C. Hingeston (London: Longman, Brown, Green, Longmans and Roberts, 1858), 314.
51 Wegman, "New Music for a World Grown Old," 233.
52 John Gower, *Tales of the Seven Deadly Sins: Being the confessio amantis* (London and New York: Routledge, 1889; reprinted London: Forgotten Books, 2013), 303.
53 See John Gower, *Confessio Amantis*, 3 vols, edited by Russell A. Peck, translated by Andrew Galloway (Kalamazoo, MI: Medieval Institute Publications, 2006).
54 Ardis Butterfield, *The Familiar Enemy: Chaucer, language and nation in the Hundred Years War* (Oxford: Oxford University Press, 2009).
55 'Que sy parfaictement avivent/leurs accors et leurs armonies/Qu'i semble de fait qu'ilz estrivent/Aux angeliques melodies'; cited and translated in Bent, "The Musical Stanzas in Martin Le Franc's *Le Champion des Dames*." Wegman's translation gives 'These [harp players] invigorate their chords and harmonies with such perfection that it seems in truth as if they were emulating the euphony of angels'; Wegman, "New Music for a World Grown Old," 240.
56 Wright and Gallagher, "Martin le Franc."

Epilogue

In the 1340s or 1350s, at the height of Anglo-French aggression, Philippe de Vitry fuelled his war of words and music – waged against his compatriot Jehan de le Mote – with a new motet: *Phi millies/O creator*. The tenor and contratenor text of *Phi millies* carried the combined lyric 'The grain lies smothered by the chaff, which the Frenchman will blow from the threshing floor'.[1] Here, as Anna Zayaruznaya has demonstrated, the well-known matins responsory 'Jacet granum' – taken from the liturgy for St Thomas of Canterbury – is used as the foundation of a piece of anti-English vitriol, exploiting textual and musical devices to emphasise its message.

In the new musical context of *Phi millies*, the plainchant was both a reminder of St Thomas's importance as popular English saint, and a satirical blow to his reputation as Englishman – born in London, certainly, but to Norman parents. Although Thomas was the first native Englishman to occupy the position of Archbishop of Canterbury, his periods of exile weakened his ethnic claim. Vitry's motet closed with a damning prediction: 'nec plus erit hoc nomen: Anglia', 'nor will there be any longer such a name as England': the English were predicted to fall to the French Crown in a humiliating defeat. He also warned others who, like le Mote, had left France to work at the court of Edward III. The anti-English zeal of Vitry's motet is made all more potent by its failure to utter 'Anglia' until the final word of the triplum, instead using endless references to those who were thought to have conquered the native English (Trojans, Saxons, Danes) as well as by the piece's distortion of the liturgical song for one of the country's most loved religious figures. Just as French motets by outspoken composers like Vitry could be political, English music – through choice of subject, use of allusions from political literature or the interplay of music and text – could play a part in the forging of ideas that were fundamental to the development of the English nation. The message of a surprisingly large portion of English-texted music and writings about English music from the period 1260–1460 is that the country was spiritually exalted, its rulers and the general population occupying a meeting place between Angle and angel.

The political dominance of the English Crown during the Middle Ages relied on more than victory in physical struggles against the French: it depended on success in a spiritual war in which the ruling Plantagenets and Lancastrians were portrayed as pious descendants of a line of 'blessed martyrs and holy kings so good', as the fifteenth-century Bury St Edmunds monk John Lydgate might say.[2] English kings were anointed by God, possessing – from the reign of Edward the Confessor onward – the special ability to heal cases of scrofula, the 'king's evil'.[3] Through its multisensory appeal, music could play a powerful role in that branding exercise. Kings could be *miles Christi*, soldiers of Christ, in the image of their heroic forebears, their wives intercessors in the manner of the Blessed Virgin Mary.

The spirit of nostalgia that made (and still makes) medieval music and culture so appealing to modern audiences likewise drew on notions of England's special place in God's creation. Lavezzo reminds us that the roots of English nationalism are not found in the nineteenth century, but much earlier, stating that 'to acquire a full understanding of the earliest representations of English community in literary artifacts, we must extend our gaze still farther back in the history of the West, to the Middle Ages'.[4] Certainly, nationalism functioned in very different ways during the centuries in which England developed into a political nation. One of the advantages of looking at questions of Englishness in relation to song from this early period is that texted music functioned not as 'history' *per se*, but as a historicising force. Motets placed their subjects into a historical perspective as part of regular devotional practice, claiming holiness for figures that may or may not have been saints – just as they may or may not have been native Englishmen.

The development, maintenance and enhancement of the concept of England as both ethnically coherent and special was the most fundamental national project of the later Middle Ages; it was also simultaneously audacious and vulnerable because it relied on a complex web of mythology, history and religious doctrine. Its success can be seen in the quiet acceptance of many of its central stories in subsequent historical writing, even to the present day, in music and in wider scholarship. Its accomplishment has also resulted in the whitewashing of English music history, which has subsequently neglected some of the messiness of sources, of repertories and of performance that have only recently become the focus of serious study.

The impact of nationalism on contemporary understanding of medieval English music has been far reaching because it has assisted writers in choosing their subject, methodology, approach and case studies. This scholarly context has created a self-fulfilling prophecy, helping to create a canon of music, and of English music in particular, with 'Sumer is icumen in' and then composer John Dunstaple at its head. In nineteenth-century Germany, Chaucer's work was once used to explain subsequent developments in German writing; Richard Utz has demonstrated that this was achieved through philological scrutiny aiming to reveal a strong, masculine and Aryan past for German literature.[5] In a musicological parallel, Dunstaple has offered a convenient model of creative genius to act as a reference point in broader European histories of musical style, not least because his music was disseminated beyond English borders. He was already lauded in the fifteenth century for heading up the English composers responsible for the latest musical innovations. Dunstaple's alleged impact on European masters could be inferred both from those that praised his music and through a particular interpretation of *contenance angloise*, one in which this phrase meant a distinctly English sound or style.

As I have shown, such mythologising of composers, works or styles has done much to distract from building an accurate picture of music and musical practices in medieval England, a problem only exacerbated by the appropriation of medieval song by composers of the past century such as Britten to create connections with English music history. Of course, it is not the role of the composer to give a balanced or objective representation of early culture. Examination of music by composers for whom medieval music has been a meaningful stimulus can, however, help us to focus our understanding of those conceptions that lie at the heart of the reception of early music over the past century. There remain plenty of opportunities to consider the exploitation of medievalism in the music of British composers from Benjamin Britten to Judith Weir, Thea Musgrave, Peter Maxwell Davies and James Dillon.

Current research is placing the sounding nature of music, musico-textual meanings in monophonic and polyphonic genres, and the roles of patrons, listeners and scribes at the heart of investigations into medieval repertoire. This book has questioned whether we might debase the formerly privileged place of the composer, the work and of questions of English style in historical narrative. I have shown the diverse ways in which English music has been variously side-lined for not fully resembling continental models, misappropriated as part of nationalistic agenda, misrepresented through anachronistic comparisons with later repertoire, and generally distorted through reliance on narrowly focused archival study. In each case, I hope also to have identified ways forward: revisiting and uncovering archival sources and making the musical evidence speak to a broader range of devotional and political texts, for example. The foundations of English musical history were laid deep in the medieval past, in the mythologising of Gerald of Wales, Matthew Paris and many other chroniclers as well as through the monophonic and polyphonic repertoire itself which engaged reflectively with its own historical position through text and the placement of chant in new musical contexts. The first course of bricks was then laid by early music historians such as Burney and Hawkins before the exponential growth of musicology as a discipline occurred hand-in-hand with nineteenth- and twentieth-century nationalisms. Excavating those layers allows us to take a fresh look at the music while also identifying our own priorities, our contemporary agenda. It is time to create new stories for medieval English music.

Notes

1 This motet's extreme anti-English sentiment has not gone unnoticed previously; see, for example, Denis Stevens, "Music in Honour of St Thomas of Canterbury," *Musical Quarterly* 56 (1970), 332. Such comments were made before the rediscovery of the musical source that has since been used by Anna Zayaruznaya to make a new edition, discussed as part of her book *The Monstrous New Art: Divided forms in the late medieval motet* (Cambridge: Cambridge University Press, 2015). The texts of the

152 *Epilogue*

     motet, found in Paris, Bibliothèque Nationale, Lat. 3343, ff.71v–72, were first described in Edmond Pognon, "Du nouveau sur Philippe de Vitry et ses amis." *Humanisme et Renaissance* 6 (1939).
2   John Lydgate referred St Edmund, King and Martyr, as 'This hooly martir, this blyssyd kyng so good'; see the edition by Anthony Bale and A. S. G. Edwards, *John Lydgate, The Lives of Ss Edmund and Fremund and the Extra Miracles of St Edmund, Edited from British Library MS Harley 2278 and Bodleian MS Ashmole 46* (Heidelberg: Universitaetsverlag Winter, 2009).
3   Frank Barlow, "The King's Evil," *English Historical Review* 95 (1980).
4   Kathy Lavezzo, ed. *Imagining a Medieval English Nation* (Minneapolis, MN: University of Minnesota Press, 2003), vii.
5   Richard J. Utz, "Inventing German(ic) Chaucer: Ideology and philology in German anglistics before 1945," *Studies in Medievalism* 8 (1996).

Appendix A

John Dunstaple and other relevant people in historical records

Table A.1: John Dunstaple, musician

This table compiles some of the key places in which composer John Dunstaple's name appears in documents from his lifetime and shortly afterwards. It is not designed to be exhaustive, since it excludes the mention of his name in music books except where he may have been involved in the copying process. I have included the reference to motets at Canterbury because their date is significant to Dunstaple's biography; no composer's name is recorded in the chronicle itself for these pieces.

Event	Listed as	Date
Two motets sung at Canterbury Cathedral, named in chronicle attributed to Thomas Elmham	No name given	21 August 1416
Inscription in Cambridge, St John's College MS 162 (F.25), f. 74, a manuscript containing hand of John Dunstaple. 'Iste libellus pertinebat Iohanne Dunstaple cum Iohanni duce Bedfordie musico'	Iohanne Dunstaple	15th-century hand
Cambridge, Emmanuel College MS 70, collection of texts relating to judicial astrology (calculation of horoscopes)	'quod Dunstaple' (f. 58, f. 118v); 'quod Dunst.' (f. 128v, f.135, f.144, f.149)	One signed item is dated 1420[1]
Owner of copy of Boethius's *De musica* and *De arithmetica* (now Oxford, Corpus Christi College 118); part 2 (*De arithmetica*) in John Dunstaple's hand	'Iohannes Dunstaple' (front) and 'Dunstaple' (rear). 'Quod Dunstaple' at end of part 2.	
One of the composers (Bent) or scribes (Thomson) of music in a now-fragmentary choirbook[2]	'quod Dunstaple'	Reign of Henry VI (1422–61)

Continued ...

154   *Appendix A*

Continued

Martin le Franc, *Le Champion des Dames*	Mentions Dunstable in relation to *contenance angloise*	*c.* 1440–2
Tinctoris, *Prohemium* to the *Proportionale*	Mentions Dunstaple as heading the English musicians responsible for a new art	*c.* 1476
Plated tomb marks John Dunstaple's death, reported in the 1618, Munday's revised version of Stow's *Survay of London* (1598)	Dunstable I, Juris Astrorum	'Mil Equater semel L trius'[3] (1618)
John of Wheathamsted, Abbot of St Albans, writes epitaph	Johannis Dunstapil	Date unknown; reported in Weever's *Funerall Monument* (1631)

Table A.2: John Dunstaple listed as Armiger or Esquire

Receives cup worth 78s. 4d. and a furred scarlet gown from Queen Joan as New Year's gift	Gifts given to John Dunstaple, an Esquire of the queen ['Johanni Dunstaple uni armigero dicte Regine pro I gonum'][4]	1427–8
John Donstaple, Esquire, nobleman, of the diocese of Lincoln	Armigero	
Inspeximus and confirmation of lands to John Dunstable, the present tenant of the lands[5]	Esquire	30 November 1435
Grant to Johannes Dunstaple, giving 'liberam warrennam in Stepilmorden et Gildenmorden in com. Cantabr' (to hold these lands in free warren, i.e. permission to hunt game on the property)[6]	Armiger	1436
Tax records NA 163/7/31/1 John Dunstaple, income of £24 plus grant of £80 from Queen Joan; holder of lands in Cambridge, Essex and London	None listed	1436

Continued . . .

Appendix A 155

Continued

National Archives, JUST 1/108/11 [now missing] Assize Record. William Hasilden, Esq. v. John Dunstaple senior, Esquire, Cambridgeshire[7]	John Dunstaple senior, Esquire	1 September 1436–31 August 1437
Exemption for life of John Dunstaple, Esquire, from being put on assizes, juries, attaints or recognitions, though the matter touch the king, and from being made mayor, sheriff, escheator, coroner, justice, constable, or collector of tenths, fifteenths, tallages or subsidies; or trier or governor of men at arms, hobelers and archers, or any other bailiff or minister of the king[8]	Esquire	25 March 1437

Granted lands in Normandy following death of John of Bedford:[9]
    The lordship of Croisy, nr. Evreux (1436–40)
    The fief of La Ruaudière (from early 1437)
    The fief of Beaumanoir (from early 1437)
    Lands in the *bailliage* of Côtentin (July 1438–?), Rouen (Sep 1439–?) and Alençon (from September 1440)
    Lands surrendered or lost after 1440
	Jehan Dunstaple escuier seignur de Croisy; Esquire [escuier] and anglois appear; in the *délai* for Beaumanoir and La Ruaudière of 5 July 1438 he is titled 'serviteur et familier domestique de Onfroy Duc de Gloucestre'[10]	Held between 1436/7 and at least 1440/1

Memorandum of acknowledgement. Robert Edolffe of London (girdler) to John Dunstaple Esquire and his assigns. Charter of all goods of Robert in England, Wales and Ireland[11]	Armiger	20 May 1439
Property in London parishes confirmed as belonging to John Dunstable[12]	Armiger	17 November 1446
Owner of Broadfield manor, Hertfordshire, granted by Richard Whaplode to John Dunstaple, his wife Margaret, Ralph Grey and Henry Wells[13]	Armiger	16 March 1449
National Archives C 1/26/309 Chancery Proceedings addressed to the Lord Chancellor. Richard and Elizabeth Barlee (niece of Edmund Caumpe) v. John Donstabill, Richard Cawdray and other feoffees, re: messuages and lands in Bassingbourn, Steeple Morden and Litlington, Cambridge	Esquire [squire] Donstabill	c.1456–9
National Archives C 1/26/576 Barlee v. Dunstable. As above but defendants listed as John Dunstable, Richard Caudrey, John Middleton	Esquire [squire] Dunstable	c.1456–9

Continued . . .

156 Appendix A

Continued

| Will of Johannes Dunstaple (Broadfield, Hertfordshire) Hertfordshire Record Office, DE/Z120/44505 | Armiger | 7 July 1459 [16th-century copy, abridged] |
| Writ of *diem clausit extremum* issued following the death of John Dunstaple | Esquire | 14 September 1459, Winchester |

Table A.3: Probably John Dunstaple Esquire

| Declaration of Robert Wylne and Thomas Chaterley yeoman [*sic*] of the Crown and the king's servants, that on Wednesday after St Martin last in St Mary's church Notyngham, they spoke with John Dunstable executor of Sir John Ryder late canon of Southwell, and declared that Sir John [Ryder] gave to his niece Johane, the wife of John Paunton, 100*l*. which Henry late cardinal of England and late bishop of Wynchestre owed to him, also that John and Johane received the said 100*l*. of the executors of the cardinal, and to this the said executor [i.e. John Dunstable] said he would 'agree him' in all points, provided that the parson of Saint Bride's in Fletestrete, London, would swear that he knew that Sir John [Ryder] made the gift as abovesaid; and after this on the Monday in Sexagesima last in Saint Bride's church the parson swore by his priesthood before Robert and Thomas that he knew and was present when Sir John gave the said 100*l*. to his niece | 4 March 1449 |

Table A.4: Other John Dunstaples

John Dunstaple of Walbrook, served as Alderman	Skinner and Alderman	1293–1307
John Dunstavylle/John Dunstaple (canon of Hereford Cathedral and prebendary of Putson Minor)[14]	Clerk	28 April 1419 (resigned post by 28 May 1440)
John Dunstaple of Gloucester; accused of abduction of Agnes, wife of Robert Barbour, with two others[15]	Chaloner[16]	Some time between 1386 and 1486
John Dunstaple and John Trendeler marked as 'Custer' [Warden] within the Coupers at the Masters of Misteries sworn in	Custer [Warden]	[2 Hen VI: 1423/4][17]
'John Dunstaple alias Gloucester' is awarded an annual rent of 40*s*. by James Berkeley, Lord of Berkeley, for 'his good and laudable service'	None	1442

Continued . . .

Continued

John Dunstaple owed money by Thomas Langford, citizen and 'curriour' of London, debt of £18[18]	Goldsmith and citizen of London	18 November 1461

Table A.5: Richard Hatfield

NA 44/31/21 Exparte Hatfeld Subject: to lands in Steeple Morden and the manors of Steeple Morden and Avenells[19] in Cambridgeshire. The document records Richard Hatfield's inheritance	None listed	1461
Richard Hatfield appointed as Sergeant Avener of the household	Esquire; Sergeant Avener of the household	20 June 1461
Will of Richard Hatfeld of Steplemorden	Esquire ['Squyer']	1467, Probate 3 July 1468
Writ of *diem clausit extremum*	Esquire	19 March 1468
Commitment with like clause and proviso of the keeping of all the manors and lands that have come into the King's hands after the death of Margaret, late the wife of Richard Hatfield Esquire and late the wife of William Hyde Esquire	Esquire	31 December 1469

Table A.6: Thomas Hatfield

Master William Hattecliffe pays £200 to the king to hold all the lands of Margaret Hatfield/Hyde after her death and after the death of Edward her heir, during the minority of Thomas	Thomas still a minor	29 December 1473
Thomas Hadfeld, *alias* Hatfelt, gentleman of Steple Mordon co. Cambridge, son of Richard Hatfeld Esquire, to Oliver Hilton, gentleman of Mamcestre co. Lancaster, his heirs and assigns. Release and quitclaim with warranty of all his rights in all messuages, lands and tenements, meadows, pastures and fields called 'Sonderland' lying in Assheton on Lune in that county, formerly of Richard his father[20]	Gentleman of Steeple Morden, confirms had inherited his father's lands in the north of England	19 February 1480/1

Continued ...

158 *Appendix A*

Continued

A case of debt. Thomas Hatfield of Steeple Morden (Debtor) and Henry Snow of London (Gentleman), £300[21]	Esquire	26 August 1483 (original hearing 10 July 1482; first term 18 May 1483)
Thomas Hatfeld, to Thomas Oxenbrigge, Gilbert Ormeston, John Smith and Nicholas Stanbery clerks, their heirs and assigns. Gift with confirmation by charter of the manors of Gilden Mordon co. Cambridge, and of Bradfield and Cumberlow Green co. Hertford, with all lands and tenements, rents, reversons and services in Stratford Langthorne and elsewhere in Essex and in the city of London: and appointment of Thomas Porter and Richard Creche as his attorneys etc. to convey seisin of the same	None listed	15 August, 1484
Thomas son of Richard Hatfeld and Thomas Rawley Esquires, to Thomas Oxenbrigge and William Wentworth Esquires, Thomas Worsley, Gilbert Ormeston, John Smyth clerks, Reynold Bray, John Denton and Thomas Aythorpe gentlemen, their heirs and assigns. Demise and enfeoffment with warranty of the manor of Steeple Mordon co. Cambridge, with all lands and tenements, meadows, lesues, pastures, commons, rents and services therein and in Litlington and Abington in that county, which they held jointly by demise of Thomas Ingram and Henry Snowe: with appointment of Richard Waverer and Richard à Coer as their attorneys	Son of Richard Hatfield Esquire	25 October 1484
Quitclaim of property (Three Kings of Cologne) Quitclaim from Thomas Hatfield to John Breton (citizen & Salter of London), John Gibbs and Thomas Goldhurst[22]	Of Steeple Morden in the County of Cambridge, Esquire and heir of Margaret Hatfield	26 October 1486
Names of various people to be intendant to Edmund Hampden as escheator, including Thomas Hafield [sic]	None	5 November 1486
Copy of fine between Henry Snow [Snawe], citizen and draper of London, and Magdalen his wife (plaintiffs), and Thomas Hatfeld, gentleman, and Elizabeth his wife (defendants), concerning manor of Broadfield[23]	Gentleman	8 July 1489

Table A.7: Edward Hatfield

NA C 1/47/280 William Hyde v. John Marchal of London (Mercer). Action brought by the said Marchall in the Common Pleas on an obligation, which was agreed to be regarded as satisfied by the surrender to Marchall of the letters patent granting to him and complainant the wardship and marriage of Edward Hatfield, son and heir of Margaret, late the wife of complainant, and the said Edward. London	Son and heir of Margaret Hyde [previously Hatfield, née Dunstaple]	1472
Grant to John Marshall, citizen and Mercer of London, and John Pulter, gentleman, of the custody of all manors and lands late of Margaret late the wife of Richard Hatfield esq and late the wife of Wiliam Hyde esq, tenant-in-chief, during the minority of the said Edward, son and heir of the said Richard and Margaret[24]	Edward still minor	20 April 1472
Writ *in diem clausit extremum* for the death of Edward Hatfield	A minor of the Kings ward	16 June 1472
NA C 140/42/50 Chancery inquisitions post mortem, Edward Hatfield, son and heir of Margaret, who was the wife of the late William Hyde, Cambridgeshire	Son and heir	1472
Grant for £200 paid to the king of Master William Hattecliffe, the king's secretary, of all the lordships, manors, lands, rents, reversions, services and other possessions late of Margaret Hyde, tenant-in-chief, late the wife of Richard Hattefield esq, deceased, and in the king's hands by the death of any ancestor of Edward, now deceased, their son and heir, or Thomas, their son and heir, to hold during the minority of the said Thomas with his custody and marriage without disparagement, and so from heir to heir[25]	Deceased	29 December 1473

Table A.8: Margaret Hatfield/Hyde (née Margaret Dunstaple)

Rent payment. Paid the 9th day of November in the first year of the reign of Henry VII Margaret Dunstable [Margarete donstabyl] for quarter rent at Michaelmas to Thomas Ingram [Yngram] 2s[26]		9 November 1485
Calendar of inquisitions post mortem reports death, 20 May 1486. Notes lands in Hertfordshire (Manor of Bradfield, worth £10, held of Robert Hyde as of his manor of Throkking;[27] 2 messuages and 30 acres of land in Stratford Langthorne, worth 100s., held of the abbot)		Died 20 May 1486, inquisition 4 November 1486

Notes

1. Rodney M. Thomson, "John Dunstable and his Books," *The Musical Times* 150 (2009), 11.
2. Thomson, "John Dunstable and his Books," 16. Bent suggests 'quod' is scribal in Cambridge, Emmanuel College MS 70 and authorial in H6; Margaret Bent, "A New Canonic *Gloria* and the Changing Profile of Dunstable," *Plainsong and Medieval Music* 5 (1996), 59.
3. Corrected by Charles Maclean to 'Anno Mil C quarter semel L tria'; "The Dunstable Inscription in London," *Sammelbände der Internationalen Musikgesellschaft*, 11. Jahrg., H. 2. (1910), 249.
4. 'To John Dunstaple, an esquire of the said Queen, for making him out of it [i.e. the sum of money] a gown of scarlet cloth [de pan(n)o?] and fur in full with a fur of Fecheux. And long green cloth for making a gown of it by the gift of the same lady (our) Queen aforesaid within the time of this account six ells of scarlet cloth [pan(n)i?], nine ells of long green cloth [pan(n)i?] by Warr'. Translation by Leofranc Holford-Strevens.
5. *Calendar of the Patent Rolls, Henry VI, Volume 2, 1429–1436*, edited by H. C. Maxwell-Lyte (London: His Majesty's Stationery Office, 1907), 495.
6. Reported in Henry Davey, "John Dunstaple," *The Musical Times* 45 (1904), 712. Davey did not believe this to be the composer. A grant of free warren sometimes came considerably later than the original grant of property.
7. This document was identified by the Public Record Office (now National Archives) as in need of permanent preservation, but it never arrived at the office. It is currently missing. Information here taken from catalogue entry.
8. *Calendar of Close Rolls, Henry VI: Volume 3, 1436–1441*, edited by H. C. Maxwell-Lyte (London: His Majesty's Stationery Office, 1907), 52; also reported by Judith Stell and Andrew Wathey. "New Light on the Biography of John Dunstable?" *Music and Letters* 62 (1981), 62, fn. 10.
9. Andrew Wathey notes that 'Dunstable's tenure of these estates can be traced for a period of almost four years until they were forcibly relinquished in the face of French military advances'; "Dunstable in France," *Music and Letters* 67 (1986), 16.
10. 'His designation as "serviteur et familier domestique" offers few insights into his function within Gloucester's household, although the term is found elsewhere in the land grants and *délais* of other armigerous household retainers'; Wathey, "Dunstable in France," 23.
11. *Calendar of the Close Rolls, Henry VI, Volume 3, 1435–1441*, edited by A. E. Stamp (London: Her Majesty's Stationery Office, 1937), 262–69. Witnesses Thomas Befewe (Mercer), Thomas Berarde (Mercer), Robert Wynchecombe (Mercer), Edward Barton (Girdler), all of London. Henry Gairstane. 'Robert Edolf' was also named in a dispute with the warden (Elys Holcote) and scholars of Merton College over the possession of deeds for the Woolsack (Wollesak) in All Hallows, Bread Street, London, at some point between 1443 and 1456, possibly 1455–56; London, National Archives, C 1/151/153 (and an indenture of the same, London, National Archives, C 1/16/622).
12. Presented to various alderman including Thomas Stokdale, probably identifiable with the Escheator of Hertfordshire and Essex in 1436 and 5 November 1439–4 November 1440 (London, National Archives, E 153/2244). It is unclear at present whether this specific property can be identified – as is implied by Wathey – with that described in the Oxford, Merton College MS 2977, in which property is listed belonging to John Hunte *alias* Tebaude. It is possible that this was John Hunte, a clerk in the king's chapel 1415–50, a man Wathey has suggested served as part of Queen Joan's chapel 1427/28; Wathey, "Dunstaple in France," 8. I have also identified that Hunte was in receipt of various corrodies (allowances for a lifetime's supply of food, clothes, housing

or care), namely: (1) having been sent to the abbot and convent of Hyde Abbey, Winchester 'to taken such maintenance as Thomas Meweys deceased had therein' (8 June 1421); (2) Meaux Abbey, following the death of royal chaplain John Burell (d. before 5 February 1423), who had held it previously; (3) Cirencester Abbey, Hunte sent to receive a corrody for life, one formerly awarded to John Somerset, on 28 January 1441; (4) in 1431 a command was issued by Humphrey Duke of Gloucester, Guardian of England: 'To J. [*sic*: Simon Sydenham] bishop of Cicestre [Chichester]. Nomination, with advice and assent of the council, of John Hunte, the king's servant, clerk of his chapel, to receive the pension wherein by reason of his new creation the bishop is bound to one of the king's clerks, until by him provided with a benefice' (24 February 1431); (5) Hunte's death appears to have been *c.* 1461, as Daniel Sheldon, the king's servant, was sent to the abbot and convent of Winchcombe, Gloucester, 'to take of that house such corrody etc as John Hunte deceased had therin' on 20 July 1461/2. In 1392, a payment of £3 3*s* 4*d* was made 'from the prioress of Haliwell for the tenement of Adam Merifeld and Thomas Exton which John Hunte holds'; A. K. McHardy, "Ecclesiastical Property in the City of London, 1392: Bread Street Ward," *The Church in London 1375–1392* (London: London Record Society, 1977), 64–68.

13   After the deaths of John and Margaret Dunstaple and Ralph Grey, the surviving owner Henry Wells left the main Broadfield manor to his cousin and heir John Fayreware, who granted it to Henry Snow of London, gentleman, and Magdalen his wife and their heirs.
14   See Richard L. Greene, "John Dunstable: A Quincentenary Supplement," *The Musical Quarterly* 40 (1954).
15   Court of Chancery, London, National Archives, C 1/68/106 (1386–1486).
16   A maker of chalons, fabric originating in Châlons-sur-Marne.
17   *Calendar of Letter-Books of the City of London. K. Henry V*, edited by Reginald Sharpe (London: J. G. Francis, 1911), 145–57, where Sharpe notes that this is undated but 'likely 1432/3', which must be an error. However, a plea in 1433/4 has Thomas Langshote accused of making false vessels by John Trendler and John Dunstaple, wardens of the Mistery. Pairs of wardens had governed the fraternity since 1422.
18   *Calendar of the Patent Rolls I. Edward I, Volume 1, 1272–1281*, edited by H. C. Maxwell-Lyte (London: Her Majesty's Stationery Office, 1901), 6.
19   Part of the parish of Gamlingay, immediately to the north of Steeple and Guilden Morden, Cambridgeshire. From 1433 until the 1540s, Avenels manor in Guilden Morden passed with Brewis Manor in Steeple Morden; A. P. Baggs, S. M. Keeling and C. A. F. Meekings, "Parishes: Steeple Morden." In *A History of the County of Cambridge and the Isle of Ely* 8, edited by A. P. M. Wright, 111–24 (London: Victoria County History, 1982).
20   "Close Rolls, Edward IV: 1478–1481," *Calendar of Close Rolls, Edward IV, Edward V, Richard III: 1476–1485*, edited by K. H. Ledward (London: Her Majesty's Stationery Office, 1954), 214.
21   London, National Archives, C 241/264/9.
22   London, Salters' Company Archives, H1/2/1/9. Quitclaim by Thomas Hatfield of Steeple Mordon Cambridge Esq., son and heir of Margarete Hatfield to John Breton Cit. and Salter Thomas Goldhurst and John Gybbes of £3 rent described H1/2/1/8 and of 38s rent from a tenement called late the Wolsak (Philip Ball Haberdasher) in All Saints Bredestrete. These rents were lately recovered from Thomas Hatfield by John Breton, Thomas Goldhurst and John Gybbes by writ of right in Guildhall before Hugh Brice Kt. Mayor and the Aldermen.
23   GB-HFr 44505.
24   *Calendar of the Patent Rolls, Edward IV, Volume II, 1468–1476*, edited by W. H. B. Bird and K. H. Ledward (London: Her Majesty's Stationery Office, 1953), 340.

Appendix A

25 *Calendar of the Patent Rolls, Edward IV, Volume II*, 416.
26 London, London Metropolitan Archives, MS 593/1, f.22v. These churchwardens' accounts (formerly London Guildhall Library, MS 593/1) cover the period 1474–1538. The Thomas Ingram in GB-HFr 44505 was probably dead by this time.
27 Throkkyng church in Hertfordshire was also the recipient of money in the will of Henry Snow, Gentleman of London (see Appendix B). The manor belonged to members of the Hyde family.

Appendix B
Hertfordshire Record Office MS 44505

The following items offer a transcription and translation of the manuscript now held as GB-HFr 44505. The source is damaged and its text originated as an effort to collate materials relating to the manor of Broadfield in Hertfordshire into a single source, presumably for some legal purpose, thus recopying them here in the early part of the sixteenth century. I am very grateful to Leofranc Holford-Strevens, who provided the transcription and translation of these documents; I have made very few changes to his texts, any remaining errors are my own.

Wrapper: Copyes of old Deeds belonging to Bradfield. 27. H. 6

Item 1: Charter of John Fray, Salter

Item 1 is a faulty copy of a document already published, so is reproduced below as it appears in Stamp's edition.[1]

15 July 1427
Westminster

Writing indented of John Fray of Hertfordshire [Hertfordshire source names him as a Salter here], disclaiming aught in the manor and advowson of Bradfelde in the County of Hertfordshire which by charter of feoffment dated at the Herne 31 January 4 Henry VI, John Tyrell of Essex Esquire gave to Humphrey earl of Stafford, John Hotoft, Lewis John and Thomas Horne, their heirs and assigns, therein naming also John Fray, but John Clerke the younger, citizen and grocer of London, and Thomas Clerke, clerk, are at this date in peaceable possession of the same by feoffment of John Clerke the elder of Erdeley, Elizabeth his wife and John Hughessone of Asshewelle to them, their heirs and assigns, but excepting and reserving to John Fray, his heirs and assigns, his right in rents and services of old time due from lands called 'Simondescroft' and Reynhale pertaining to his lordship of Coderede, and from 9 acres of meadow called 'Greyesmede' pertaining to his lordship of Russenden, and his right in 'Symondescroft', Reynhale and 'Greyesmede', all being parcel of the manor of Bradfelde; confirmation of the estate of John Clerke the younger and Thomas Clerke, and quitclaim to them, their heirs and assigns, of the said manor and advowson, with the exceptions aforesaid. Dated 16 July 5 Henry VI.

Item 2: Abridged will of John Dunstaple, Esquire

This document is very highly abridged and abbreviated, so for ease of comparison for those consulting the original, line numbers have been retained for the transcription.

7 July 1459
Broadfield, Hertfordshire

1 Hec est ultima voluntas mei Johannis Dunstaple armigeri indentata facta apud
2 Bradfeld in Comitatu Hertfordscirie vijo die mensis Julij anno domini millesimo
3 quadringentesimo quinquagesimo nono et anno RR Henrici
4 Sexti post conquestum xxxvijo. Quoad disposicionem omnium et singlorum
5 maneriorum terrarum et tenementorum meorum cum pertinenciis ubicumque infra regnum
6 Anglie existentium in quibus diuerse persone ad usum meum ex grandi
7 fiducia et ad meam denominacionem feoffati existunt. Videlicet
8 Imprimis volo quod dicti feoffati mei incontinenter post discessum

//

1 meum permittant et paciantur Margarettam uxorem meam percipere Et
2 habere ad totam vitam suam absque impeticione calumpnia Seu
3 implacitacione vasti feuda exitus reven' et profitua provenientia
4 de omnibus illis manerijs terris et tenementis meis cum pertinenciis que habeo tam
5 in Com'[itatu] herts quam extra Item Que quidem vero manoria terrae et
6 tenenenta predicta cum pertinenciis predicta Margaretta tenet ad terminam vite
7 sue conmuniter cum alijs personis ad mei denominacionem. Et insuper
8 volo quod eadem Margaretto uxor mea incontinenter post discessum
9 meum Si per eam ad hoc faciendum dicti feoffati requisiti fuerint
10 habeat solam Seisinam et possessionem omnium et singlorum predictorum
11 maneriorum terrarum et tenementorum meorum cum pertinenciis in predictis' Comitatu
12 herts et extra Item Tenendo eedem Margarette et assignatis suis
13 ad totam vitam suam et executoribus suis per unum annum integrum
14 ultra absque impeticione calumpnia Seu implacitacionem vasti
15 Ita quod post discessum eiusdem Margarette et post dictum ann[um] ultra
16 volo quod feoffati mei predicti inde per cartam Indentatam faciant statum
17 Margarette filie mee habendum et tenendum sibi et heredibus de
18 corpore suo per Ricardum Hatf[e]ld armigerum virum suum legitime procreatis
19 Et Si contingat prefatam Margarettam filiam meam sine heredibus
20 de corpore suo per predictum Ricardus virum suum legitime procreatis

21 obiere [*mistake for* obire] tunc omnia predicta maneria terre et tenementa cum pertinenciis integre
22 remaneant eedem Margarette filie mee et heredibus de corpore
23 suis legitime procreatis. Et si contingat ipsam Margaretto filiam
24 meam sine heredibus de corpore suo legitime procreatis obiere extunc
25 volo quod omnia tenementa que habeo in Com[itatu] Essex per executores et feoffatos
26 meos vendantur. Et quod pecunia ex hui(us)modi vendicione percepta
27 inter Abbatem monasterij de Stratford Langthorne et Priorissam
28 Prioratus de Stratford at Bowe adtunc existentes per executores
29 meos equaliter participaretur et distribuatur etc.

This is the indented last will of me, John Dunstaple, Esquire, made at Broadfield in the County of Hertfordshire, the seventh day of July in the year of our Lord 1459 and the 37th year of the reign of King Henry the sixth after the Conquest. As to the disposition of all and sundry of my manors, lands and tenements, with their appurtenances, wherever they are within the kingdom of England, in which divers persons to my benefit from great trust and at my nominations are feoffees. Namely. [Names omitted] Firstly I will that my said feoffees shall immediately after my decease permit and allow Margaret my wife to receive and keep for the whole of her life without hindrance, claim, or impleading for waste the fiefs, proceeds, revenues and profits issuing from all those my manors, lands and tenements with their appurtenances that I have as well in the County of Hertfordshire as outside it etc. Item Which manors, lands and tenements aforementioned with their appurtenances the aforenamed Margaret holds to the end of her life in common with the other persons at my nomination. And furthermore I will that the same Margaret my wife immediately after my decease if the said feoffees shall have been required to do this by her shall have sole seisin and possession of all and sundry of the aforesaid my lands and tenements with their parts in the aforenamed County of Hertfordshire and outside. Item the same Margaret and her assigns holding for the whole of her life and her executors for one whole year further without hindrance, claim or impleading for waste. So [error for Item?] that after the decease of the same Margaret and after the said further year I will that my feoffees aforementioned then by indented charter make an estate for Margaret my daughter to have and to hold for herself and the heirs of her body lawfully begotten by Richard Hatfield, Esquire, her husband. And if it should happen that the aforementioned Margaret my daughter dies without heirs of her body lawfully begotten by the aforesaid Richard her husband then all my aforenamed manors, lands and tenements with their appurtenances shall remain entirely with the same Margaret my daughter and heirs of her body lawfully begotten. And if it should happen that the said Margaret my daughter dies without heirs of her body lawfully begotten then I will that all my tenements that I have in the County of Essex shall be sold by my executors and feoffees. And that the money received from such sale shall be shared and divided equally by my executors between the Abbot of the monastery of Stratford Langthorne[2] and the Prioress of the Priory of Stratford-at-Bow[3] for the time being etc.

Item 3: Henry and Magdalen Snow v. Thomas and Elizabeth Hatfield

8 July 1489
Westminster

Hec est finalis Concordia facta in curia domini R apud West[monasterium] a die Sci Johnannis Baptiste in xv dies anno regnorum Henrici R'Anglie et France Septimi a conquestu quinto etc inter henricum Snawe civem et parmarium Londoniensem et Magdalenam uxorem eius querentes et Thomam Hatfeld generosum et Elizabetham uxorem eius deforcientes de manerio de Bradfeld etc unde placitum etc Scilicet quod predicti Thomas et Elizabetha recognouerunt predicta manerium etc. esse ius imprimis Henrici et illa remiserunt etc de ipsis Thoma et Elizabeth et heredibus imprimis Thome predictis henrice et Magdalen et heredibus imprimis Henrici [in perpetuum]. Et cetera.

This is the final agreement made in the court of the Lord King at Westminster a fortnight [15 days as in *quinze jours*] after the day of St John the Baptist[4] in the fifth year of the reigns [in England and France] of Henry king of England and France, the seventh after the conquest etc., between Henry Snow,[5] citizen and shieldmaker [elsewhere he is styled as Draper] of London, and Magdalen his wife the plaintiff and Thomas Hatfeld, gentleman[6], and Elizabeth his wife the deforciants [defendants] concerning the manor of Broadfield, about which the case [was] pleaded [between them], namely that the aforenamed Thomas and Elizabeth recognized the aforesaid manor etc. to be the right above all of Henry and returned them etc. from the said Thomas and Elizabeth and the heirs especially of Thomas to the afternamed Henry and Magdalen and the heirs especially of Henry. Et cetera.

Item 4: Richard Whaplode and John Suthrey grant Steeple Morden to John and Margaret Dunstaple, Ralph Grey and Henry Wells

16 March 1448/49

Omnibus Xsti fidelibus et cetera Johannes Fayreware de Myldenale in Com[itatu] Suffolk Husbondman etc Cum Richardus Whapled viccarius cederit de Steplemordon et Joh[ann]es Suthrey per quandam cartam suam cuius data est apud Bradfeld xvio die Marcii anno RR' Henrici Sexti post conquestum xxviio [1449] dimiserunt et cetera Johanni Dunstaple armigero et Margarette ux[or]i eius Radolpho Grey et predicto Henrico Welles manerium de Bradefeld etc habendum et tenendum predictum manerium etc prefato Johanni Dunstaple et Margarette uxori eius Rado' et [item incomplete]

To all Christ's faithful *etc* John Fairware of Meldenale in the County of Suffolk, Husbandman, etc. Whereas Richard Whaplode, vicar, has withdrawn from Steeple Morden and John Suthrey by a certain charter of his which is dated at Bradfield the 16th day of March in the 27th year of the reign of King Henry the sixth after the conquest have granted *etc* to John Dunstaple, Esquire, and to Margaret his wife, to Ralph Grey,[7] and to the aforementioned Henry Wells the manor of Broadfield etc. to have and to hold the aforenamed manor to the aforesaid John Dunstaple and Margaret his wife, Ralph [Grey] and [item incomplete].

Notes

1   "Close Rolls, Henry VI: July 1427," *Calendar of Close Rolls, Henry VI, Volume 1 1422–1429*, edited by A. E. Stamp (London: His Majesty's Stationery Office, 1933).
2   Stratford Langthorne Abbey was a house of Cistercian monks.
3   Stratford-at-Bow Priory was a house of Benedictine nuns.
4   Literally: 'From St John the Baptist's day to fifteen days', but that would suggest a period of time. The Nativity of John the Baptist falls on 24 June.
5   Thomas Hatfield and Henry Snow were cousins. Henry Snow's will, made 3 August 1496, indicates that by his later life he was styled as Gentleman (London, National Archives PROB 11/10).
6   Thomas Hatfield here styled Gentleman; at other times styled Esquire.
7   Ralph Grey, John Leventhorpe and Thomas Bawd, Esquire also released land to four men in the parish of St Sepulchre Without Newgate in the ward of Farringdon Without in 1444/5 (London, National Archives, E 326/2176). Ralph Grey of Brent Pelham in Hertfordshire also owned the Manor of Alswick in Layston. In 1464/5, following Ralph's death, this property passed from John Leventhrop senior and Elizabeth Grey, Ralph's wife, to her son Richard Hatfield; the document was witnessed by various people including both William and George Hyde (London, National Archives DE/H/643). A William Hyde was later the second husband of John Dunstaple's daughter Margaret. Other documents in the National Archives are testament to further landholding. It is possible that this Ralph Grey was the man who in 1453 signed the petition to build King's College, Cambridge.

Appendix C
Property owned by John Dunstaple and his heirs

London and Essex properties (from *c.* 1434/5)

Land and rents in Stratford Langthorne, Essex: these passed from John Dunstaple to his daughter Margaret, to her son Thomas Hatfield.

Group of London properties (see GB-Lma Husting Roll 175): Probably acquired in 1434/5, and certainly held by 1445. Included the unnamed tenancy in the parish of St Stephen, Walbrook (which passed to John Dunstaple's daughter Margaret), The Woolsack, and The Three Kings of Cologne (*alias* The White Bull).

Cambridgeshire properties (from 1435)

Brewis manor, Steeple Morden
Avenels manor, which descended with Brewis manor
Gilden Morden
Abingdon and Litlington
Bassingbourn

Normandy properties (held between 1436/7 and 1440/1)

The lordship of Croisy, nr. Evreux (1436–40)
The fief of La Ruaudière (from early 1437)
The fief of Beaumanoir (from early 1437)
Lands in the *bailliage* of Côtentin (July 1438–?), Rouen (Sep 1439–?) and Alençon (from September 1440)

Hertfordshire properties (1449 onwards)

Broadfield manor in Hertfordshire (Bradfeild, Bradfeld). Broadfield comprised parts that were split and inherited by different people: Cumberlow [Comberlow, Cumberlawe Green] also called Mounseys (two messuages; 30 acres of land, pasture and meadow) in the parish of Rushden [Rishden]. Associated also with Cottered.

Bibliography

Antiphonale Sarisburiens: A reproduction in facsimile of a manuscript of the thirteenth century. Edited by Walter H. Frere. Reprint, Farnborough, 1966.
Calendar of the Fine Rolls, Volume 29, Henry VI, 1452–1461. Edited by C. T. Flower. London: His Majesty's Stationery Office, 1939.
Calendar of Close Rolls, Henry VI: Volume 1, 1422–1429. Edited by A. E. Stamp. London, His Majesty's Stationery Office, 1933.
Calendar of Close Rolls, Henry VI: Volume 3, 1436–1441. Edited by H. C. Maxwell-Lyte. London: His Majesty's Stationery Office, 1907.
Calendar of Close Rolls, Henry VI: Volume 4, 1441–1447. Edited by A. E. Stamp. London: His Majesty's Stationery Office, 1937.
Calendar of Close Rolls, Henry VI: Volume 5, 1447–1454. Edited by C. T. Flower. London: His Majesty's Stationery Office, 1947.
Calendar of Close Rolls, Edward IV, Edward V, Richard III: 1476–1485. Edited by K. H. Ledward. London: Her Majesty's Stationery Office, 1954.
Calendar of Inquisitions Post Mortem, Henry VI. Edited by M. L. Holford, S. A. Mileson, C. V. Noble and Kate Parkin. Woodbridge: Boydell and Brewer, 2010.
Calendar of Letter-Books of the City of London. K. Henry V. Edited by Reginald Sharpe. London: J. G. Francis, 1911.
Calendar of Papal Registers Relating to Great Britain and Ireland, Volume 8, 1427–1447. Edited by J. A. Twemlow. London: His Majesty's Stationery Office, 1909.
Calendar of the Patent Rolls I. Edward I, Volume 1, 1272–1281. Edited by H. C. Maxwell-Lyte. London: Her Majesty's Stationery Office, 1901.
Calendar of the Patent Rolls, Henry VI, Volume 2, 1429–1436. Edited by H. C. Maxwell-Lyte. London: His Majesty's Stationery Office, 1907.
Calendar of the Patent Rolls I: Edward IV, Volume I, 1461–1467. Edited by H. C. Maxwell-Lyte. London: Her Majesty's Stationery Office, 1897.
Calendar of the Patent Rolls, Edward IV, Volume II, 1468–1476. Edited by W. H. B. Bird and K. H. Ledward. London: Her Majesty's Stationery Office, 1953.
Calendar of Wills Proved and Enrolled in the Court of Husting, London: Part 2, 1358–1688. Edited by R. R. Sharpe. London: Her Majesty's Stationery Office, 1890.
Le Codex F.160 de la Bibliothèque de la Cathédrale de Worcester, Antiphonaire Monastique (XIIIe siècle). Paléographie Musicale 12. Solesmes: Monks of Solesmes, 1997. First published 1922, Tournai: Desclée; repr. 1972, Berne: Lang.
Allen, Warren Dwight. *Philosophies of Music History: A study of general histories of music 1600–1960*, 2nd edn. New York: Dover Publications, 1962.
Allmand, Christopher T. *Lancastrian Normandy, 1415–1450: The history of a medieval occupation*. Oxford: Clarendon Press, 1983.

Bibliography

Aveling, Judith. "The Late Medieval Mass and Office of the Holy Name of Jesus in England: Sources, development and practice." PhD diss., Bangor University, 2015.

Baggs, A. P., S. M. Keeling and C. A. F. Meekings. "Parishes: Steeple Morden." In *A History of the County of Cambridge and the Isle of Ely 8*, edited by A. P. M. Wright, 111–24. London: Victoria County History, 1982.

Bagnall Yardley, Anne. *Performing Piety: Musical culture in medieval English nunneries*. New York: Palgrave Macmillan, 2006.

Baillie, Hugh. "Squares." *Acta Musicologica* 32 (1960): 178–93.

Bale, Anthony. *The Jew in the Medieval Book: English antisemitisms, 1350–1500*. Cambridge: Cambridge University Press, 2006.

——. trans. *A Book of Margery Kempe*. Oxford: Oxford University Press, 2015.

Bale, Anthony and A. S. G. Edwards, eds. *John Lydgate, The Lives of Ss Edmund and Fremund and the Extra Miracles of St Edmund*, Edited from *British Library MS Harley 2278 and Bodleian MS Ashmole 46*. Heidelberg: Universitaetsverlag Winter, 2009.

Barlow, Frank. *The Life of King Edward who Rests at Westminster, Attributed to a Monk of St Bertin*. London: Thomas Nelson and Sons, 1962.

——. *Edward the Confessor*. London: Eyre and Spottiswoode, 1970.

——. "The King's Evil." *English Historical Review* 95 (1980): 1–27.

Barnwell, Paul, Claire Cross and Ann Rycraft, eds. *Mass and Parish in Late Medieval England: The use of York*. Reading: Spire Books, 2005.

Barth, Fredrik. *Ethnic Groups and Boundaries: The social organisation of culture difference*. London: George Allen and Unwin, 1960.

Bartlett, Robert. *England Under the Norman and Angevin Kings 1075–1225*. Oxford: Clarendon Press, 2000.

Beaven, Alfred P. "Aldermen of the City of London: Walbrook ward." In *The Aldermen of the City of London Temp. Henry III–1912*, edited by Alfred P. Beaven, 216–24. London: E. Fisher, 1908.

Bennett, Michael J. "Richard II and the Wider Realm." In *Richard II: The Art of Kingship*, edited by Anthony Goodman and James L. Gillespie, 187–204. Oxford: Clarendon Press, 1999.

Bent, Ian. "The English Chapel Royal Before 1300." *Proceedings of the Royal Musical Association* 90 (1963): 77–95.

Bent, Margaret. "Sources of the Old Hall Manuscript." *Proceedings of the Royal Musical Association 94th Sess.* (1967–8): 19–35.

——. "The Old Hall Manuscript: A palaeographical study." PhD diss., University of Cambridge, 1969.

——. "The Transmission of English Music 1300–1500: Some aspects of repertory and presentation." In *Studien zur Tradition in Der Musik: Kurt von Fischer zum 60. Geburtstag*, edited by Hans Heinrich Eggebrecht and Max Lütolf, 65–83. Munich: Musikverlag Emil Katzbichler, 1973.

——. "A Lost English Choirbook of the Fifteenth Century." *International Musicological Society: Report of the 11th Congress, Copenhangen, 1972, 2 vols*, edited by H. Glahn, Søren Sørensen and Peter Ryom, 257–62. Copenhagen: Wilhelm Hansen, 1974.

——, ed. *Two 14th-Century Motets in Praise of Music*. Newton Abbot: Antico edition, 1977.

——. "Rota Versatilis – Towards a reconstruction." In *Source Materials and the Interpretation of Music, A Memorial Volume to Thurston Dart*, edited by Ian Bent, 65–98. London: Stainer and Bell, 1981.

———. "The Progeny of Old Hall: More leaves from a royal English choirbook." In *Gordon Athol Anderson, 1929–81, In Memoriam*, edited by Luther Dittmer, 1–54. Henryville, Ottawa, and Binningen: Institute of Mediaeval Music, 1984.

———. "The Late-Medieval Motet." In *Companion to Medieval and Renaissance Music*, edited by Tess Knighton and David Fallows, 114–19. London: Dent and Sons, 1992.

———. "A New Canonic Gloria and the Changing Profile of Dunstable." *Plainsong and Medieval Music* 5 (1996): 45–67.

———. "The Musical Stanzas in Martin Le Franc's Le Champion des Dames." In *Music and Medieval Manuscripts: Paleography and Performance. Essays Dedicated to Andrew Hughes*, edited by John Haines and Randall Rosenfeld, 91–127. Aldershot: Ashgate, 2004.

———. "The Earliest Fifteenth-Century Transmission of English Music to the Continent." In *Essays on the History of English Music: Sources, style, performance, historiography. In honour of John Caldwell*, edited by Emma Hornby and David Maw, 83–96. Woodbridge: Boydell and Brewer, 2010.

———. "Dunstaple, John (d. 1453)." *Oxford Dictionary of National Biography*. Oxford University Press, 2004; online ed, May 2006. Accessed 15 November 2015, www.oxforddnb.com/view/article/8286.

———. "Dunstaple, John." *Grove Music Online. Oxford Music Online*. Oxford University Press. Accessed 21 December 2015, www.oxfordmusiconline.com/subscriber/article/grove/music/08331.

———. "Old Hall Manuscript." *Grove Music Online. Oxford Music Online*. Oxford University Press. Accessed 21 December 2015, www.oxfordmusiconline.com/subscriber/article/grove/music/20296.

Bent, Margaret and Ian Bent. "Dufay, Dunstable, Plummer – A New Source." *Journal of the American Musicological Society* 22 (1969): 394–424.

Bent, Margaret and Roger Bowers. "The Saxilby Fragment." *Early Music History* 1 (1981): 1–28.

Bergeron, Katherine and Philip V. Bohlman, eds. *Disciplining Music: Musicology and its canons*. Chicago and London: University of Chicago Press, 1992.

Besseler, Heinrich. *Die Musik des Mittelalters und der Renaissance*. Potsdam: Bücken, 1930.

Binski, Paul. *Westminster Abbey and the Plantagenets: Kingship and the representation of power 1200–1400*. New Haven and London: Yale University Press, 1995.

Blasina, James. "Music and Gender in the Medieval Cult of St. Katherine of Alexandria, c. 1050–1400." PhD diss., Harvard University, 2015.

Bliss, W. H., ed. *Calendar of Papal Registers Relating to Great Britain and Ireland, II, 1305–42*. London: Her Majesty's Stationery Office, 1895. Accessed 7 August 2015, www.british-history.ac.uk/cal-papal-registers/brit-ie/vol2/pp290-296.

Bowers, Roger. "Choral Institutions within the English Church: Their constitution and development 1340–1500." DPhil diss., University of East Anglia, 1975.

———. "Some Observations on the Life and Career of Lionel Power." *Proceedings of the Royal Musical Association* 102 (1975–1976), 103–27.

———. "Obligation, Agency, and Laissez-faire: The Promotion of Polyphonic Composition for the Church in Fifteenth-Century England." In *Music in Medieval and Early Modern Europe*, edited by Iain Fenlon, 1–19. Cambridge: Cambridge University Press, 1981.

———. "Fixed Points in the Chronology of English Fourteenth-Century Polyphony." *Music and Letters* 71 (1990): 313–15.

———. "Review of Music in the Royal and Noble Households in Late Medieval England, by Andrew Wathey." *Music and Letters* 73 (1992): 638–41.

Bibliography

———. "To Chorus from Quartet: The performing resource for English church polyphony, c. 1390–1559." In *English Choral Practice, 1400–1650*, edited by John Morehen, 1–47. Cambridge: Cambridge University Press, 1995.

———. *English Church Polyphony: Singers and Sources from the 14th to the 17th Century*. Aldershot: Ashgate, 1999.

Breen, Edward. "The Performance Practice of David Munrow and the Early Music Consort of London." PhD diss., King's College, London, 2014.

Britten, Benjamin. "A Note on the Spring Symphony." *Music Survey* 2 (1950): 237.

Bukofzer, Manfred. "'Sumer is icumen in': A Revision." *University of California Publications in Music* 2 (1944): i–vi, 79–113.

———. "Two Fourteenth-Century Motets on St Edmund." *Studies in Medieval and Renaissance Music*, 17–33. New York: Norton and Company, 1950.

———. "John Dunstable: A quincentenary report." *The Musical Quarterly* 40 (1954): 29–49.

———. "Popular and Secular Music in England." In *The New Oxford History of Music 3: Ars Nova and the Renaissance, 1300–1540*, edited by Anselm Hughes and Gerald Abraham, 107–33. London: Oxford University Press, 1960.

———, ed. "John Dunstaple: Complete Works". *Musica Britannica 8*. Revised by Margaret Bent, Ian Bent and Brian Trowell. London: Stainer & Bell, 1970.

Burney, Charles. *A General History of Music from the Earliest Ages to the Present Period*. London: 1776–89. Edited by Frank Mercer in 2 vols. London: G. T. Foulis, 1935. Reprinted New York: Dover, 1957.

Burstyn, Shai. "Gerald of Wales and the Sumer Canon." *The Journal of Musicology* 2 (1983): 13–50.

———. "Is Gerald of Wales a Credible Musical Witness?" *The Musical Quarterly* 70 (1986): 155–69.

Braswell, Laurel. "Saint Edburga of Winchester: A Study of Her Cult, AD 950–1500, With an Edition of the Fourteenth-Century Middle English and Latin Lives." *Mediaeval Studies*, 33 (1971): 292–333.

Bray, Jennifer R. "Concepts of Sainthood in Fourteenth-Century England." *Bulletin of the John Rylands Library*, Manchester 66 (1984): 40–77.

Bretschneider, Wolfgang. "Bewundert-verstoßen-wiederentdeckt: Die Sequenz 'Dies irae'. Ein musiktheologischer Beitrag." *Bibel und Kirche* 63 (2008): 233–7.

Brothers, Thomas. "Contenance Angloise and Accidentals in Some Motets by Du Fay." *Plainsong and Medieval Music* 6 (1997): 21–51.

Brown, Howard Mayer. *Music in the Renaissance*. Englewood Cliffs, NJ: Prentice Hall, 1976.

Busse Berger, Anna Maria. *Medieval Music and the Art of Memory*. Berkeley and Los Angeles: University of California Press, 2005.

Butterfield, Ardis. *The Familiar Enemy: Chaucer, language and nation in the hundred years war*. Oxford: Oxford University Press, 2009.

Caldwell, John. *Medieval Music*. London: Hutchinson, 1978.

———. *The Oxford History of English Music: From the Beginnings to c. 1715, 2 vols*. Oxford: Oxford University Press, 1991.

———. "St Ethelbert, King and Martyr: His cult and office in the West of England." *Plainsong and Medieval Music* 10 (2001): 39–46.

Capgrave, John. *The Chronicle of England*. Edited by F. C. Hingeston. London: Longman, Brown, Green, Longmans and Roberts, 1858.

Carapetyan, Armen. "Editorial: In reply to an incorrect statement." *Musica Disciplina* 3 (1949): 45–54.

Carey, Hilary M. "Judicial Astrology in Theory and Practice in Later Medieval Europe." *Studies in History and Philosophy of Biological and Biomedical Sciences* 41 (2010): 90–8.
Carlson, David R. "The Civic Poetry of Abbot John Whethamstede of St. Albans." *Mediaeval Studies* 61 (1999): 205–42.
Caxton, William. *The Golden Legend or Lives of the Saints Compiled by Jacobus de Voragine, Archbishop of Genoa*, 1275; Englished by William Caxton, Westminster, first Latin edition published 1470, English translation 1483.
Chaney, William A. *The Cult of Kingship in Anglo-Saxon England: The transition from Paganism to Christianity*. Manchester: Manchester University Press, 1970.
Chappell, William, ed. *A Collection of National English Airs, Consisting of Ancient Song, Ballad*. London: Chappell: 1838.
———. *Popular Music of the Olden Time*. London: Cramer, Beale & Chappell, 1844.
Cheung Salisbury, Matthew. "The Use of York: Characteristics of the Medieval Liturgical Office." *Borthwick Papers*, 113. York: University of York, 2008.
———. *The Secular Liturgical Office in Late Medieval England*. Turnhout, Belgium: Brepols, 2015.
Cheung Salisbury, Matthew, Andrew Hughes and Heather Robbins. *Cataloguing Discrepancies: The printed York Breviary of 1493*. Toronto: University of Toronto Press, 2011.
Cheung Salisbury, Matthew, Sally Harper and John Harper, eds. *Lady Mass According to the Use of Salisbury, Early English Church Music EC58*. London: British Academy, forthcoming for 2016.
Citron, Marcia. *Gender and the Musical Canon*. Cambridge: Cambridge University Press, 1993.
Clark, Anne L., ed. *Elizabeth of Schönau: The complete works*. New York: Paulist Press, 2000.
Clark, James G. *A Monastic Renaissance at St Albans: Thomas Walsingham and his circle, c. 1350–1440*. Oxford and New York: Clarendon Press, 2004.
———. "Nicholas Trevet." *Oxford Dictionary of National Biography* (Accessed 22 January 2008) www.oxforddnb.com/view/article/27744, accessed 16 September 2016.
———. "Trevet, Nicholas (b. 1257x65, d. in or after 1334)." In *Oxford Dictionary of National Biography*, online edn, edited by Lawrence Goldman. Oxford: Oxford University Press, 2004. Accessed 23 December 3015 www.oxforddnb.com/view/article/27744.
Clayton, Mary. *The Cult of the Virgin Mary in Anglo-Saxon England*. Cambridge: Cambridge University Press, 1990.
Cole, Suzanne. *Thomas Tallis and his Music in Victorian England*. Woodbridge: Boydell and Brewer, 2008.
Colton, Lisa. "Music in Pre-Reformation York: A New Source and Some Thoughts on the York Masses." *Plainsong and Medieval Music* 12 (2003): 71–88.
———. "The Articulation of Virginity in the Medieval *Chanson de nonne*." *Journal of the Royal Musical Association* 133 (2008): 159–88.
———. "Music and Identity in Medieval Bury St Edmunds." In *St Edmund, King and Martyr: Changing images of a medieval saint*, edited by Anthony Bale, 87–110. Woodbridge: Boydell, 2009.
———. "Languishing for Provenance: *Zelo tui langueo* and the search for women's polyphony in England." *Early Music* 39 (2011): 315–26.
———. "Sumer is icumen in." *Grove Music Online. Oxford Music Online*. Oxford University Press. Accessed 16 October 2014, www.oxfordmusiconline.com/subscriber/article/grove/music/27110.

176 Bibliography

——. "'Sowndys and melodiis': Perceptions of sound and music in the later middle ages." In *Cultural Histories of Noise, Sound and Listening in Europe, 1300–1918*, edited by Ian Biddle and Kirsten Gibson, 19–30. Abingdon, UK: Routledge, 2016.

——. "Music, text and structure in fourteenth-century music, the case of *Ave miles celestis curie*." *Early Music* 45 (forthcoming for 2017).

Cook, James. "The Style of Walter Frye and an Anonymous Mass in the Lucca Choirbook." *Music and Letters* 96 (2015): 1–27.

Coote, Lesley A. *Prophecy and Public Affairs in Later Medieval England*. Woodbridge: Boydell and Brewer, 2000.

Cottle, Basil. *The Triumph of English 1350–1400*. London: Blandford Press, 1969.

Coussemaker, Charles Edmond Henri De. *L'art harmonique aux XIIè et XIIIè siècles*. Paris: A. Durand et Didron, 1865.

Crook, John. *The Architectural Setting of the Cult of Saints in the Early Christian West c. 300–1200*. Oxford: Clarendon Press, 2000.

Crowest, Frederick. *The Story of British Music (From the Earliest Times to the Tudor Period)*. London: Richard Bentley, 1896.

Cullum, Patricia H. "Virginitas and Virilitas: Richard Scope and his Fellow Bishops." In *Richard Scrope: Archbishop, rebel, martyr*, edited by P. J. P. Goldberg, 86–99. Donington: Shaun Tyas, 2007.

Cumming, Julie E. *The Motet in the Age of Du Fay*. Cambridge: Cambridge University Press, 1999.

Curtis, Gareth. "Stylistic Layers in the English Mass Repertory *c.* 1400–1450." *Proceedings of the Royal Musical Association* 109 (1982–1983): 23–38.

Curtis, Gareth and Andrew Wathey. "Fifteenth-Century English Liturgical Music: A list of the surviving repertory." *RMA Research Chronicle* 27 (1994): 1–69.

Davey, Henry. "John Dunstaple." *The Musical Times* 45 (1904): 712–14.

——. *History of English Music*. London, Curwen and Sons, 1895; 2nd edn, 1921.

Davies, Robert R. *The First English Empire: Power and identities in the British Isles 1093–1343*. Oxford: Oxford University Press, 2000.

Davies, Virginia. *Clergy in London in the Late Middle Ages: A register of clergy ordained in the diocese of London based on episcopal ordination lists, 1361–1539*. London: University of London Centre for Metropolitan History, 2000.

Davison, Archibald T. and Willi Apel, eds. *Historical Anthology of Music. Oriental, medieval and renaissance music*. Cambridge, MA: Harvard University Press, 1946.

Dean, Ruth J. "Elizabeth, Abbess of Schönau, and Roger of Ford." *Modern Philology* 41 (1944): 209–20.

Deeming, Helen. "Music in English Miscellanies of the Twelfth and Thirteenth Centuries." DPhil diss., University of Cambridge, 2004.

——. "The Song and the Page: Experiments with form and layout in manuscripts of medieval Latin song." *Plainsong and Medieval Music* 15 (2006): 1–27.

——. "The Sources and Origin of the 'Agincourt Carol'", *Early Music* 35 (2007): 23–38.

——, transcr. and ed. *Songs in British Sources c. 1150–1300. Musica Britannica* 95. London: Stainer and Bell, 2013.

——. "Music and Contemplation in the Twelfth-Century Dulcis Jesu memoria." *Journal of the Royal Musical Association* 139 (2014): 1–39.

——. "An English Monastic Miscellany: The Reading Manuscript of Sumer is icumen in." In *Manuscripts and Medieval Song: Inscription, performance, context*, edited by Helen Deeming and Elizabeth Eva Leach, 141–62. Cambridge: Cambridge University Press, 2015.

Dent, Edward, J. "The Relation of Music to Human Progress." *Musical Quarterly* 14 (1928): 307–19.
Dillon, Emma. *Medieval Music-Making and the Roman de Fauvel*. Cambridge: Cambridge University Press, 2002.
——. *The Sense of Sound: Musical meanings in France, 1260–1330*. Oxford and New York: Oxford University Press, 2012.
Dobson, Eric J. and Frank Ll. Harrison, eds. *Medieval English Songs*. New York: Cambridge University Press, 1979.
Duffin, Ross W. "The Sumer Canon: A new revision." *Speculum* 63 (1988): 1–21.
Duggan, Anne J., ed. *Kings and Kingship in Medieval Europe*. King's College London Medieval Studies 10. Exeter: Short Run Press, 1993.
Dumitrescu, Theodor. *The Early Tudor Court and International Musical Relations*. Aldershot: Ashgate, 2007.
Drake, George Warren J., ed. "Motetti de passione, de cruce, de sacramento, de Beata Virgine et huiusmodi B: Venice, 1503." *Monuments of Renaissance Music* 11. Chicago: University of Chicago, 2002.
Edwards, Warwick. "Polyphony in Thirteenth-Century Scotland." In *'Our Awin Scottis Use': Music in the Scottish Church up to 1603*, edited by Sally Harper and Isobel Woods Preece, 225–71. Glasgow: Universities of Glasgow and Aberdeen, 2000.
Emden, Alfred Brotherton. *A Biographical Register of the University of Oxford to AD 1500, 3 vols*. Oxford: Clarendon Press, 1957–9.
Everist, Mark. "Anglo-French Interaction in Music c. 1170–c.1300." *Revue Belge de Musicologie* 46 (1992): 5–22.
——. "Reception Theories, Canonic Discourses, and Musical Value." In *Rethinking Music*, edited by Nicholas Cook and Mark Everist, 378–402. London and New York: Oxford University Press, 1999.
Fallows, David. *Dufay*. London: J. M. Dent, 1982.
——. "The Contenance Angloise: English influence on continental composers of the fifteenth century." *Renaissance Studies* 1 (1987): 189–208.
——. "Dunstable, Bedyngham and O rosa bella." *The Journal of Musicology* 12 (1994), 287–305.
——, ed. *Secular Polyphony 1380–1480*. Musica Britannica 97. London: Stainer and Bell, 2014.
Fauser, Annegret. "The Scholar Behind the Medal: Edward J. Dent (1876–1957) and the politics of music history." *Journal of the Royal Musical Association* 139 (2014): 235–61.
Forrest Kelly, Thomas. *Early Music: A very short introduction*. Oxford: Oxford University Press, 2011.
Frere, Walter Howard, "The Newly Found York Gradual." *Journal of Theological Studies* 2 (1901), 578–86.
——., ed. *Antiphonale Sarisburiense: A reproduction in facsimile from early manuscripts with a dissertation and analytical index*. London: Gregg Press, 1901–1924; reprinted Farnborough, 1966.
Fuller, Thomas. *The Worthies of England*. London: J. G., W. L. and W. G., 1662.
Geary, Patrick J. *Phantoms of Remembrance: Memory and oblivion at the end of the first millennium*. Princeton, NJ: Princeton University Press, 1994.
Genensky, Marsha and Johanna M. Rose, *CD liner notes to Hildegard von Bingen, 11,000 Virgins: Chants for the feast of St. Ursula, Anonymous 4*. Harmonia Mundi, 907200, 1997.
Goehr, Lydia. *The Imaginary Museum of Musical Works*. Oxford: Clarendon Press, 1992.

Bibliography

Goodman, Anthony. *Margery Kempe and Her World*. London: Longman, 2002.
Gower, John. *Tales of the Seven Deadly Sins: Being the Confessio Amantis*. London and New York: Routledge, 1889; Reprint. London: Forgotten Books, 2013.
Graesse, Thomas, ed. *Legenda Aurea*. Leipzig: Impensis Librariae Arnoldianae, 1850.
Greene, Richard L. "John Dunstable: A quincentenary supplement." *The Musical Quarterly* 40 (1954): 360–3.
——, ed. *The Early English Carols*, 2nd edn. Oxford: Clarendon Press, 1977.
Görlach, Manfred. *The Textual Tradition of the South English Legendary. Leeds texts and monographs, New series 6*. Leeds: University of Leeds, 1974.
Griffiths, Ralph A. "Monarchy and Kingship." In *Medieval England: An encyclopaedia*, edited by Paul E. Szarmach, M. Teresa Tavormina and Joel T. Rosenthal, 520–1. New York and London: Garland, 1998.
Grout, Donald J. *A History of Western Music*. New York: W. W. Norton, 1960.
Haines, John. "The Arabic Style of Performing Medieval Music." *Early Music* 29 (2001): 369–78.
——. *Eight Centuries of Troubadours and Trouvères: The changing identity of medieval music*. Cambridge: Cambridge University Press, 2004.
——. *Music in Films on the Middle Ages: Authenticity vs. fantasy*. New York: Routledge, 2014.
——. "The Revival of Medieval Music." In *The Cambridge History of Medieval Music*, edited by Mark Everist and Thomas Forrest Kelly, 2 vols. Cambridge: Cambridge University Press, 2017.
——. "Medievalist Music and Dance." In *The Oxford Handbook of Victorian Medievalism*, edited by Corinna Wagner and P. Parker, pages tbc. Oxford: Oxford University Press, 2016.
Hallam, Elizabeth M. "Royal Burial and the Cult of Kingship in France and England, 1060–1330." *Journal of Medieval History* 8 (1982): 359–80.
Hamilton, Elina G. "Walter of Evesham's De speculatione musicae: Authority of music theory in medieval England." *Musica Disciplina* 58 (2014): 153–66.
Handschin, Jacques. "The Summer Canon and its Background: I." *Musica Disciplina* 3 (1949): 55–94.
——. "The Summer Canon and its Background: II." *Musica Disciplina* 5 (1951): 65–113.
Hankeln, Roman. "Reflections of War and Violence in Early and High Medieval Saints' Offices." *Plainsong and Medieval Music* 23 (2014): 5–30.
Hankeln, Roman and James Borders. "Forward," *Plainsong and Medieval Music* 23 (2014): 1–3.
Harman, R. Alec, ed. *Thomas Morley: A plain and easy guide to practical music*. New York: Norton, 1952.
Harper, John. *The Forms and Orders of Western Liturgy from the Tenth to the Eighteenth Century*. Oxford: Clarendon Press, 1991.
Harrison, Frank Ll. *Music in Medieval Britain*. London: Routledge and Kegan Paul, 1958.
——. "Benedicamus, Conductus, Carol: A newly-discovered source." *Acta Musicologica* 37 (1965): 35–48.
——. "Ars Nova in England: A new source," *Musica Disciplina* 21 (1967): 67–85.
——. "Polyphonic Music at the Chapel of Edward III." *Music and Letters* 59 (1978): 420–8.
Harrison, Frank Ll., and Peter M. Lefferts, eds. *Motets of English Provenance. Polyphonic Music of the Fourteenth Century* 15. Monaco: Editions L'Oiseau-Lyre, 1980.
Harrison, Frank Ll. and Roger Wibberley, eds. *English Polyphonic Music of the Late Thirteenth and Early Fourteenth Centuries. Early English church music 26*. London: Stainer and Bell, 1981.

Harriss, Gerald L., ed. *Henry V: The practice of kingship*. Oxford: Oxford University Press, 1985.
Hawkins, John. *A General History of the Science and Practice of Music, 4 vols*. London: T. Payne and Son, 1776; edited and reprinted with additional introduction by Charles Cudworth. New York: Dover Publications, 1963.
Higgins, Paula. "Musical 'Parents' and their 'Progeny': The discourse of creative patriarchy in early modern Europe." In *Music in Renaissance Cities and Courts: Studies in Honor of Lewis Lockwood*, edited by Jessie Ann Owens and Anthony M. Cummings, 169–86. Warren, MI: Harmonie Park Press, 1997.
Hiley, David. "The Norman Chant Traditions–Normandy, Britain, Sicily." *Proceedings of the Royal Musical Association* 107 (1980–81): 1–33.
——. "The Rhymed Sequence in England: A preliminary survey." In *Musicologie medieval: Notations et sequences, Actes de la table ronde du C.N.R.S. à l'Institut de Recherche et d'Histoire des Textes, 6–7 septembre 1982*, edited by Michel Huglo, 227–46. Paris, Librairie Honoré Champion, 1987.
——, ed. *Oxford Bodleian Library MS. Lat. liturg. b. 5 (The York Gradual)*. Ottawa: Insitute of Mediaeval Music, 1995.
Hohler, Christopher. "Reflections on Some Manuscripts Containing Thirteenth-Century Polyphony." *Journal of the Plainsong and Medieval Music Society* 1 (1978): 2–38.
Hoppin, Richard. *Medieval Music*. New York: Norton, 1978.
Horne, Joyce M., ed. "Prebendaries: Putson Minor." In *Fasti Ecclesiae Anglicanae 1300–1541: Volume 2, Hereford Diocese*, 47–48. London: Athlone Press, 1962.
Horstmann, Carl, ed. *Altenglische Legenden*. Paderborn: F. Schöningh, 1875.
——. *The Early South English Legendary. Early English text society, Original series 87*. London: Trübner, 1887.
Howell, Margaret J. "The Children of Henry III and Eleanor of Provence." In *Thirteenth Century England 4*, edited by P. R. Coss and S. G. Lloyd, 57–72. Woodbridge: Boydell and Brewer, 1992.
Howlett, David. "Studies in the Works of John Whethamstede." DPhil diss., University of Oxford, 1975.
Hughes, Andrew. "Antiphons and Acclamations: The politics of music in the coronation service of Edward II, 1308." *Journal of Musicology* 6 (1988): 150–68.
——. "The Monarch as the Object of Liturgical Veneration." In *Kings and Kingship in Medieval Europe*, edited by Anne J. Duggan, 375–424. Exeter: Short Run Press, 1993.
——. "British Rhymed Offices: A catalogue and commentary." In *Music in the Medieval English Liturgy*, edited by Susan Rankin and David Hiley, 239–84. Oxford: Clarendon Press, 1993.
——. "Coronation Ceremony, Music and Ritual of." In *Medieval England: An Encyclopaedia*. Edited by Paul E. Szarmach, M. Teresa Tavormina and Joel T. Rosenthal, 209–10. New York and London: Garland, 1998.
Hughes, Andrew and Margaret Bent, eds. *The Old Hall Manuscript. Corpus Mensurabilis Musicae 46, 3 vols*. [Rome]: American Institute of Musicology, 1969–73.
Huot, Sylvia. *Allegorical Play in the Old French Motet*. Stanford: Stanford University Press, 1997.
Hurry, Jamieson Boyd. *Sumer Is Icumen In*. London: Novello, 1913; 2nd edn, 1914.
Husmann, Heinrich and Gilbert Reaney. "The Origin and Destination of the 'Magnus liber organi'." *The Musical Quarterly* 49 (1963): 311–30.
Kantorowicz, Ernst H. *Laudes Regiae: A study in liturgical acclamations and mediaeval ruler worship, with a study of the music of the laudes and musical transcriptions*

180 Bibliography

by Manfred F. Bukofzer. Berkeley and Los Angeles: University of California Press, 1946.
——. *The King's Two Bodies*. Princeton: Princeton University Press, 1957.
Kaye, Philip R. *The 'Contenance Angloise' in Perspective: A study of consonance and dissonance in continental music, c. 1380–1440*. New York and London: Garland, 1989.
Kenney, Sylvia. *Walter Frye and the Contenance Angloise*. New Haven and London: Yale University Press, 1964.
Kern, Fritz. *Kingship and Law in the Middle Ages*. Translated by S. B. Chrimes. New York: Frederick A. Praeger Publishers, 1957.
Kirkman, Andrew. "Some Early Fifteenth-Century Fauxbourdons by Dufay and his Contemporaries: A study in liturgically-motivated musical style." *Tijdschrift van de Vereniging voor Nederlandse Muziekgeschiedenis* 40 (1990): 3–35.
——. "The Style of Walter Frye and an Anonymous Mass." *Early Music History* 15 (1992): 191–223.
——. *The Cultural Life of the Early Polyphonic Mass: Medieval context to modern revival*. Cambridge: Cambridge University Press, 2010.
Klaniczay, Gábor. *Holy Rulers and Blessed Princesses: Dynastic cults in medieval central Europe*. Translated by Eva Pálmai. Cambridge: Cambridge University Press, 2002.
Kleinberg, Aviad M. "Proving Sanctity: Selection and authentication of saints in the later middle ages." *Viator* 20 (1989): 183–205.
Knapp, Janet. "Conductus." *Grove Music Online. Oxford Music Online*. Oxford University Press. Accessed 16 November 2015, www.oxfordmusiconline.com/subscriber/article/grove/music/06268.
Lake, Justin. "Authorial Intention in Medieval Historiography." *History Compass* 12 (2014): 344–60.
Lang, Paul Henry. "Communication." *Journal of the American Musicological Society* 2 (1949): 202–5.
Larwood, Jacob, and John Camden Hotten. *The History of Signboards from the Earliest Times to the Present Day*. London: Chatto and Windus, 1866; 12th edn, 1908.
Lavezzo, Kathy, ed. *Imagining a Medieval English Nation*. Minneapolis, MN: University of Minnesota Press, 2003.
Leach, Elizabeth Eva. *Sung Birds: Music, nature, and poetry in the later middle ages*. Ithaca: Cornell University Press, 2007.
——. *Guillaume de Machaut: Secretary, poet, musician*. Ithaca: Cornell University Press, 2011.
——. *Seeing Sens: Guillaume de Machaut and de Melun*. Published online: 2012. Accessed 10 August 2015 http://users.ox.ac.uk/~musf0058/MachautMelun.html.
Leech-Wilkinson, Daniel. *The Modern Invention of Medieval Music: Scholarship, ideology, performance*. Cambridge: Cambridge University Press, 2002.
Lefferts, Peter M. "The Motet in England in the 14th Century." *Current Musicology* 28 (1979): 55–75.
——. "Text and Context in the Fourteenth-Century English Motet." *L'ars nova italiana del trecento* 6 (1984): 169–92.
——. *The Motet in England in the Fourteenth Century*. Michigan: Ann Arbor, 1986.
——. "English Music Theory in Respect to the Dating of Polyphonic Repertoire in England, 1320–1399." In *Atti del XIV congresso della Società Internazionale di Musicologia, Bologna, 1987: Transmissione et recezione delle forme di cultura musicale*, 3 vols, edited by Angelo Pompilio, III, 653–58. Turin: Edizioni di Torino, 1990.

———. *Robertus de Handlo Regulae and Johannes Hanboys Summa. A new critical text and translation*. Lincoln, Nebraska, and London: University of Nebraska Press, 1991.
———. "England." In *Cambridge Companion to Medieval Music*, edited by Mark Everist, 107–120. Cambridge: Cambridge University Press, 2011.
Lefferts, Peter M. and Margaret Bent, compilers. "New Sources of English Thirteenth- and Fourteenth-Century Polyphony." *Early Music History* 2 (1982): 273–362.
Le Franc, Martin. *Le Champion des Dames, 5 vols*. Edited by Robert Deschaux. Paris: Honore Champion, 1999.
Legge, M. Dominica. "'La Lumiere as Lais': A postscript." *The Modern Language Review* 46 (1951): 191–5.
Lewis, Katherine J. "'Rule of lyf alle folk to sewe': Lay responses to the cult of St Katherine of Alexandria in late-medieval England, 1300–1530." DPhil diss., University of York, 1996.
———. *The Cult of St Katherine of Alexandria in Late Medieval England*. Woodbridge: Boydell, 2002.
Losseff, Nicky. *The Best Concords: Polyphonic music in thirteenth-century England*. New York: Garland, 1994.
Luard, Henry Richard, ed. and trans. *Lives of Edward the Confessor, I: La Estoire de Seint Aedward Le Rei; II: Vita Beati Edvardi Regis et Confessoris; III: Vita Aeduuardi Regis Qui Apud Westmonasterium Requiescit*. London: Longman, 1858.
———. *The Chronicle of Thomas Wykes. Annales Monastici 4*. Rolls series 36. London: Longman, 1869; repr. New York: Kraus Reprint, 1964.
Lyell, Laetitia and Frank D. Watney, eds. *Acts of Court of the Mercers' Company 1453–1527*. Cambridge: Cambridge University Press, 1936; repr. 2012.
MacCracken Henry N., ed. *The Minor Poems of John Lydgate*. London: Oxford University Press, 1911; repr. 1961.
McHardy, A. K. *The Church in London 1375–1392*. London: London Record Society, 1977.
Maclean, Charles. "The Dunstable Inscription in London." *Sammelbände der Internationalen Musikgesellschaft*, 11. Jahrg., H. 2. (1910): 232–49.
McInnes, Louise. "The Social, Political and Religious Contexts of the Late Medieval Carol: 1360–1520." PhD diss., University of Huddersfield, 2014.
McKisack, May. *The Fourteenth Century, 1307–1399*. Oxford: Clarendon Press, 1959.
McNiven, Peter. "Scrope, Richard (c.1350–1405)." In *Oxford Dictionary of National Biography*. edited by H. C. G. Matthew and Brian Harrison. Oxford: Oxford University Press, 2004. Online edn. Edited by Lawrence Goldman, May 2008. Accessed 23 December 2015 www.oxforddnb.com/view/article/24964.
Marks, Richard. *Image and Devotion in Late Medieval England*. Stroud: Sutton Publishing, 2004.
Marr, Peter. "The Melody of 'Sumer is icumen in'." *The Musical Times* 108 (1967): 1104–6.
Mateer, David and Elizabeth New. "'In Nomine Jesu': Robert Fayrfax and the Guild of the Holy Name in St Paul's Cathedral." *Music and Letters* 81 (2000): 507–19.
Maxwell, Kate. 'When Here is Now and Now is Then: Bridging the gap in time with "Sumer Is Icumen In".' In *Building Bridges for Multimodal Research: International perspectives on theories and practice of practices of multimodal analysis*. Edited by Janina Wildfeuer. Bern: Peter Lang, 2015.
Meyvaert, Paul. "John Erghome and the Vaticinium Roberti Bridlington." *Speculum 41* (1966): 656–64.
Morgan, Nigel. "The Coronation of the Virgin by the Trinity and Other Texts and Images of the Glorification of Mary in Fifteenth-Century England." In *England in the Fifteenth Century*, edited by Nicholas Rogers, 223–41. Stamford: Paul Watkins, 1994.

Morgan, Philip. "Of Worms and War: 1380–1558." In *Death in England: An illustrated history*, edited by Peter C. Jupp, and Clare Gittings, 119–46. Manchester: Manchester University Press, 1999.
Morley, Thomas. *A Plain and Easy Guide to Practical Music*. Edited by Alec Harman. New York: Norton, 1952.
Mountney, Hugh. *The Three Holy Kings*. Leominster: Gracewing, 2003.
Nelson, Janet L. and Peter W. Hammond. "Coronation." In *Medieval England, An encyclopaedia*, edited by Paul E. Szarmach, M. Teresa Tavormina and Joel T. Rosenthal, 207–9. New York and London: Garland, 1998.
Nosow, Robert. *Ritual Meanings in the Fifteenth-Century Motet*. Cambridge: Cambridge University Press, 2012.
Nuttall, P. Austen. *A History of the Worthies of England by Thomas Fuller, 3 vols*. London: Thomas Tegg, 1840.
Obst, Wolfgang. " 'Svmer is icumen in' – A Contrafactum?" *Music and Letters* 64 (1983): 151–61.
Ord, Craven. "An Account of the Entertainment of Henry the Sixth at the Abbey of Bury St. Edmunds." *Archaeologia* 15 (1806): 65–71.
Ormrod, Mark. "The Personal Religion of Edward III." *Speculum* 64 (1989): 849–77.
Page, Christopher. *Discarding Images: Reflections on Music and Culture in Medieval France*. Oxford: Oxford University Press, 1993.
———. "An English Motet of the Fourteenth Century in Performance." *Early Music* 25 (1997): 7–32.
———. *CD liner notes to Christopher Page dir. Masters of the Rolls: Music by English composers of the fourteenth century*. Hyperion, CDA67098, 1999.
Palti, Kathleen. " 'Synge we now alle and sum': Three fifteenth-century collections of communal song: A study of British Library, Sloane MS 2593; Bodleian Library, MS Eng. poet. e.1; and St John's College, Cambridge, MS S.54." PhD diss., University College, London, 2008.
Petrina, Alessandria. *Cultural Politics in Fifteenth-Century England: The case of Humphrey Duke of Gloucester*. Leiden, Netherlands: Brill, 2004.
Pfaff, Richard W. *New Liturgical Feasts in Later Medieval England*. Oxford: Clarendon Press, 1970.
———. *The Liturgy in Medieval England: A history*. Cambridge: Cambridge University Press, 2009.
Pirrotta, Nino. "On the Problem of 'Sumer is icumen in'." *Musica Disciplina* 2 (1948): 205–16.
Planchart, Alejandro Enrique, ed. *Embellishing the Liturgy: Tropes and polyphony*. Aldershot: Ashgate, 2009.
Pognon, Edmond. "Du nouveau sur Philippe de Vitry et ses amis." *Humanisme et Renaissance* 6 (1939), 48–55.
Powicke Frederick L., ed. *The Life of Ailred Abbot of Rievaulx by Walter Daniel*. London: Thomas Nelson and Sons, 1950.
Raine, James, ed. *The Historians of the Church of York and its Archbishops, Rolls series 71, 3 vols*. London: Longman, 1879–94; repr. Cambridge: Cambridge University Press, 2012.
Randall Upton, Elizabeth. *Music and Performance in the Later Middle Ages*. New York: Palgrave Macmillan, 2013.
Raynor, Henry. *Music in England*. London: Robert Hale, 1980.
Reames, Sherry L. "Liturgical Offices for the Cult of St. Thomas Becket." In *Medieval Hagiography: An anthology*, edited by Thomas Head, 561–93. New York: Garland, 2000.

——. "Reconstructing and Interpreting a Thirteenth-Century Office for the Translation of Thomas Becket." *Speculum* 80 (2005): 118–70.
Reese, Gustave. *Music in the Middle Ages*. London: J. M. Dent, 1940.
Riches, Samantha J. E. *St George: Hero, martyr and myth*. Stroud: Sutton, 2000.
Ridyard, Susan Janet. "St Edburga at Pershore: A case of mistaken identity?" In *The Royal Saints of Anglo-Saxon England: A study of West Saxon and East Anglian cults*, 129–39. Cambridge, Cambridge University Press: 1988.
Rockstro, W. S. "Schools of Composition §XVI The Early English Schools (1226–1625)," in *A Dictionary of Music and Musicians, 4 vols*. Edited by George Grove, III, 268–77. London: Macmillan, 1890.
——. "Sumer is icumen in." In *A Dictionary of Music and Musicians, 4 vols*. Edited by George Grove, III, 765–8. London: Macmillan, 1890.
Roscow, Gregory H. "What is 'Sumer is icumen in'?" *The Review of English Studies, New series* 50 (1999): 188–95.
Rosenthal, Joel T. "Edward the Confessor and Robert the Pious: 11th century kingship and biography." *Mediaeval Studies* 33 (1971): 7–20.
Roskell, J. S., L. Clark and C. Rawcliffe, eds. *The History of Parliament: The House of Commons 1386–1421*. Woodbridge: Boydell and Brewer, 1993.
Roth, Cecil. *A History of the Jews in England*, 3rd Edn. Oxford: Clarendon Press, 1978.
Rothenberg, David J. *The Flower of Paradise: Marian devotion and secular song in medieval and renaissance Europe*. Oxford: Oxford University Press, 2011.
Sanders, Ernest H. "Tonal Aspects of 13th-Century Polyphony." *Acta Musicologica* 37 (1965): 19–34.
——. "Review of Répertoire International des Sources Musicales, B IV2: Manuscripts of Polyphonic Music (c. 1320–1400), by Gilbert Reaney." *Music and Letters* 51/4 (1970), 458–59.
——. "The Medieval Motet." In *Gattungen der Musik in Einzeldarstellung: Gedenkschrift Leo Schrade*, edited by Wulf Arlt, 497–573. Berne: Francke Verlag, 1973.
——, ed. *English Music of the Thirteenth and Early Fourteenth Centuries. Polyphonic Music of the Fourteenth Century 14*. Paris and Monaco: L'Oiseau-Lyre, 1979.
——. "English Polyphony in the Morgan Library Manuscript." *Music and Letters* 61 (1980): 172–76.
——. "Sumer Is Icumen In." *Grove Music Online*. Grove Music Online. *Oxford Music Online*. Oxford University Press. Accessed 21 December 2015; Stable URL to the current entry "Sumer is icumen in" provides a link to Sanders's previous version www.oxfordmusiconline.com/subscriber/article/grove/music/27110.
Sanders, Ernest, Frank Harrison and Peter M. Lefferts, eds. *English Music for Mass and Office. Polyphonic Music of the Fourteenth Century 17*. Monaco: Editions L'Oiseau-Lyre, 1986.
Sandon, Nicholas. "Fragments of Medieval Polyphony at Canterbury Cathedral." *Musica Disciplina* 30 (1976): 37–53.
——. *The Use of Salisbury: The proper of the Mass from Advent to Septuagesima*. Newton Abbot: Antico Edition, 2000.
Saul, Nigel. "Richard II and Westminster Abbey." In *Cloister and the World: Essays in Medieval History in Honour of Barbara Harvey*, edited by John Blair and Brian Golding, 196–218. Oxford: Clarendon Press, 1996.
Scheifele, Eleanor L. "Richard II and the Visual Arts." In *Richard II: The art of kingship*, edited by Anthony Goodman and James Gillespie, 187–204. Oxford: Clarendon Press, 1999.

Schmitz, Oskar Adolf Hermann. *Das Land ohne Musik*. Munich: G. Müller, 1914.
Schofield, Bertram. "The Provenance and Date of 'Sumer is icumen in'." *Music Review* 9 (1948): 81–6.
Sheingord Pamela and Marcelle Thiébaux, trans. "The Passion of Saint Ursula (Regnante Domino)." *Vox Benedictina* 6 (1989): 257–92. Reprinted: Toronto: Peregrina Publishing, 1991.
Shephard, Tim and Lisa Colton, eds. *Sources of Identity: Makers, owners and users of music sources before 1600*. Turnhout: Brepols, forthcoming.
Slocum, Kay. *Liturgies in Honour of Thomas Becket*. Toronto: University of Toronto Press, 2004.
Smaill, Adele. "Medieval Carols: Origins, forms, and performance contexts." PhD diss., University of Michigan, 2003.
Spiegel, Gabrielle M. "The Cult of St Denis and Capetian Kingship." In *Saints and their Cults: Studies in religious sociology, folklore and history*, edited by Stephen Wilson, 141–68. Cambridge: Cambridge University Press, 1983.
Stell, Judith, and Andrew Wathey. "New light on the biography of John Dunstable?" *Music and Letters* 62 (1981): 60–3.
Stevens, Denis. "Music in Honour of St Thomas of Canterbury." *Musical Quarterly* 56 (1970): 311–48.
Stokes, Martin. "Introduction: Ethnicity, identity and music." In *Ethnicity, Identity and Music: The musical construction of place*, edited by Martin Stokes, 1–28. Oxford: Berg, 1994.
Strohm, Paul, ed. *Hochon's Arrow: The social imagination of fourteenth-century texts*. Princeton: Princeton University Press, 1992.
——. *England's Empty Throne: Usurpation and the language of legitimation, 1399–1422*. New Haven and London: Yale University Press, 1998.
Strohm, Reinhard. *The Rise of European Music 1380–1500*. Cambridge: Cambridge University Press, 1993.
——. "Looking Back at Ourselves: The problem with the musical work-concept." In *The Musical Work: Reality or invention*, edited by Michael Talbot, 128–52. Liverpool: Liverpool University Press, 2000.
——. "Music, Humanism, and the Idea of a 'Rebirth' of the Arts." In *Music as Concept and Practice in the Late Middle Ages*, edited by Reinhard Strohm, and Bonnie Blackburn, 346–405. Oxford: Oxford University Press, 2001.
Strohm, Reinhard and Bonnie Blackburn, eds. *Music as Concept and Practice in the Late Middle Ages*. Oxford: Oxford University Press, 2001.
Summers, William John. "The Effect of Monasticism on Fourteenth-Century Polyphony." In *La Musique et Le Rite Sacre et Profane*, edited by C. Jaques, 104–42. Strasbourg: University of Strasbourg, 1986.
——. "To Trope or Not To Trope? Or, how was the English Gloria performed?" In *Music in Medieval Europe: Studies in Honour of Bryan Gillingham*. Edited by Terence Bailey and Alma Santosuosso, 95–111. Aldershot: Ashgate, 2007.
Sutton, Ann F. *The Mercery of London: Trade, goods and people, 1130–1578*. Aldershot: Ashgate, 2005.
Swanson, Rodney N. *A Calendar of the Register of Richard Scrope, Archbishop of York, 1398–1405, 2 vols*. York: Borthwick Institute of Historical Research, 1981 and 1985.
Talbot, Michael. "Introduction." In *The Musical Work: Reality or invention?*, edited by Michael Talbot, 1–13. Liverpool: Liverpool University Press, 2000.
Taylor, Andrew. *Textual Situations: Three medieval manuscripts and their readers*. Philadelphia: University of Pennsylvania Press, 2002.

Taylor Andrew and A. E. Coates. "The Dates of the Reading Calendar and the Summer Canon," *Notes and Queries* 243 (1998): 22–4.

Temperley, Nicholas. "Review [Untitled] of The Oxford History of English Music: Volume 1: From the beginnings to *c*. 1715 by John Caldwell." *Notes* 49 (1992): 541–3.

Thomson, R. M. "The Music for the Office of St Edmund King and Martyr." *Music and Letters* 65 (1984): 189–93.

———. "John Dunstaple and his Books." *The Musical Times* 150 (2009): 3–16.

Trowell, Brian. "A Fourteenth-Century Ceremonial Motet and its Composer." *Acta Musicologica* 29 (1957): 65–75.

Turville-Petre, Thorlac. *England the Nation: Language, literature and identity, 1290–1340*. Oxford: Clarendon Press, 1996.

Utz, Richard J. "Inventing German(ic) Chaucer: Ideology and philology in German Anglistics before 1945." *Studies in Medievalism* 8 (1996): 5–26.

Voragine, Jacobus de. *The Golden Legend, Readings on the Saints, 2 vols*. Translated by William Granger Ryan. Princeton, NJ: Princeton University Press, 1993.

Walker Bynum, Caroline. *Holy Feast and Holy Fast: The religious significance of food to medieval women*. Berkeley and Los Angeles: University of California Press, 1987.

Walters Robertson, Anne. *Guillaume de Machaut and Reims: Context and meaning in his musical works*. Cambridge: Cambridge University Press, 2002.

Warner, Marina. *Alone of All Her Sex: The myth and the cult of the Virgin Mary*. New York: Vintage Books, 1976.

Warren, Eleanor Margaret. "Community and Identity in the Shadow of York Minster: The medieval chapel of St Mary and the Holy Angels." PhD diss., University of Leeds, 2013.

Wathey, Andrew. "Dunstable in France." *Music and Letters* 67 (1986): 1–36.

———. "Lost Books of Polyphony in England: A list to 1500." *RMA Research Chronicle* 21 (1988): 1–20.

———. *Music in the Royal and Noble Households in Late Medieval England: Studies of sources and patronage*. London and New York: Garland, 1989.

———. "The Peace of 1360–1369 and Anglo-French Musical Relations." *Early Music History* 9 (1990): 129–74.

———. "Matheus de Sancto Johanne." *Grove Music Online*. *Oxford Music Online*. Oxford University Press. Accessed 21 December 2015, www.oxfordmusiconline.com/subscriber/article/grove/music/18061.

Watts, John. *Henry VI and the Politics of Kingship*. Cambridge: Cambridge University Press, 1996.

Weber, William. "The History of Musical Canon." In *Rethinking Music*, edited by Mark Everist and Nicholas Cook, 336–55. London and New York: Oxford University Press, 1999.

Weever, John. *Antient Funeral Monuments of Great-Britain, Ireland, and the Islands Adjacent*. London: W. Tooke, 1631.

Wegman, Rob C. "New Music for a World Grown Old: Martin Le Franc and the Contenance Angloise." *Acta Musicologica* 75 (2003): 201–41.

———. "Johannes Tinctoris and the 'New Art'." *Music and Letters* 84 (2003): 171–88.

———. "The Other Josquin." *Tijdschrift van de Koninklijke Vereniging voor Nederlandse Muziekgeschiedenis* 58 (2008): 33–68.

Werf, Hendrik Van der. "Anonymous IV as Chronicler." *Musicology Australia* 15 (1992): 3–13.

White, James G. *The Churches and Chapels of Old London, with a Short Account of those who have Ministered in them*. London: C. E. Gray, 1901.

── . *History of the Ward of Walbrook in the City of London: Together with an account of the Aldermen*. London: Printed for Private Circulation, 1904. Repr. London: Forgotten Books, 2013.

Williamson, Amy. "Genre, Style and Repertory in Thirteenth-Century Insular Polyphony." PhD diss., University of Southampton, in preparation.

Williamson, Magnus. "Liturgical Polyphony in the Pre-Reformation English Parish Church: A provisional list and commentary." *Royal Musical Association Research Chronicle* 38 (2005): 1–43.

Windeatt, Barry, ed. *The Book of Margery Kempe*. London: Longman: 2000.

Winstead, Karen A. *Virgin Martyrs: Legends of sainthood in late medieval England*. Ithaca and London: Cornell University Press, 1997.

── . *John Capgrave: The life of Saint Katherine*. Kalamazoo, Michigan: Medieval Institute Publications, 1999.

Winters, Ben. *Erich Wolfgang Korngold's* The Adventures of Robin Hood: *A film score guide*. Lanham, MD: Scarecrow Press, 2007.

Wogan-Browne, Jocelyn. *Saints' Lives and Women's Literary Culture c. 1150–1300: Virginity and its authorizations*. Oxford: Oxford University Press, 2001.

Wooldridge, Harry Ellis. *The Oxford History of Music 1*. Oxford: Clarendon Press, 1901.

Wright, Peter. "Binchois in England: Some questions of style, influence, and attribution in his sacred works." In *Binchois Studies*, edited by Andrew Kirkman and Dennis Slavin, 87–118. Oxford: Oxford University Press, 2000.

Wright, Craig and Sean Gallagher. "Martin le Franc." *Grove Music Online. Oxford Music Online*. Oxford University Press. Accessed 21 December 2015, www.oxfordmusiconline. com/subscriber/article/grove/music/17928.

Wright, Thomas. *Political Poems and Songs Relating to English History, Composed During the Period from The Accession of Edward III to that of Richard III, 2 vols. Rolls series 14*. London: Longman, 1859–61.

── , ed. *The Historical Works of Giraldus Cambrensis*. London: George Bell & Sons, 1863.

Wulstan, David. "Sumer is icumen in: A perpetual puzzle canon?" *Plainsong and Medieval Music* 9 (2000): 1–17.

Youngs, Deborah. *Humphrey Newton (1466–1536): An early Tudor gentleman*. Woodbridge: Boydell, 2008.

Yri, Kirsten. "Noah Greenberg and the New York Pro Musica: Medievalism and the Cultural Front." *American Music* 24 (2006): 421–44.

Zayaruznaya, Anna. *The Monstrous New Art: Divided forms in the late medieval motet*. Cambridge: Cambridge University Press, 2015.

Zon, Bennett. *Music and Metaphor in Nineteenth-Century British Musicology*. Aldershot: Ashgate, 2000.

Index

Aelred of Rievaulx (1110–67) 47
Aethelweard, Ealdorman 7
Agincourt Carol 41–2
Alanus, Johannes 126–8
Albanus roseo rutilat (Dunstaple) 90
allegorical lyrics 54–5
Allen, Warren Dwight 19
Alle psallite cum luya/Alleluya 32
angels/Angles in medieval texts 136–43
anonymity in English music 124–6
antiphons 42–3, 74–5, 91, 141–2, 147, 40
Archbishops: (St) Richard Scrope of York 72, 75–9, 106; St Thomas of Canterbury 43, 137, 149
Are post libamina/Nunc surgunt 142
ars nova 125–6
astronomy and astrology, John Dunstaple 90
Augustine of Canterbury, St 138, 140–1, 147, 36
Augustine par angelis 140, 147, 36
authorship 8, 65–6, 79–80; anonymity in English music 124–6; authorial presence and value 68–73, *71*; and the cult of St Edburga 72, 73–5; genre and liturgical function 67–8; mythologising of 150–1; Richard Scrope's impact on York liturgy 75–9; *see also* Dunstaple, John (c. 1390–1453/1459?)
Ave miles celestis curie/Ave rex gentis 29, 141
'Ave rex gentis anglorum' (Garnier of Rebais) 141–2

Bach, P. D. Q. 30
Barlow, Frank 42
Bede 137–9
Bent, Margaret 67, 86, 92, 119, 120, 127, 136, 142

Berger, Busse 25
Biblical characters: Esther and Judith 54, 56–7, 62, 50; John the Baptist 90–1
Biblical imagery 46–7
Binchois, Gilles 70, 91, 133, 136, 145
Blessed Virgin Mary cult 42; *Singularis laudis digna* 52–7
Board, Ernest (1877–1934) *18*, 19, 27–8
books *see* codices/books
Bowers, Roger 44–5, 56–7, 58, 68–9, 92, 94–5, 127
Braswell, Laurel 74
Bread Street, London 103–7
Bridlington Prophecies 55–6, 57
Britain/England distinction 7–8, 11, 33, 140
Britten, Benjamin 32–3, 38, 81
Broadfield, Hertfordshire 93, 97–8, 103, 106, 163–7, 169; Broadfield Manor House 101–2, *101*, 113, 74
Brown, James (1923–2004) 2
Bukofzer, Manfred 24, 25, 28, 29, 30
Burney, Charles (1726–1814) 20, 21, 23–4
Burstyn, Shai 24
Bury St Edmunds, Abbey of 40, 43, 120, 141–2

Caldwell, John 4, 69, 70
Cambridge Companion to Medieval Music 4
canon (*chace*; *caccia*), forms of; *see also* 'Sumer is icumen in'
'canon' of Western music, concept of 13–14, 21–2; 'Sumer is icumen in' and English music history 22–7, *25*
Canterbury Cathedral 57, 86; St Augustine 138, 140–1, 147, 36; St Thomas 43, 76, 77, 137, 149

Index

Cantigas da Santa Maria 39
cantilenae: *Regem regum collaudemus* 44–5, 51–2; *Singularis laudis digna* 44, 45, 52–7
cantus firmus settings 21, 67, 141
Capgrave, John (1393–1464) 7, 142
Carey, Hilary 90
carols 3, 41–2, 141; *Sancta Virgo Maria* 54
'Carpe Diem' (The Fugs) 31
Caxton, William (*c.* 1422–91) 139–40
Champion des Dames, Le (le Franc) 9, 70, 133–6, 144–5; *see also* contenance angloise
Chappell, William 15, 17, 28
Charter of John Fray, Salter 163
Christus vincit 43
Chronica Pontificum Ecclesiae Eboracensis 75, 76–7
Citron, Marcia 27
Civitas nusquam conditur/T. Cibus esurientum/Cives celestis curie 44, 46–7, 48–51, *49–51*
classical music, using medieval music 1–2, 32, 33, 151
codices/books: composer portraits 70, *71*, 81, 28; manuscripts as sources of identity 118–21; Old Hall Manuscript 66, 69–70, 72, 119–20, 142; power of 39–40; Squarcialupi Codex 39, 70; *see also* authorship
Cole, Suzanne 22, 27
composer attributions *see* authorship
composer biographies 72, 82, 34–5; *see also* Dunstaple, John (*c.* 1390–1453/1459?)
composer portraits 70, *71*, 81, 28
conductus genre 57–8, 67
Confessio amantis (Gower) 143–4
confessors, personal 106–7
contenance angloise 9, 133–4, 144–5; angles and Angles in medieval texts 136–43; meaning of 'contenance' 143–4; rereading le Franc's poem 134–6; *see also* Dunstaple, John (*c.* 1390–1453/1459?)
Coote, Lesley 55
copying practices 66, 119–20, 131, 37
coronation ceremonies 42–4, 59–60
counterpoint 85, 135; *see also* contenance angloise; 'Sumer is icumen in'
Crécy, Battle of (1346) 54–6
Crowest, Frederick 23–4
Cullum, Patricia H. 78

Cumming, Julie 58
Curtis, Gareth 133

d'Abernon, Pierre (d. 1293) 120
d'Amerval, Éloi 146, 23
Daniel, Walter 47
Davey, Henry 85, 123–4
Davies, Robert 6
Deeming, Helen 26
De flore martirum/Deus tuorum militum/Ave rex gentis 141
Dent, Edward J. 5
Descendi in ortum meum (Dunstaple) 109, 7
Digital Image Archive of Medieval Music 4–5
Dufay, Guillaume 70, 133, 136, 145
Dufay Collective 32
Duffin, Ross 24
Dunstaple, John (*c.* 1390–1453/1459?) 3, 8, 9, 85–7, 107–8, 133, 144, 150–1, *153–7*; acquisition of properties 99–102, *101*, 166, 169; heirs 102–4, *102*; motets 86, 90, 91–2, 109, 9; The Three Kings of Cologne, Bread Street 104–7; tomb at St Stephen's, Walbrook 87–93, 110, 24, 110, 26; will 93–9, *96*, 164–5; *see also* contenance angloise
Durham Cathedral 120–1

Edburga of Pershore, St (d. 960) 72, 73–5
Edmund, St 29, 43, 77, 141–2
Edward the Confessor (d. 1066) 42–52, *49–51*, 59
Edward II (d. 1327) 45, 55–6
Edward III (d. 1377) 44, 45, 52; *Singularis laudis digna* 52–7
Eleven Thousand Virgins cult 77–8
Elisabeth of Schönau 78
embellishment 68
Emerson, Lake and Palmer 2
emotionalism 123–4
endemic English music 121
'Englishness' 5–8, 15, 117–18, 124, 150; Britain/England distinction 7–8, 11, 33, 140; *see also* contenance angloise; national identity
Enguerrand VII (d. 1397) 57
Erghome, John 55–6, 57
Esther (Hester; biblical figure) 54, 56–7, 62, 50
Estoire de Seint Aedward (Paris) 46, 47
ethnicity in English music 124–6; *Sub Arturo plebs* 126–8

Fallows, David 3, 135–6
Fantasia on Greensleeves (Vaughan Williams) 15
Festival of Britain (1951) 2
Flanders, Michael 15, 17, 19
folk music 15; 'Sumer is icumen in' as folk music 31–3
France: French music 121, 123, 124, 125–6, 128–9; meaning of 'contenance' 143–4
Fray, John 163
Fugs, The 31
Fuller, Thomas 88–9

Garnier (or Warner) of Rebais, Abbot 141, 147, 40
Gawetron, William 55, 112
General History of Music, A (Burney) 20
Gerald of Wales (*c.* 1146–*c.* 1223) 23–4
German literature 150
Goehr, Lydia 22
Goldhurst, Thomas 104
Gower, John 143–4
'great works/pieces' paradigm 24, 27
Greenberg, Noah (1919–66) 2
Greene, Richard L. 94
'Greensleeves' 14–15, *16–17*, 19
Gregory, St 137–41
Grout, Donald J. 32
Grove Dictionary of Music and Musicians 19

hagiography *see* saints
Haines, John 15, 17
Handschin, Jacques 24–5, 28, 30, 124
Hankeln, Roman 6, 59
harmony 21, 23, 122–3
Harrison, Frank Ll. 3, 26, 28–9, 67–8, 126
Hatfield, Edward (d. 1472) *159*
Hatfield, Margaret/Hyde (née Margaret Dunstaple, d. 1486) 97, 102–4, *102*, 113, 74, *159*
Hatfield, Richard (d. 1467) 102–3, *102*, 113, 73, *157*
Hatfield, Thomas (b. 1462) *102*, 103–4, *157–8*, 166
Hawkins, John (1719–89) 20
'hearing' Mass 129, 1
Henry III (d. 1272) 43, 46, 141–2
Henry V (d. 1422) 41–2, 119–20
Henry VI (d. 1471) 142
Henry VIII (d. 1547) 14
Hester (Esther; biblical figure) 54, 56–7, 62, 50

Hiley, David 77
Hilliard Ensemble 29
historiae 6, 73
Historiam Ecclesiasticam Gentis Anglorum (Bede) 137–9
History of English Music (Davey) 85, 123–4
Hoccle, Agnes 98
Holst, Gustav 15
Holy Name of Jesus cult 77, 105, 107
Hoppin, Richard 32, 125–6, 135
Hotten, John Camden 104
Howes, Frank 33
Humphrey Duke of Gloucester 87
Hundred Years War 54–5
Hurry, Jamieson Boyd 19
Husting Roll 175, Metropolitan Archives, London 96–7, *96*, 99

identity *see* national identity
imitatio 136, 144–5
indigenous English music 121–4
Ingram, Thomas 97
'Inter natos mulierum' 91

'Jacet granum' 149
Joan of Navarre (d. 1437) 87, 94, 95, 115, 100
John, Duke of Bedford (d. 1435) 86, 88, 100
John of Salisbury 42
John of Wheathamstead 87, 89–92, 111, 30
John the Baptist, St 90–1
'Jubilemus pia mente' 105
Judith (biblical figure) 54, 56–7, 62, 50

Kantorowicz, Ernst H. 43
Katherine of Alexandria, St 74–5
Kaye, Philip 135
Kempe, Margery (*c.* 1373–after 1439) 117
Kent *see* Canterbury Cathedral
kingship, sainthood and liturgical ceremony 40–4, 59–60; music for Edward the Confessor 44–52, *49–51*, 59
Kirkman, Andrew 21
Knapp, Janet 57–8

Lang, Paul Henry 25
Larwood, Jacob 104
Lavezzo, Kathy 150
Leach, Elizabeth Eva 20
Lefferts, Peter 4, 10, 13, 58, 67, 74, 121–2

le Franc, Martin 9, 70, 133–6, 144–5; *see also contenance angloise*
Legenda Aurea (Voragine) 139–40
Lewis, Katherine 6
Liber de arte contrapuncti (Tinctoris) 133, 136
liturgical music 3–4, 6, 66, 91, 105–6, 120–1, 125, 149–50; angels/Angles in medieval texts 136–43; genre and liturgical function 67–8; kingship and sainthood 40–4, 59–60; music for Edward the Confessor 43, 44–52, *49–51*, 59; Richard Scrope and York liturgy 75–9; 'Sumer is icumen in' as both sacred and secular 27–30; *see also* authorship
livery companies, London 104–6
Losseff, Nicky 124
Ludwig, Friedrich 25
Lumiere as Lais, La (d'Abernon) 120

Machaut, Guillaume de 70
McInnes, Louise 3
McKisack, May 45
Maclean, Charles 88, 93–4
manuscripts as sources of identity 118–21
Marian music *see* Blessed Virgin Mary cult
Marr, Peter 24, *25*, 29
Mass 21, 66; 'hearing' Mass 129n1; Mass of the Three Kings 105, 107
'medieval music', as term 2–3
Medieval Music (Hoppin) 125
melodiousness 123
Mikkalos ('Michalus') 90
Minot, Laurence 55
missals 105, 107
monasteries *see* religious institutions
motets 3, 6, 29, 63, 71, 120–2, 150; *Are post libamina/Nunc surgunt* 142; authorship and liturgical function 67–8; *Civitas nusquam conditur* 44, 46–7, 48–51, *49–51*; in honour of St Augustine and St Gregory 140–1, 147, 36; in honour of St Edmund 29, 141; of John Dunstaple 86, 90, 91–2, 109, 9; *Phi millies/O creator* 149; and politics 58–60; *Rota versatilis* 72; *Sub Arturo plebs* 126–8; *Virgo regalis fidei* 74–5
'multi-local' identity 121, 130
Munday, Anthony 88
Munrow, David (1942–76) 2
Music in England (Raynor) 123

Music in Medieval Britain (Harrison) 3, 126
Music in the Middle Ages (Reese) 122–3
Music in Western Civilization (Lang) 25
My Lady Greensleeves (Rossetti) 14–15, *16–17*
mythologising of authorship 150–1

national identity 5–8, 11, 33, 15, 117–18, 128–9, 150; ethnicity and anonymity in English music 124–8; manuscripts as sources of identity 118–21; native, endemic and indigenous English music 121–4; *see also contenance angloise*
Nemo accendit lucernam 47
'new art' 133
nobility *see* kingship, sainthood and liturgical ceremony
Norman Conquest 7
Nosow, Robert 86
notational developments 69
nunneries *see* religious institutions

Obst, Wolfgang 22
Old Hall Manuscript 66, 69–70, 72, 119–20, 142
Osbert of Clare 7
Oxford History of English Music (Caldwell) 4

Page, Christopher 53
Paris, Matthew 46, 47
Perspice Christicola see 'Sumer is icumen in'
Pfaff, Richard 105
Philippa of Hainault 56
Phi millies/O creator (de Vitry) 149
Pictures at an Exhibition (Emerson, Lake and Palmer) 2
plainchant 3, 59, 66, 68, 72, 140–2, 149; antiphons 42, 74–5, 91, 141–2, 147, 40; *Christus vincit* 43
Policraticus (John of Salisbury) 42
politics of musical expression 5–6, 40, 57–60; kingship and liturgical ceremony 40–4, 59–60; music for Edward the Confessor 44–52, *49–51*, 59; *Singularis laudis digna* 44, 45, 52–7
polyphonic genres 3–4, 6, 21, 24, 91, 109, 7, 123; *see also* authorship; *contenance angloise*; motets; national identity
pop music, classical music as part of 2
Popular Music of the Olden Time (Chappell) 15, 17, 28

Pound, Ezra 30
Preco preheminencie (Dunstaple) 86, 90, 91–2, 109, 9
Proportionale musices (Tinctoris) 133, 136
psalms 70, 73–4
Psalter of Henry VI 70
Ptolemy (d. *c.* 168) 90
puns, on angels/Angles in medieval texts 136–43

Raynor, Henry 123–4
'Reading rota' *see* 'Sumer is icumen in'
Reese, Gustave 32, 122–3, 124
Regem regum collaudemus 44–5, 51–2
Regina caeli 28–9
religion: cult of the Blessed Virgin Mary 42, 52–7; *see also* liturgical music; religious institutions
religious institutions 40, 120–1; Abbey of Bury St Edmunds 43, 141–2; Canterbury Cathedral 43, 57, 76–7, 86, 137, 138, 140–1, 147, 36, 149; Durham Cathedral 120–1; Westminster Abbey 43, 47–8, 52, 57; Winchester Cathedral 73; York Minster 72, 75–9; *see also* liturgical music; St Stephen's, Walbrook
Richard I (d. 1199) 43
Richard II (d. 1400) 43, 52
Robin Hood, The Adventures of (film, 1938) 31
rock music, classical music as part of 2
Rockstro, William S. 19, 20, 26
Rolle, Richard (d. 1349) 70, *71*, 81, 28
Roman influences 23–4
Romanticism 123–4
rondellus techniques 67
Roscow, Gregory H. 28
Rossetti, Dante Gabriel 14–15, *16–17*
Rota versatilis 72
round (*rota*), forms of *see* 'Sumer is icumen in'
royalty *see* kingship, sainthood and liturgical ceremony
Ryman, James 54

St Albans 57, 87, 111; John of Wheathamstead 87, 89–92, 111
St Augustine of Canterbury 138, 140–1, 147
St Edburga of Pershore (d. 960) 72, 73–5
St Edmund 29, 43, 77, 141–2
St Gregory 137–41

St John the Baptist 90–1
St Katherine of Alexandria 74–5
St Mary Woolchurch, Walbrook 103
saints 6, 9; kingship and liturgical ceremony 40–4, 59–60; music for Edward the Confessor 44–52, *49–51*; puns on angels/Angles in medieval texts 136–43; (St) Richard Scrope 72, 75–9
St Stephen's, Walbrook 97–9, 100, 104; John Dunstaple's tomb 87–93, 110
St Thomas of Canterbury (Thomas à Becket) 43, 76, 77, 137, 149
St Ursula and the Eleven Thousand Virgins 77–8
Salve Regina 42
Sancta Virgo Maria 54
Sancto Johanne, Matheus de (d. after 10 June 1391) 142
Sanders, Ernest H. 24, 29, 56, 68, 72, 124
Sarum missals 105
Scrope, Richard, Archbishop of York (*c.* 1350–1405) 72, 75–9
'Scrupulosa' 75, 77, 78–9
secularisation of sacred music 27–30
Shouldham, Norfolk 120
Sigismund (d. 1437) 142–3
Singularis laudis digna 44, 45, 52–7
Snow, Henry and Magdalen 166
Solaris ardor Romuli 140–1
South English Legendary 75, 139
'Spe mercedis' 75, 77, 79
Spring Symphony (Britten) 33
Squarcialupi Codex 39, 70
Steeple Morden, Cambridgeshire 92, 95, 99, 100–3, *102*, 166–7
Stell, Judith 87, 94–5
Stokes, Martin 118
Story of British Music, The (Crowest) 23–4
Stow, John 87, 88
Strohm, Paul 59
Strohm, Reinhard 3–4, 69, 70, 72, 127–8, 135, 146
Sub Arturo plebs (Alanus) 126–8
'Sumer is icumen in' 1, 3, 5, 15, 17, *18*, 19–22, 33–4; and English music history 22–7, *25*; lyrics 13; parodies of 30–1; in popular and folk culture 30–3; sacred versus secular elements 27–30
Sumer is icumen in (Board) *18*, 27–8
Summers, William 66
Survey of London (Stow) 87

Talbot, Michael 65–6
'Talent m'a pris' 20
Tallis, Thomas 22
Thomas à Becket (St Thomas of Canterbury) 43, 76, 77, 137, 149
Thomson, Rodney M. 87, 141
Three Kings of Cologne, Bread Street, London 104–7
Tinctoris, Johannes 133, 136
tonality 24, 122–3
Trevet, Nicholas (1257/65–1334) 78
Trowell, Brian 127–8
Trukyll, William 97–9
Turville-Petre, Thorlac 6

Urania, daughter of Zeus 90
Ursula and the Eleven Thousand Virgins 77–8
Utz, Richard 150

Vaughan Williams, Ralph 15
Veni sancte spiritus (Dunstaple) 86, 109
Villette, Jacques 146
Virgin Mary *see* Blessed Virgin Mary cult
Virgo regalis fidei 74–5
Vita Aedwardi Regis 45–6
Vitry, Philippe de 120, 149
voice-leading, English approaches to 122
Voragine, Jacobus de 139–40

Wales 23
Warner, Marina 42
Wathey, Andrew 87, 94–5, 97, 142
Weever, John 89
Wegman, Rob C. 133–4, 136, 143
Wells, Henry 105–7
Westminster Abbey 43, 47–8, 52, 57
Whaplode, Richard 101–2, 166–7
whistling 31, 38, 73
White, James 98
White Bull *see* Three Kings of Cologne, Bread Street, London
Whittingham, Robert (d. 1452) 88, 98, 100
Wiche, Alice and Hugh 106, 107, 114, 115
Wicker Man, The (film, 1973) 31
Winchester Cathedral 73
Wogan-Browne, Jocelyn 74
Wulstan, David 29
Wykes, Thomas (1222–93) 48

York liturgy 72, 75–9
York Mystery Plays 2
Youngs, Deborah 92

Zayaruznaya, Anna 149
Zon, Bennett 23